The Facts On File
JUNIOR
VISUAL
DICTIONARY

A British CIP catalogue record for this book is available from the British Library.

Australian CIP data available on request from Facts On File.

Facts On File books are available at special discounts when purchased in bulk quantities for businesses, associations, institutions or sales promotions. Please call our Special Sales Department in Oxford at 0865 728399.

JUNIOR VISUAL DICTIONARY

Original edition in English :
Copyright © 1990 by Éditions Québec/Amérique Inc.

For information contact:
Facts On File Limited.
Collins Street
Oxford OX4 1XJ
United Kingdom

Facts On File Pty Ltd.
Talavera & Khartoum Rds
North Ryde NSW 2113
Australia

ISBN : 0-8160-2335-2

Printed and bound in Canada on acid-free paper.

This book was produced on a Macintosh computer from Apple Computer Inc.

The Facts On File
JUNIOR
VISUAL
DICTIONARY

JEAN-CLAUDE CORBEIL
ARIANE ARCHAMBAULT
MARTIN MANSER

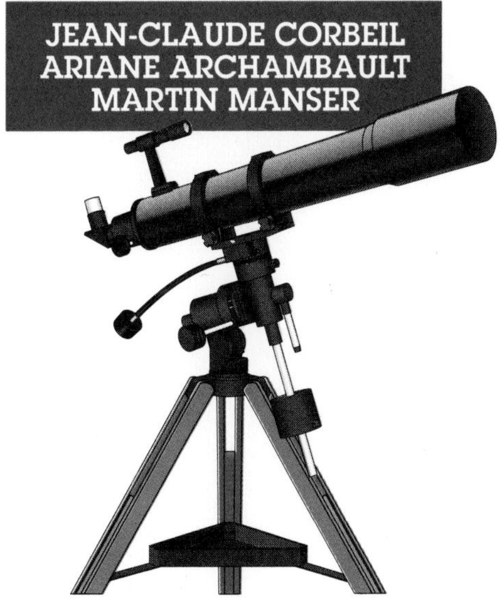

Director of Computer Graphics:
François Fortin

Art Director:
Jean-Louis Martin

Computer Graphic Artists:
Jacques Perrault,
Benoît Bourdeau,
Anne Tremblay

Computer Copy Editing:
Anik Lapointe

Facts On File
New York • Oxford • Sydney

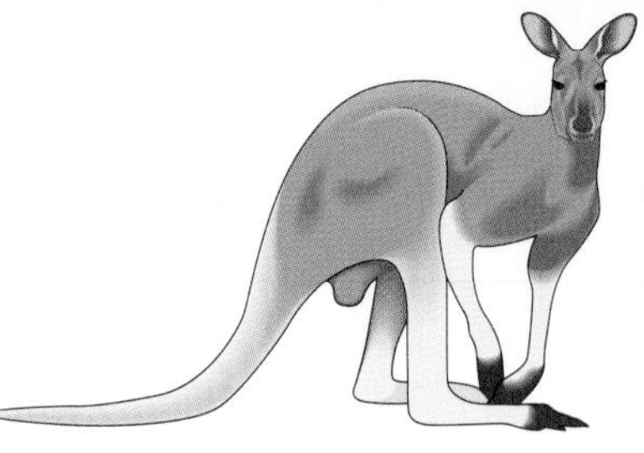

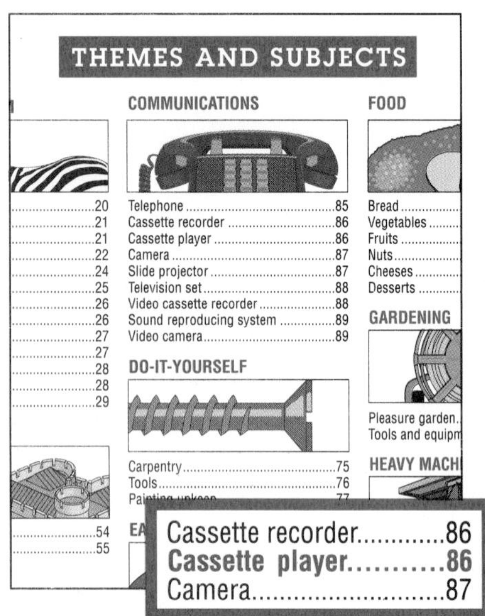

THEMES AND SUBJECTS

COMMUNICATIONS

FOOD

DO-IT-YOURSELF

GARDENING

HEAVY MACHI

1

STARTING FROM THE LIST OF THEMES AND SUBJECTS

The list of themes and subjects (pages 6 and 7) lists every topic of interest in the dictionary and specifies the page where you will find the corresponding picture.

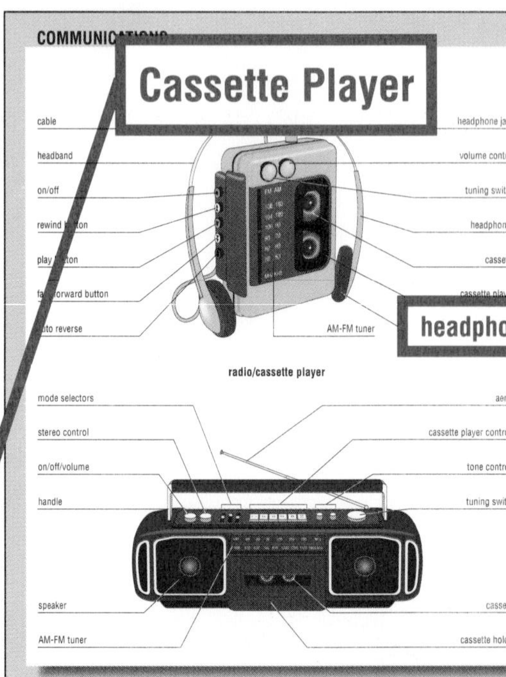

COMMUNICATIONS

Cassette Player

cable
headband
on/off
rewind button
play button
fast forward button
auto reverse

headphone jack
volume control
tuning switch
headphone
cassette
cassette player

AM-FM tuner

headpho

radio/cassette player

mode selectors
stereo control
on/off/volume
handle

speaker

AM-FM tuner

aeri
cassette player contro
tone contro
tuning switc

cassett

cassette holde

86

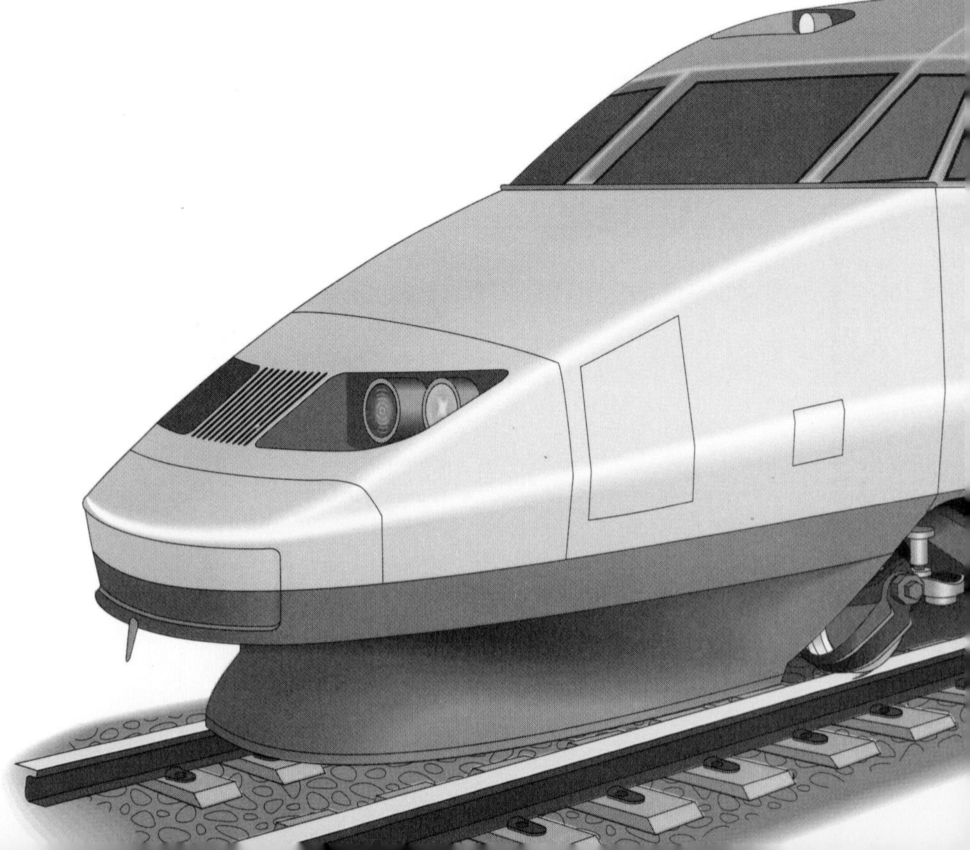

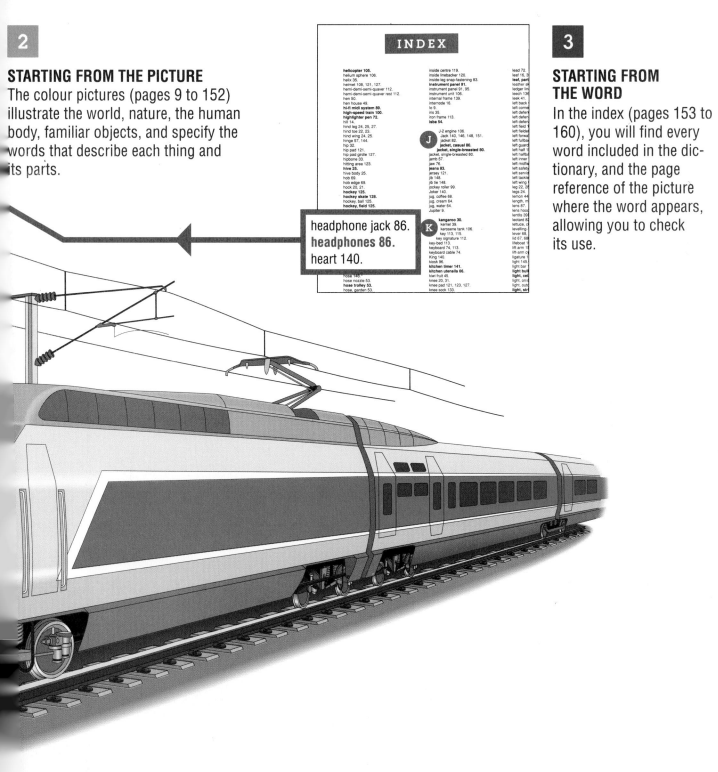

2

STARTING FROM THE PICTURE

The colour pictures (pages 9 to 152) illustrate the world, nature, the human body, familiar objects, and specify the words that describe each thing and its parts.

3

STARTING FROM THE WORD

In the index (pages 153 to 160), you will find every word included in the dictionary, and the page reference of the picture where the word appears, allowing you to check its use.

INDEX

helicopter **105.**
helium sphere 106.
helix 35.
helmet 108, 121, 127.
hemi-demi-semi-quaver 112.
hemi-demi-semi-quaver rest 112.
hen 50.
hen house 49.
hi-fi midi system 89.
high-speed train 100.
highlighter pen 72.
hill 14.
hind leg 24, 25, 27.
hind toe 22, 23.
hind wing 24, 25.
hinge 57, 144.
hip 32.
hip pad 121.
hip pad girdle 127.
hipbone 33.
hitting area 123.
hive 25.
hive body 25.
hob 69.
hob edge 69.
hock 20, 21.
hockey 125.
hockey skate 128.
hockey, ball 125.
hockey, field 125.

headphone jack 86.
headphones 86.
heart 140.

hose 146.
hose nozzle 53.
hose trolley 53.
hose, garden 53.

inside centre 119.
inside linebacker 120.
inside-leg snap-fastening 83.
instrument panel 91.
instrument panel 91, 95.
instrument unit 106.
internal frame 139.
internode 16.
Io 9.
iris 35.
iron frame 113.
isba 54.

J
J-2 engine 106.
Jack 140, 146, 148, 151.
jacket 82.
jacket, casual 80.
jacket, single-breasted 80.
jacket, single-breasted 80.
jamb 57.
jaw 76.
jeans 83.
jersey 121.
jib 148.
jib tie 148.
jockey roller 99.
Joker 140.
jug, coffee 68.
jug, cream 64.
jug, water 64.
Jupiter 9.

K
kangaroo 30.
kernel 39.
kerosene tank 106.
key 113, 115.
key signature 112.
key-bed 113.
keyboard 74, 113.
keyboard cable 74.
King 140.
kiosk 96.
kitchen timer 141.
kitchen utensils 66.
kiwi fruit 45.
knee 20, 31.
knee pad 121, 123, 127.
knee sock 133.

lead 72.
leaf 16, 3
leaf, part
leather sk
ledger lin
leech 136
leek 41.
left back
left corne
left defen
left defen
left field
left fielde
left forwa
left fullba
left guard
left half 1
left halfba
left inner
left midfie
left safety
left servic
left wing
leg 22, 2
legs 24.
lemon 44
length, m
lens 87.
lens hood
lentils 39
leotard 8
lettuce, c
levelling-
lever 68.
lid 67, 68
lifeboat 1
lift arm 1
lift-arm c
ligature 1
light 145.
light bar
light bulb
light, cei
light, on/
light, outo
light, str

THEMES AND SUBJECTS

ANIMAL KINGDOM

Horse 20
Dog....................................21
Cat 21
Bird 22
Butterfly 24
Honeybee and hive 25
Lobster 26
Snail 26
Fish 27
Frog 27
Turtle 28
Venomous snake 28
Wild animals 29

ARCHITECTURE

Traditional houses 54
Castle.................................55

CLOTHING

Trainer 78
Men's clothing 79
Sweaters.............................81
Women's clothing 82
Children's clothing 83
Personal articles 84

COMMUNICATIONS

Telephones 85
Cassette recorder 86
Cassette player 86
Camera 87
Slide projector 87
Television............................88
Video cassette recorder 88
Hi-fi midi system 89
Video camera.......................89

DO-IT-YOURSELF

Carpentry............................75
Tools 76
Painting upkeep ....,77

EARTH

Continents 12
Coastal features 13
Volcano..............................13
Cave 14
Mountain 14
Weather 15

FARM

Farm buildings.....................49
Farm animals 50

FOOD

Bread 37
Vegetables 38
Fruit 43
Nuts 46
Cheeses 47
Desserts 48

GARDENING

Garden................................51
Tools and equipment 52

HEAVY MACHINERY

Fire engines 146
Cranes 148
Bulldozer 149
Wheel loader.......................150
Dumper truck 151
Hydraulic shovel 151

HOUSE

Exterior of a house 56
Door and window 57
Stairs.................................58
Bathroom............................59
Chair and table....................60
Bed and linen......................62
Lights 63
Crockery 64
Cutlery 65
Kitchen utensils 66
Cooking utensils 67
Domestic appliances.............68
Electric cooker 69
Fridge-freezer 70

HUMAN BODY

Body 31
Skeleton..............................33
Mouth and teeth 34
Ear.....................................35
Eye.....................................35
Hand...................................36
Nose 36

THEMES AND SUBJECTS

MEASURING DEVICES

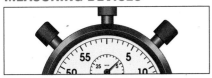

Measure of time 141
Measure of weight 142
Measure of distance 143
Measure of length 143
Measure of temperature 143

MUSIC

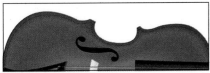

Musical notation 112
Upright piano 113
Classical guitar 114
Violin 114
Saxophone 115
Trumpet 115
Drums 116
Electric guitar 116
Orchestra 117

OPTICAL INSTRUMENTS

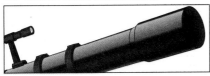

Binoculars 144
Reflecting telescope 145
Refracting telescope 145

SCHOOL

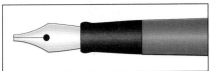

Plane surfaces, solids and colours 71
School supplies 72
Microcomputer 74
Pocket calculator 74

SPACE

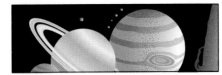

Planets of the solar system 9
Phases of the Moon 10
Sun 10
Comet 11
Stars 11

SPORTS

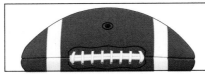

Soccer 118
Rugby union 119
American football 120
Baseball 122
Cricket 124
Hockey 125
Ice hockey 126
Skating 128
Basketball 129
Tennis 130
Downhill skiing 132
Cross-country skiing 133
Diving 134
Swimming 134
Skin diving 135
Windsurfing 136
Archery 137
Darts 137
Camping 138
Indoor games 140

SYMBOLS

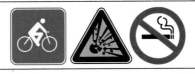

Road signs 152
Public signs 152

TRANSPORT

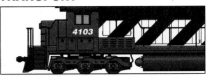

Road transport
Car 90
Caravan 93
Tractor unit 94
Motorcycle 95
Petrol station 96
Bridges 97
Bicycle 98
Rail transport
High-speed train 100
Locomotive 100
Types of freight wagons 101
Maritime transport
Passenger liner 102
Submarine 103
Air transport
Long-range aircraft 104
Helicopter 105
Space transport
Rocket 106
Space shuttle 107

VEGETABLE KINGDOM

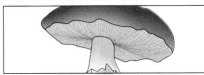

Parts of a plant 16
Parts of a leaf 17
Parts of a flower 17
Parts of a tree 18
Parts of a mushroom 19

WEAPONS

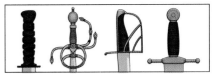

Armour 108
Swords and daggers 109
Crossbow 109
Pistol 110
Revolver 110
Tank 111

planets of the solar system

Europa

Ganymede

Io

Callisto

Titan

Jupiter

Saturn

Sun

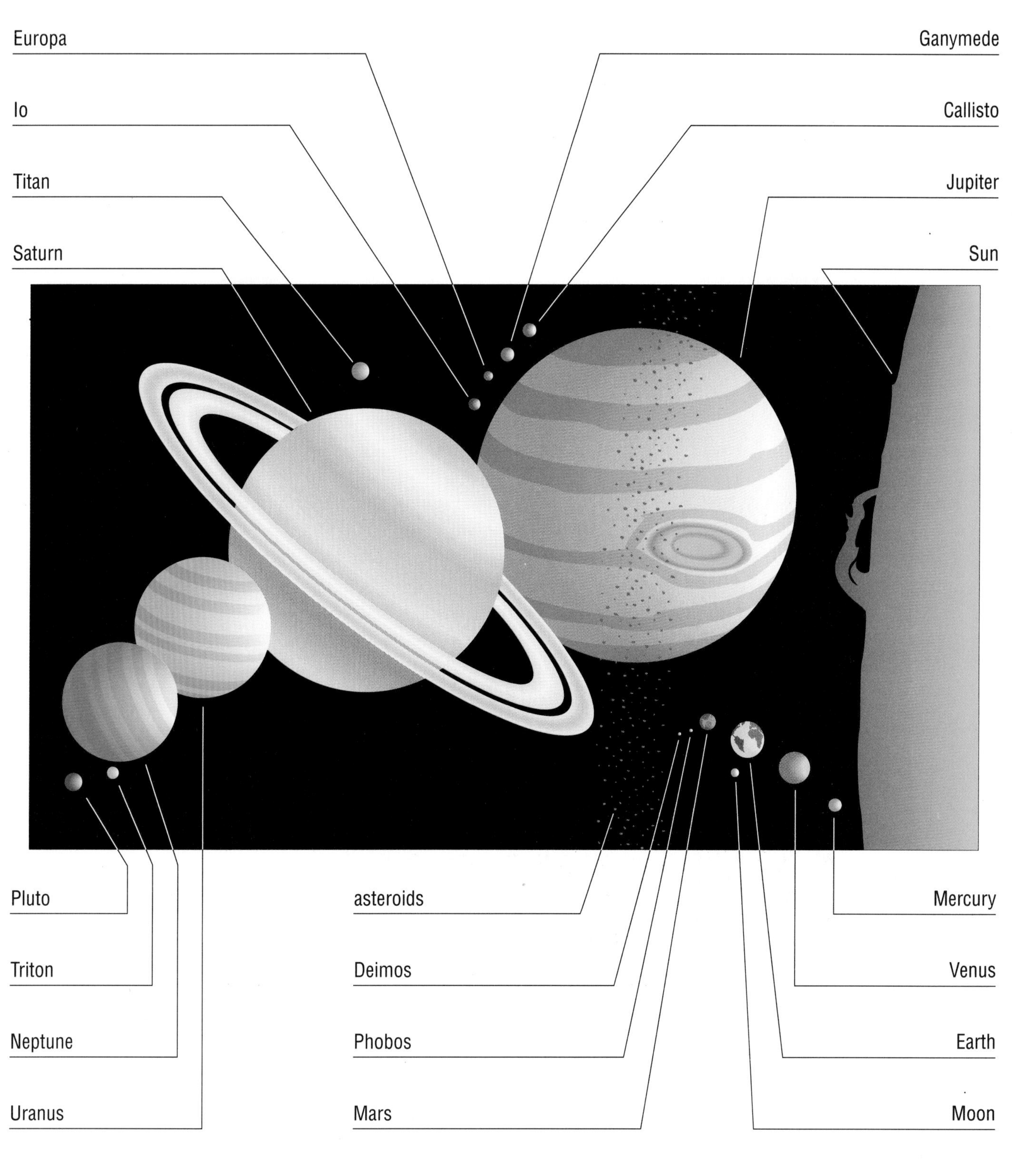

Pluto

Mercury

Triton

asteroids

Venus

Neptune

Deimos

Earth

Uranus

Phobos

Mars

Moon

Sun

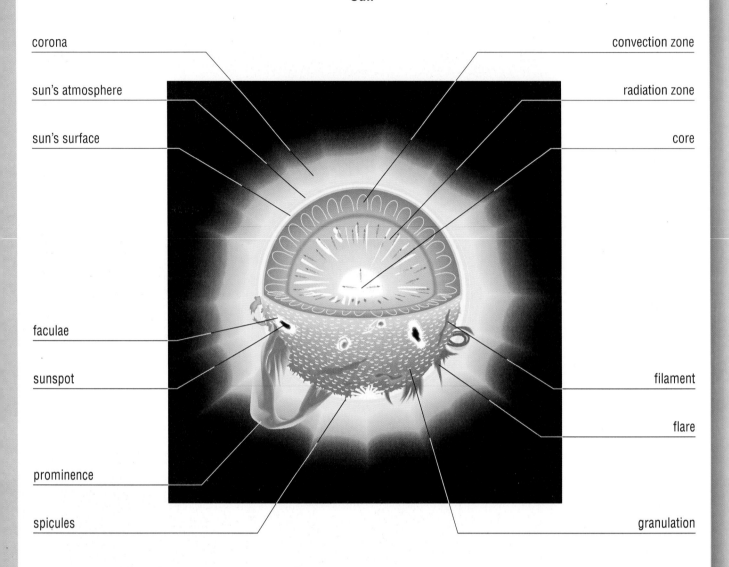

corona

sun's atmosphere

sun's surface

faculae

sunspot

prominence

spicules

convection zone

radiation zone

core

filament

flare

granulation

phases of the Moon

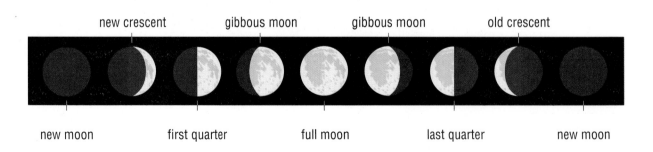

new crescent

gibbous moon

gibbous moon

old crescent

new moon

first quarter

full moon

last quarter

new moon

comet

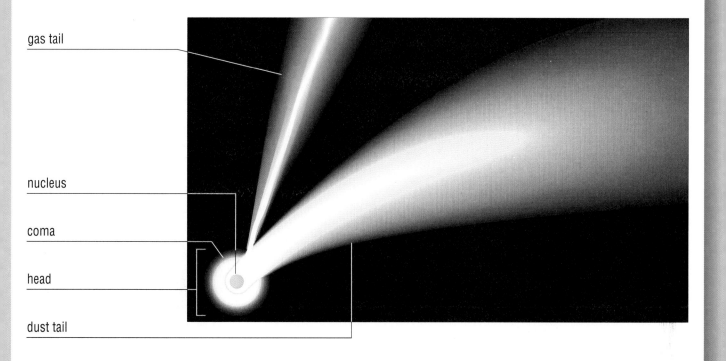

gas tail

nucleus

coma

head

dust tail

stars

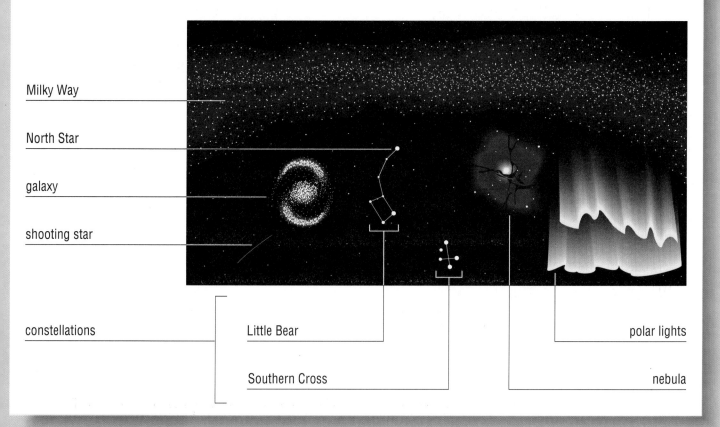

Milky Way

North Star

galaxy

shooting star

constellations

Little Bear

Southern Cross

polar lights

nebula

EARTH

continents

Arctic

Europe

Atlantic Ocean

North America

Black Sea

Asia

China Sea

Oceania

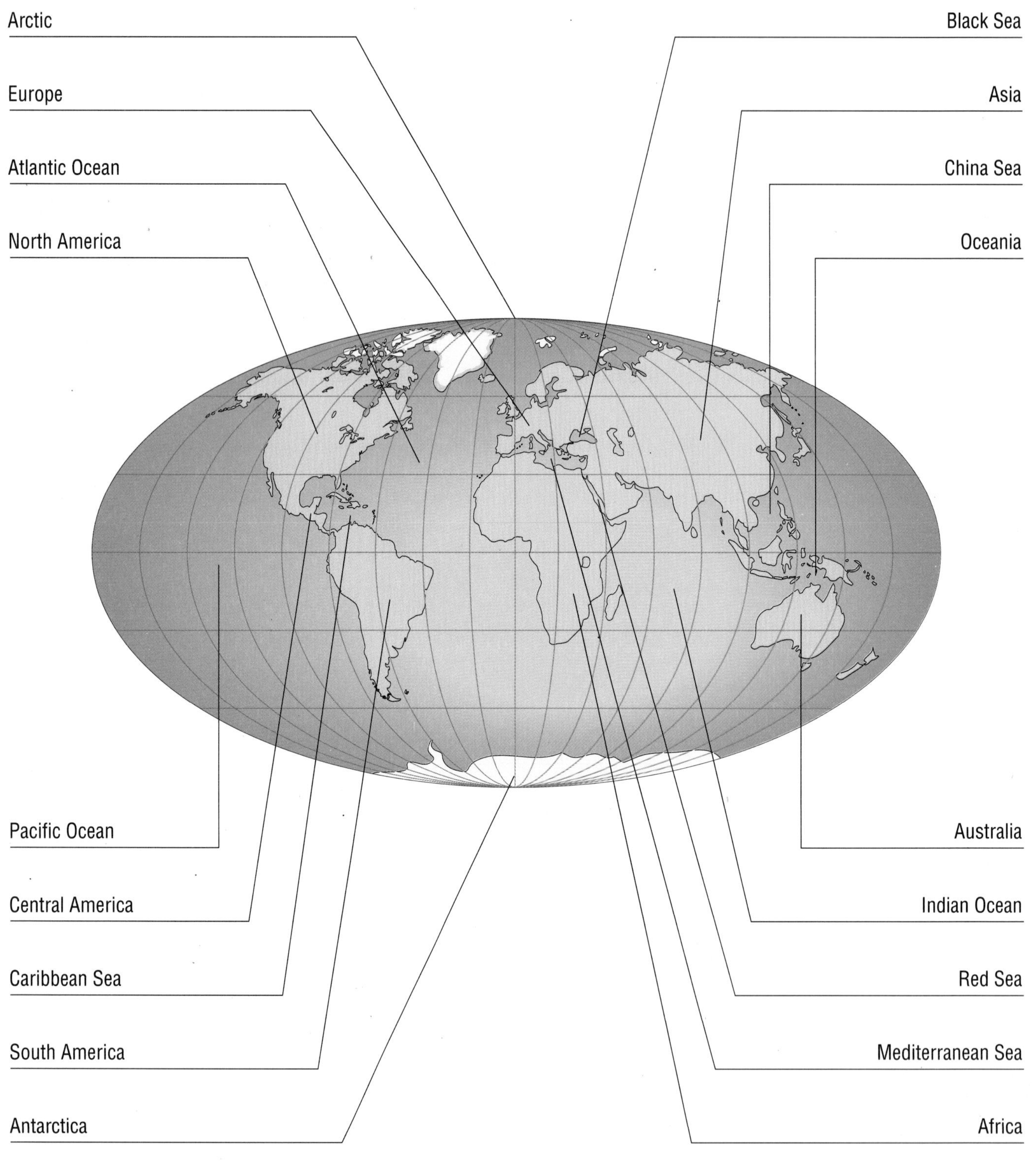

Pacific Ocean

Central America

Caribbean Sea

South America

Antarctica

Australia

Indian Ocean

Red Sea

Mediterranean Sea

Africa

volcano

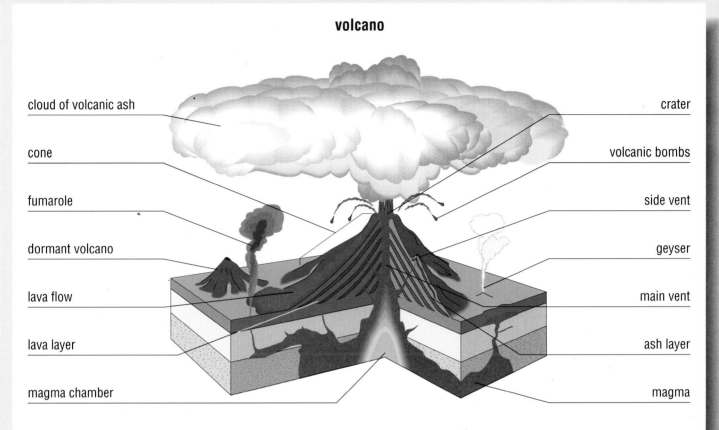

cloud of volcanic ash

cone

fumarole

dormant volcano

lava flow

lava layer

magma chamber

crater

volcanic bombs

side vent

geyser

main vent

ash layer

magma

coastal features

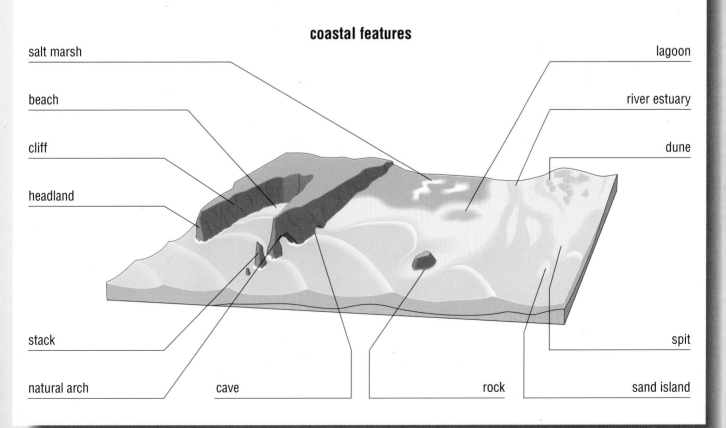

salt marsh

beach

cliff

headland

stack

natural arch

cave

rock

lagoon

river estuary

dune

spit

sand island

EARTH

mountain

summit

perpetual snow

spur

mountain slope

plateau

mountain torrent

waterfall

hill

ridge

crest

peak

pass

cliff

forest

valley

lake

cave

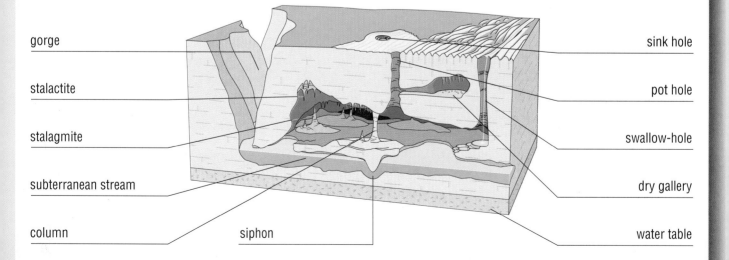

gorge

stalactite

stalagmite

subterranean stream

column

siphon

sink hole

pot hole

swallow-hole

dry gallery

water table

weather

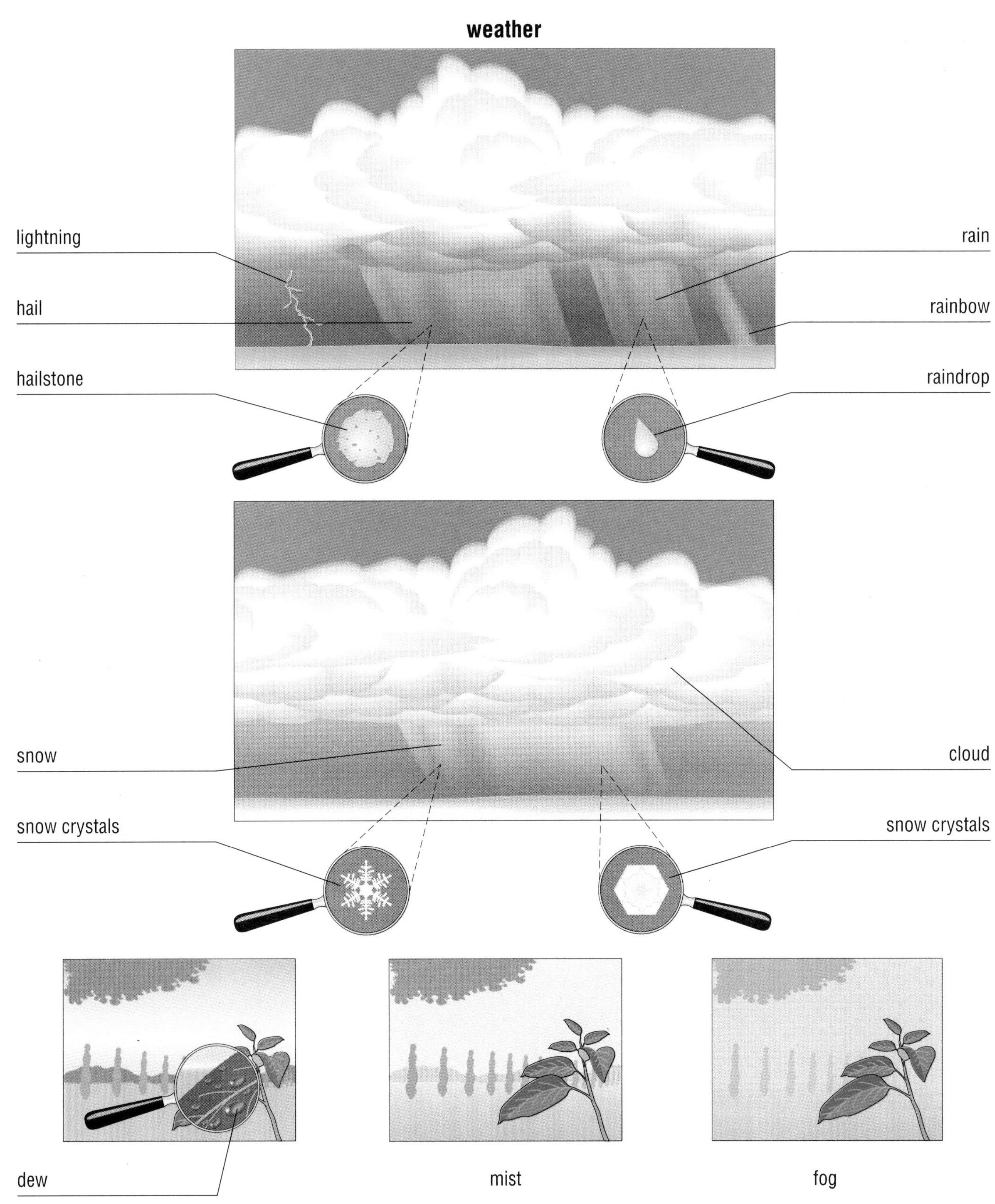

lightning

hail

hailstone

rain

rainbow

raindrop

snow

cloud

snow crystals

snow crystals

dew

mist

fog

VEGETABLE KINGDOM

parts of a plant

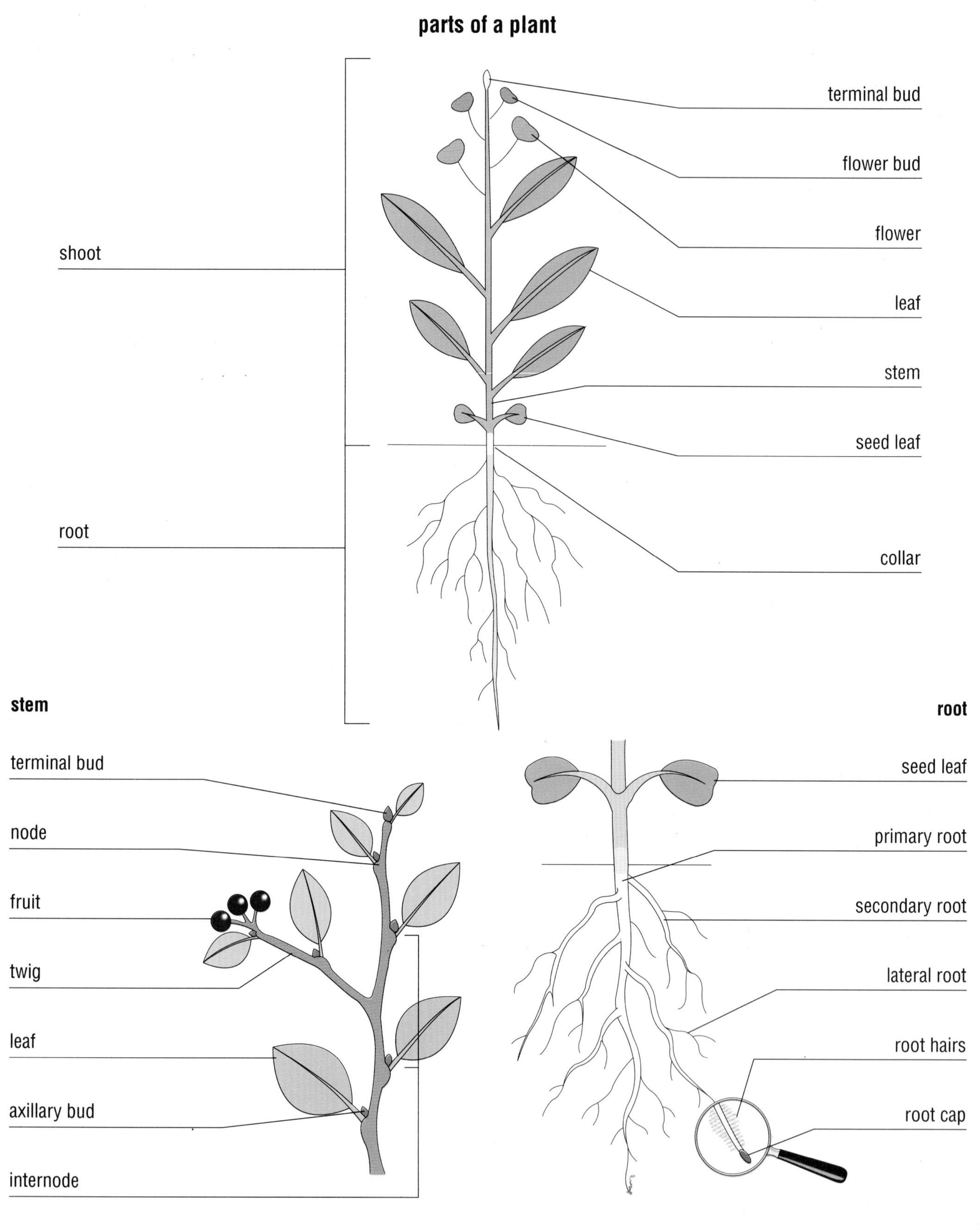

shoot

root

terminal bud

flower bud

flower

leaf

stem

seed leaf

collar

stem

terminal bud

node

fruit

twig

leaf

axillary bud

internode

root

seed leaf

primary root

secondary root

lateral root

root hairs

root cap

parts of a leaf

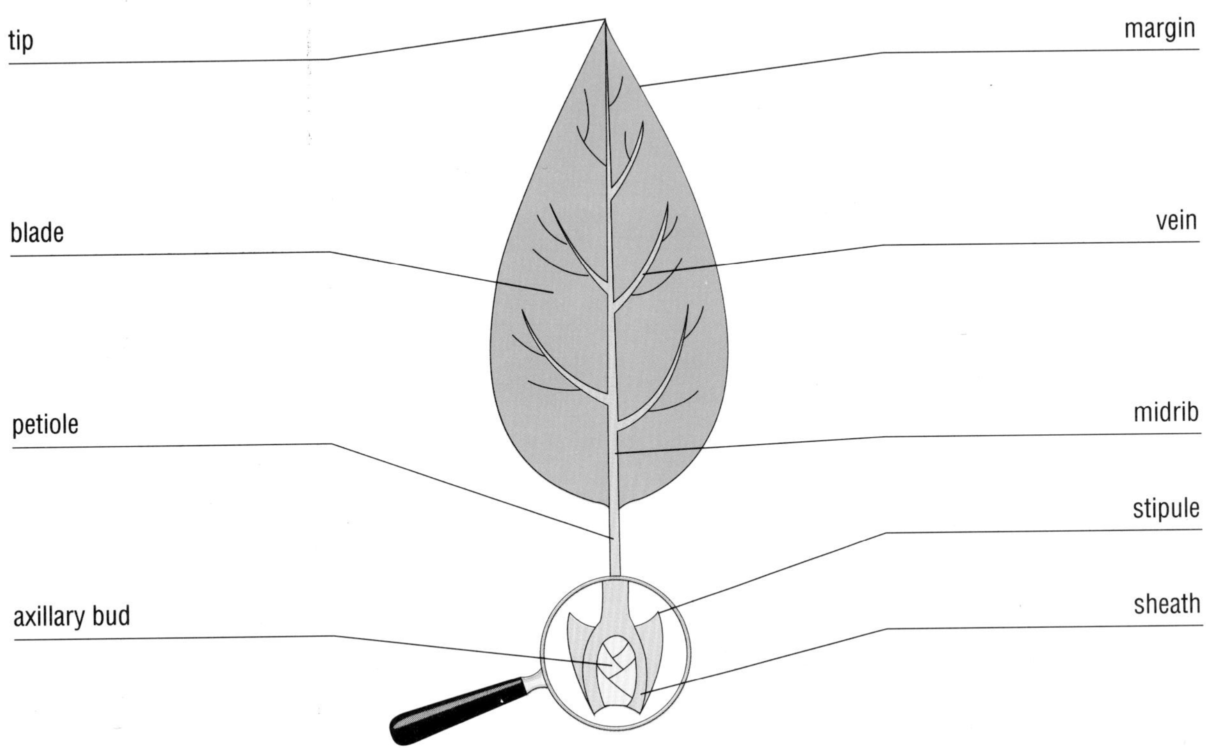

tip

margin

blade

vein

petiole

midrib

stipule

axillary bud

sheath

parts of a flower

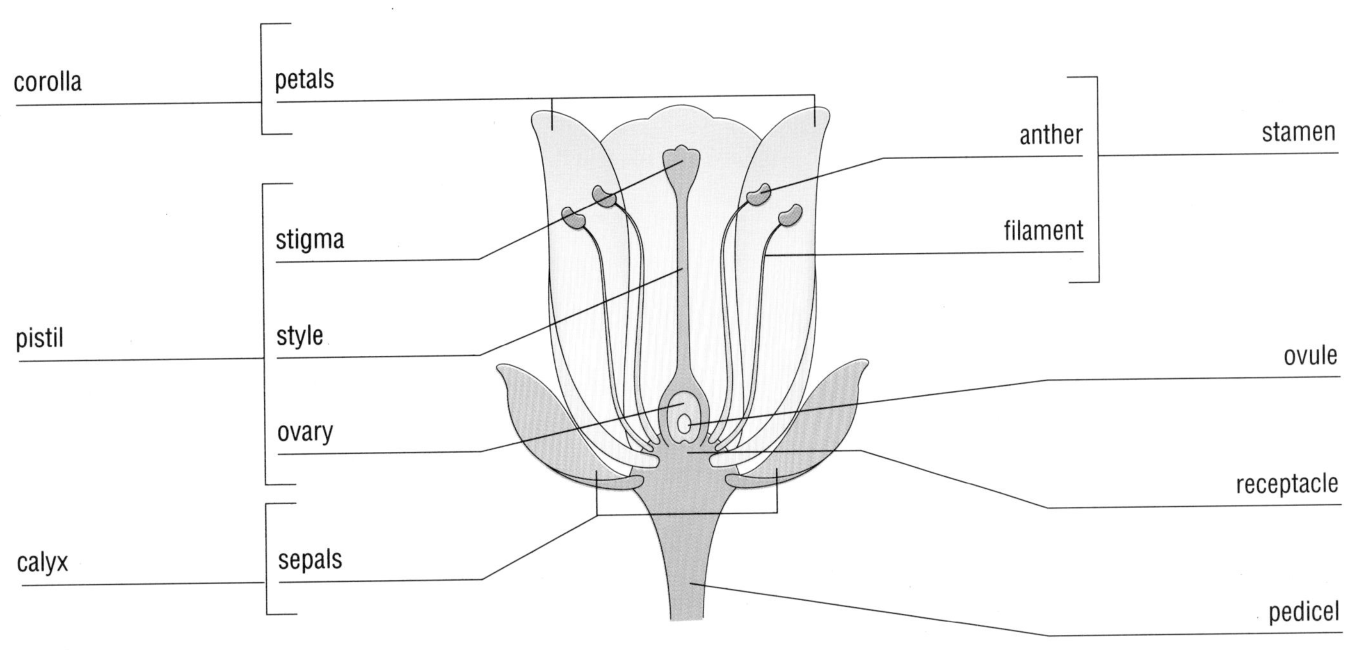

corolla

petals

anther

stamen

filament

pistil

stigma

style

ovule

ovary

receptacle

calyx

sepals

pedicel

VEGETABLE KINGDOM

parts of a tree

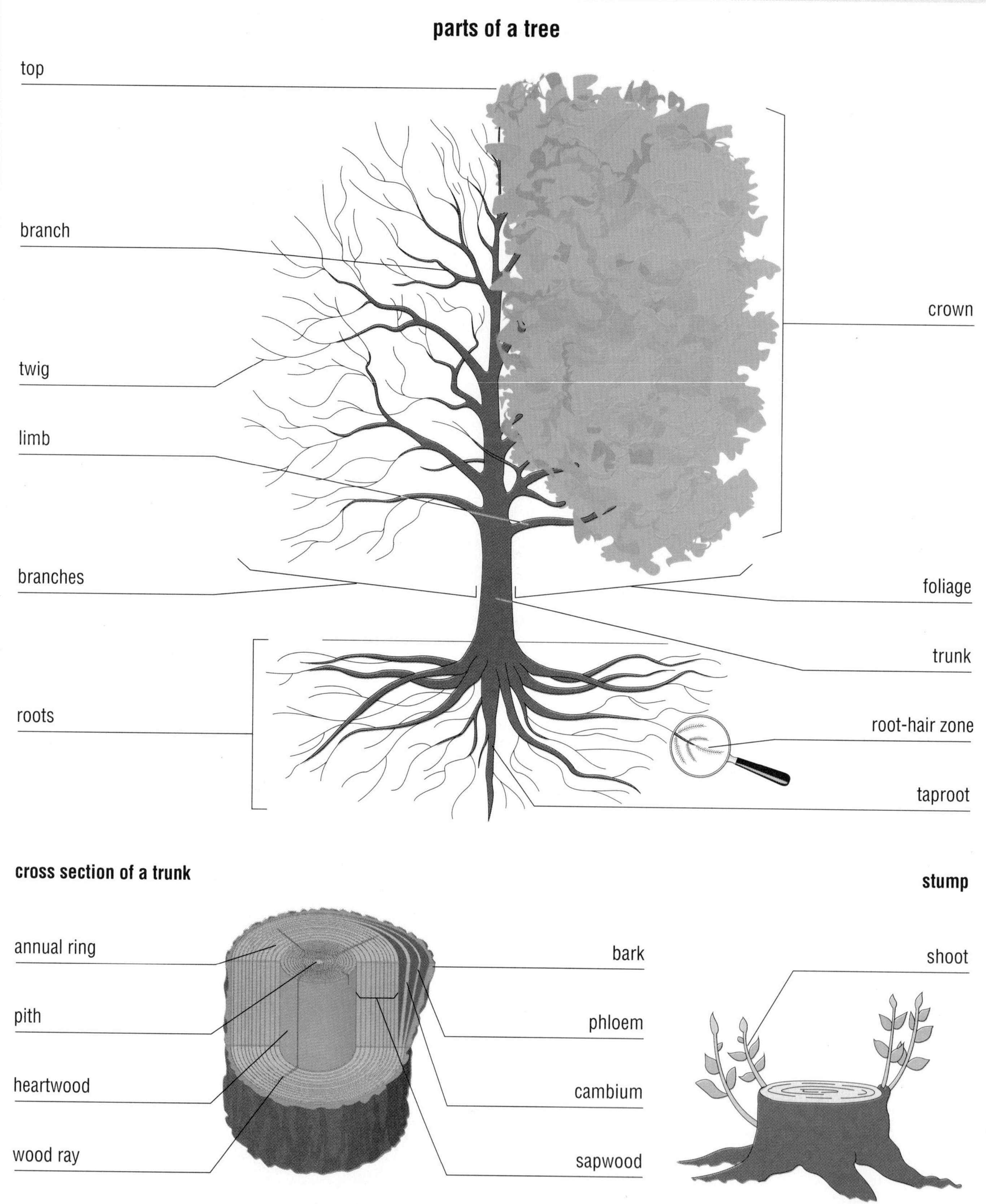

top

branch

twig

limb

branches

roots

crown

foliage

trunk

root-hair zone

taproot

cross section of a trunk

annual ring

pith

heartwood

wood ray

bark

phloem

cambium

sapwood

stump

shoot

parts of a mushroom

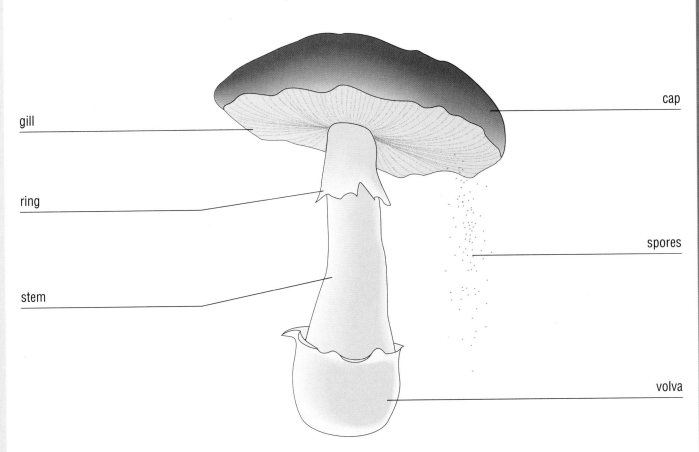

cap

gill

ring

spores

stem

volva

edible mushroom

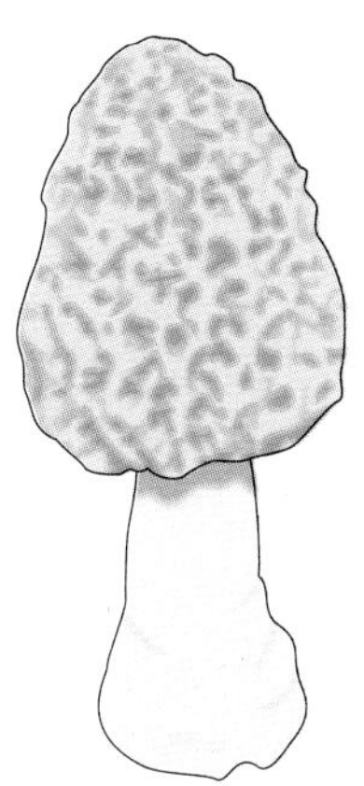

morel

poisonous mushroom

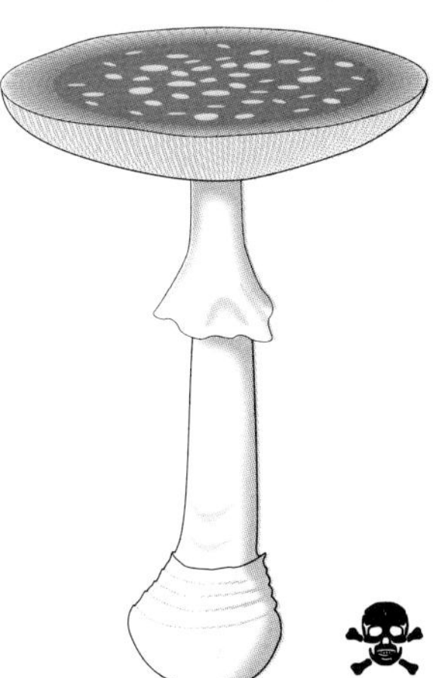

fly agaric

deadly poisonous mushroom

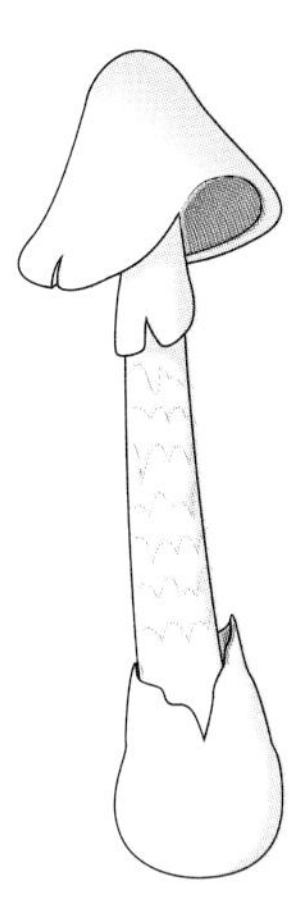

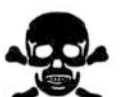

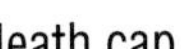

death cap

horse

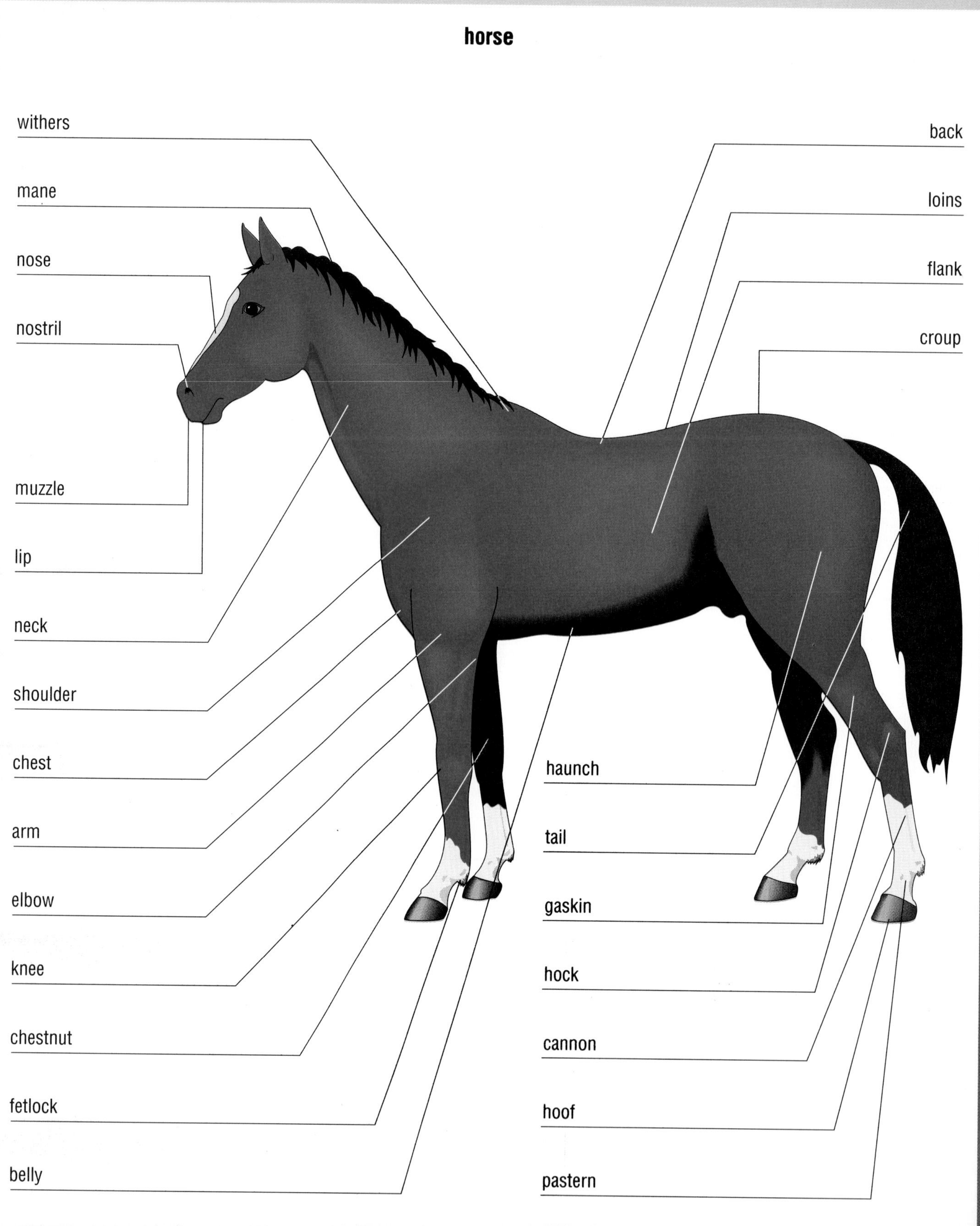

withers

mane

nose

nostril

muzzle

lip

neck

shoulder

chest

arm

elbow

knee

chestnut

fetlock

belly

haunch

tail

gaskin

hock

cannon

hoof

pastern

back

loins

flank

croup

dog

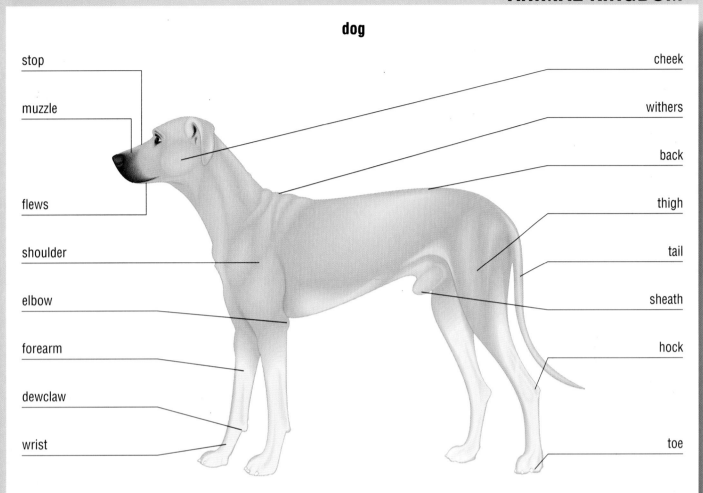

stop

muzzle

flews

shoulder

elbow

forearm

dewclaw

wrist

cheek

withers

back

thigh

tail

sheath

hock

toe

cat

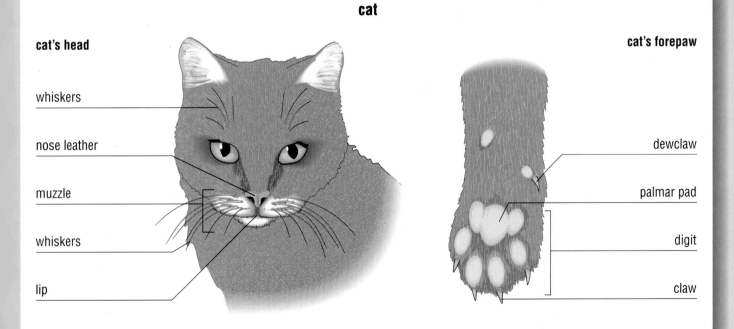

cat's head

whiskers

nose leather

muzzle

whiskers

lip

cat's forepaw

dewclaw

palmar pad

digit

claw

bird

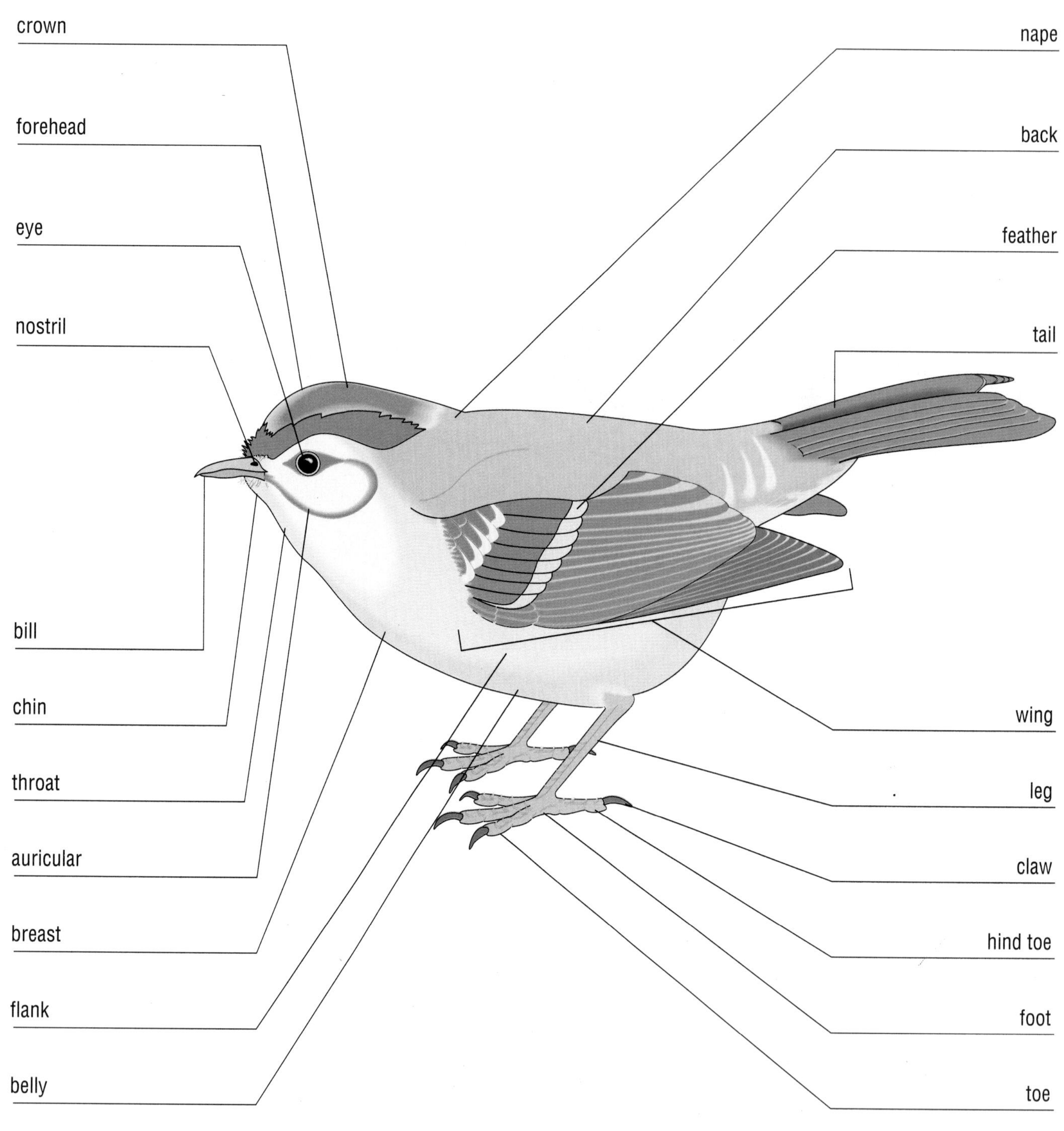

crown

forehead

eye

nostril

bill

chin

throat

auricular

breast

flank

belly

nape

back

feather

tail

wing

leg

claw

hind toe

foot

toe

major types of bills

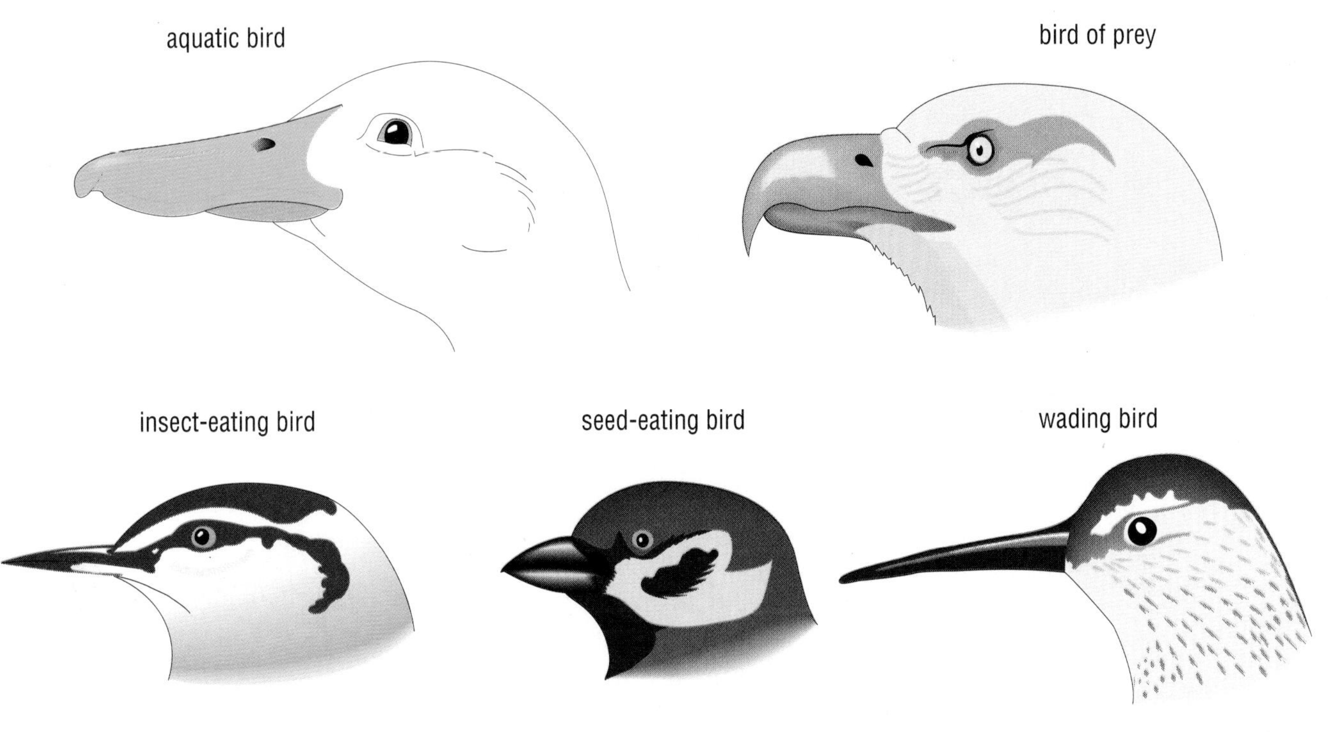

aquatic bird

bird of prey

insect-eating bird

seed-eating bird

wading bird

major types of feet

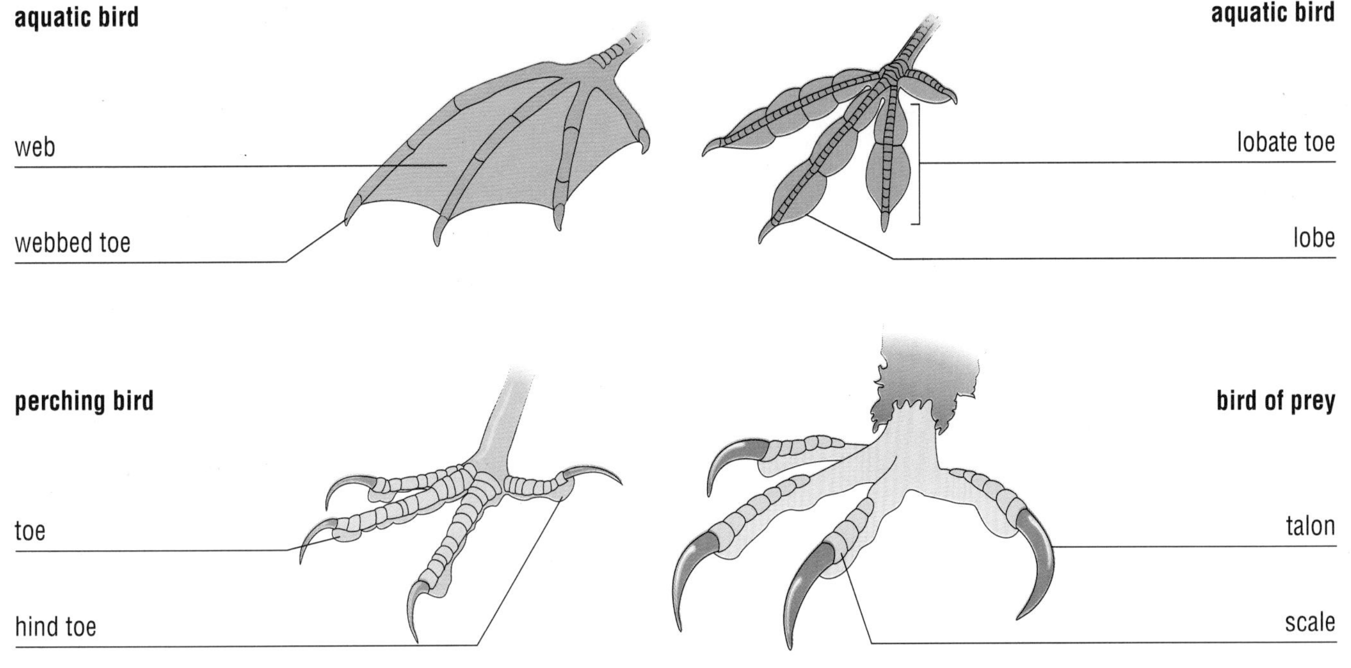

aquatic bird

web

webbed toe

aquatic bird

lobate toe

lobe

perching bird

toe

hind toe

bird of prey

talon

scale

ANIMAL KINGDOM

butterfly

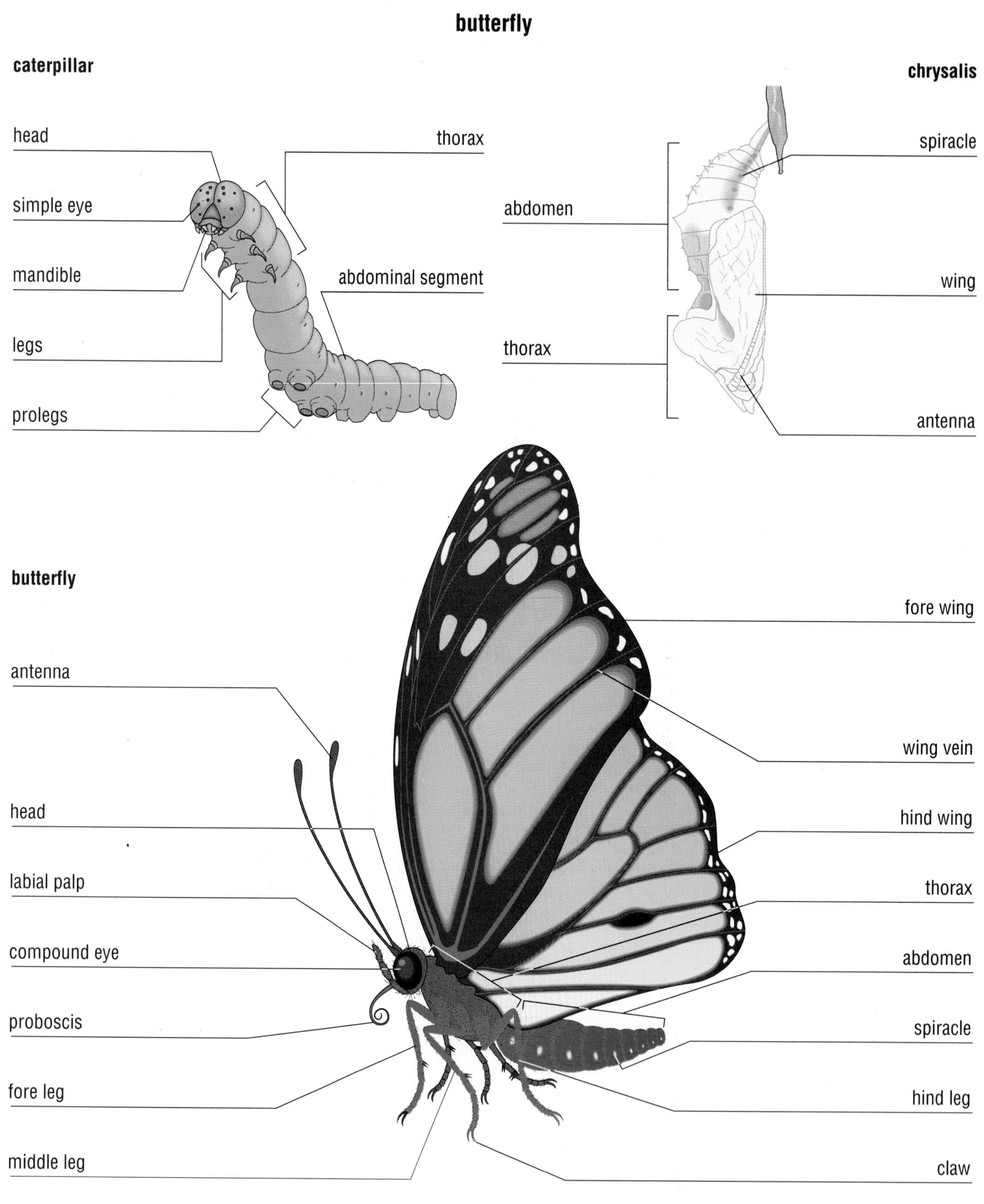

caterpillar

head

simple eye

mandible

legs

prolegs

thorax

abdominal segment

chrysalis

spiracle

abdomen

wing

thorax

antenna

butterfly

antenna

head

labial palp

compound eye

proboscis

fore leg

middle leg

fore wing

wing vein

hind wing

thorax

abdomen

spiracle

hind leg

claw

honeybee

hind wing

abdomen

pollen basket

hind leg

sting

middle leg

fore wing

head

simple eye

antenna

compound eye

mandible

fore leg

hive

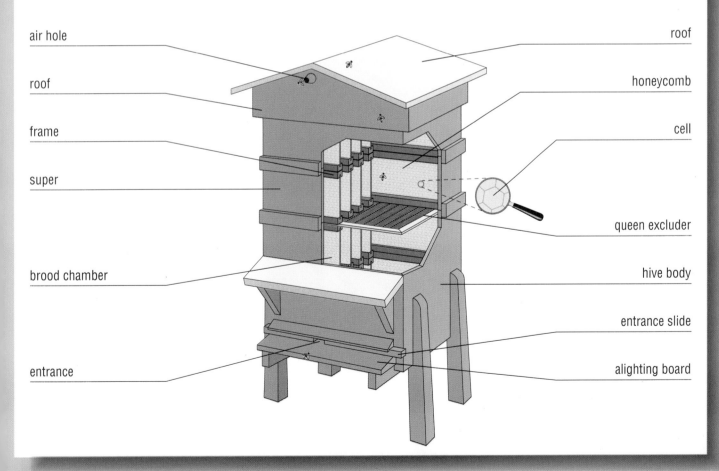

air hole

roof

frame

super

brood chamber

entrance

roof

honeycomb

cell

queen excluder

hive body

entrance slide

alighting board

ANIMAL KINGDOM

gastropod: snail

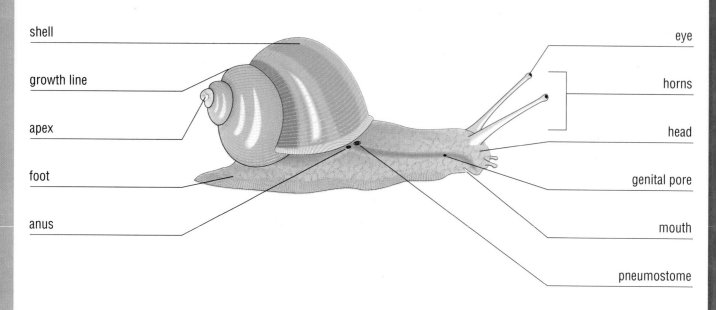

shell

growth line

apex

foot

anus

eye

horns

head

genital pore

mouth

pneumostome

crustacean: lobster

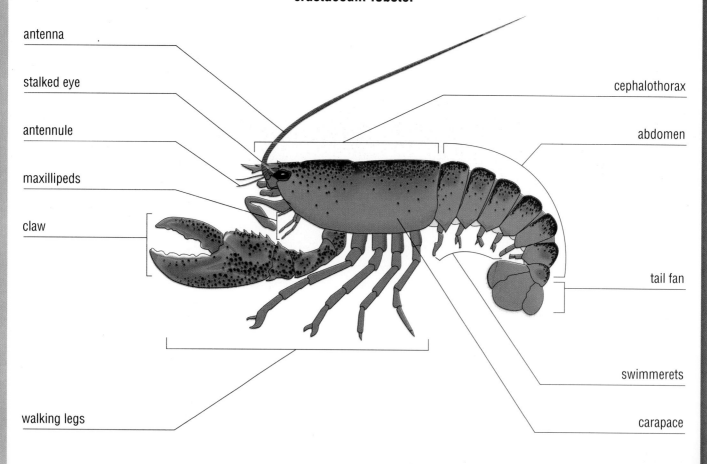

antenna

stalked eye

antennule

maxillipeds

claw

cephalothorax

abdomen

tail fan

swimmerets

walking legs

carapace

amphibian: frog

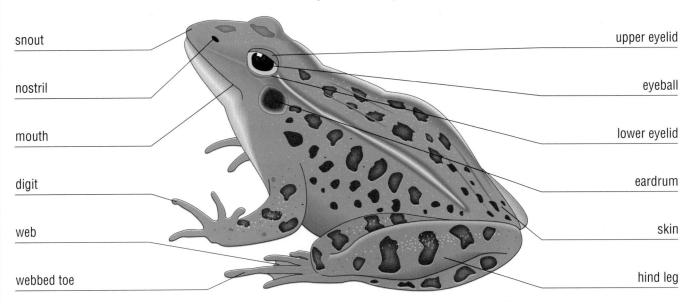

snout

nostril

mouth

digit

web

webbed toe

upper eyelid

eyeball

lower eyelid

eardrum

skin

hind leg

fish

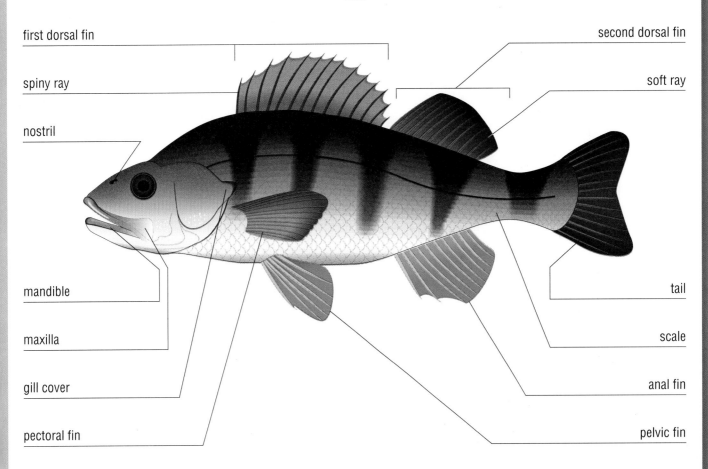

first dorsal fin

spiny ray

nostril

mandible

maxilla

gill cover

pectoral fin

second dorsal fin

soft ray

tail

scale

anal fin

pelvic fin

ANIMAL KINGDOM

turtle

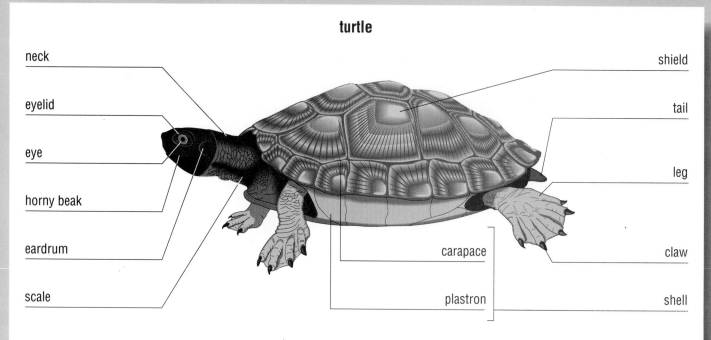

neck

eyelid

eye

horny beak

eardrum

scale

shield

tail

leg

claw

shell

carapace

plastron

venomous snake

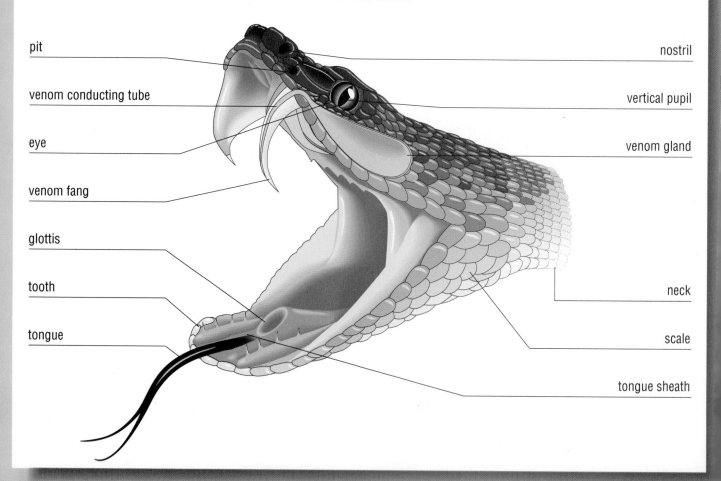

pit

venom conducting tube

eye

venom fang

glottis

tooth

tongue

nostril

vertical pupil

venom gland

neck

scale

tongue sheath

wild animals

lion

rhinoceros

zebra

crocodile

elephant

giraffe

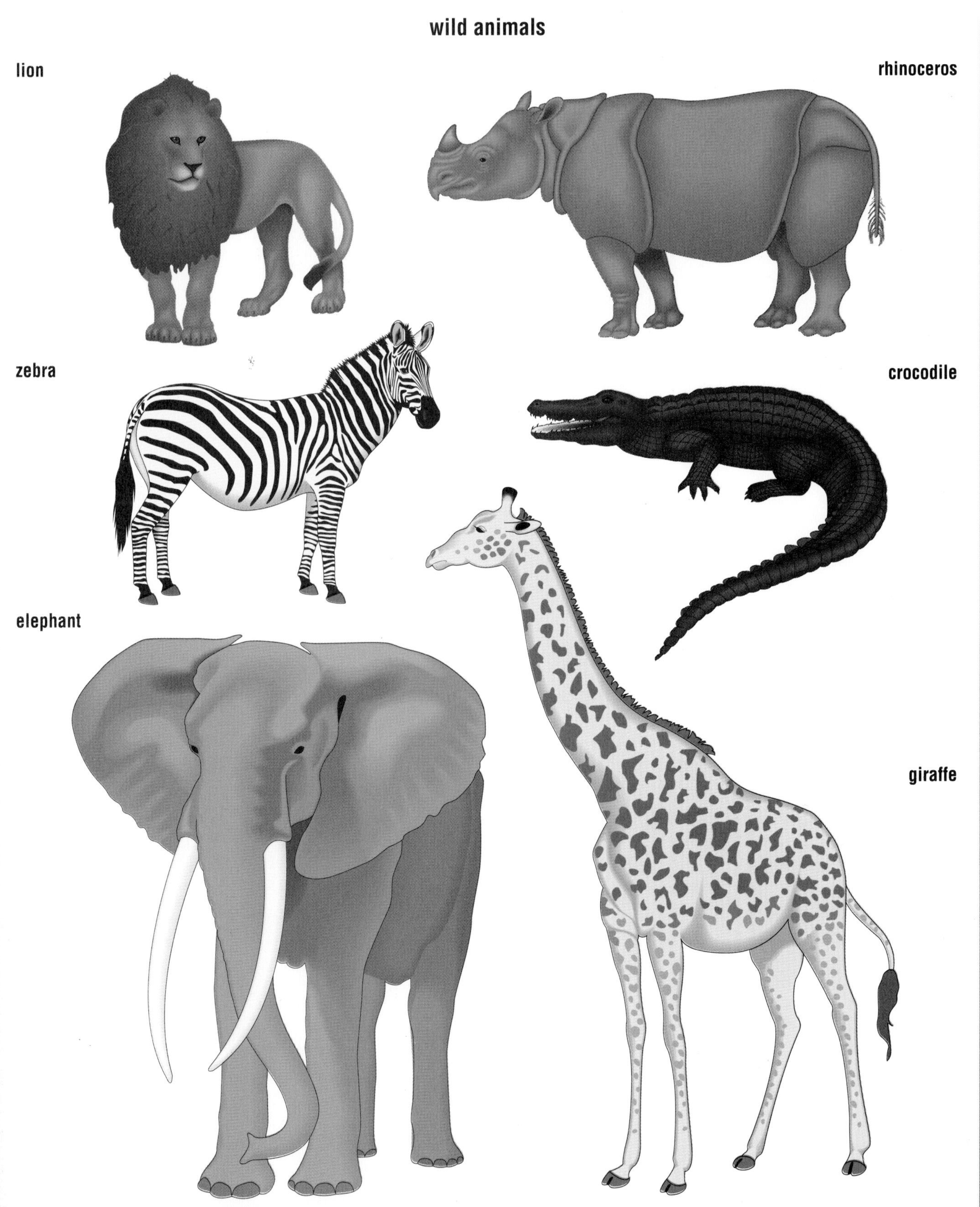

ANIMAL KINGDOM

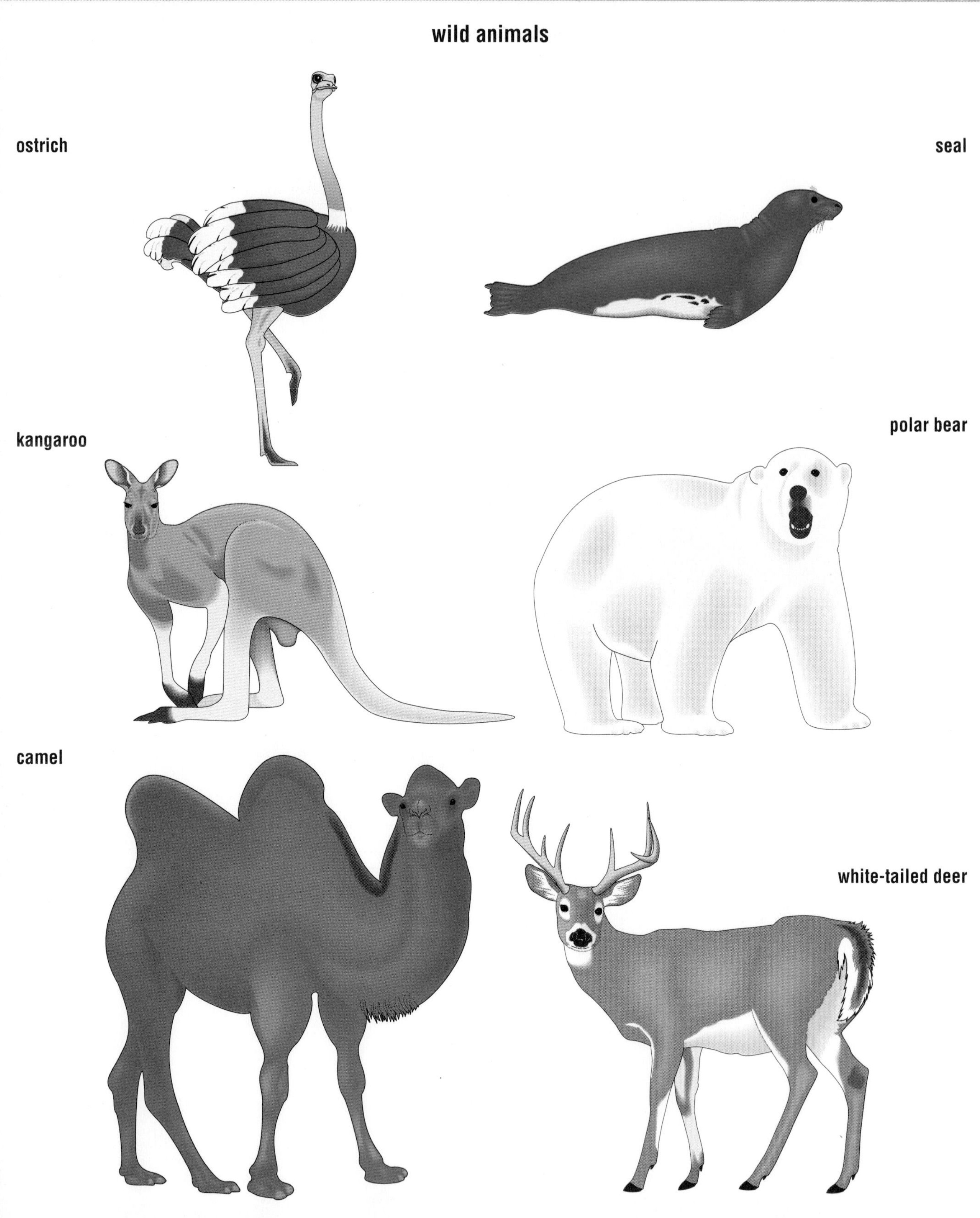

wild animals

ostrich

seal

kangaroo

polar bear

camel

white-tailed deer

body, front view

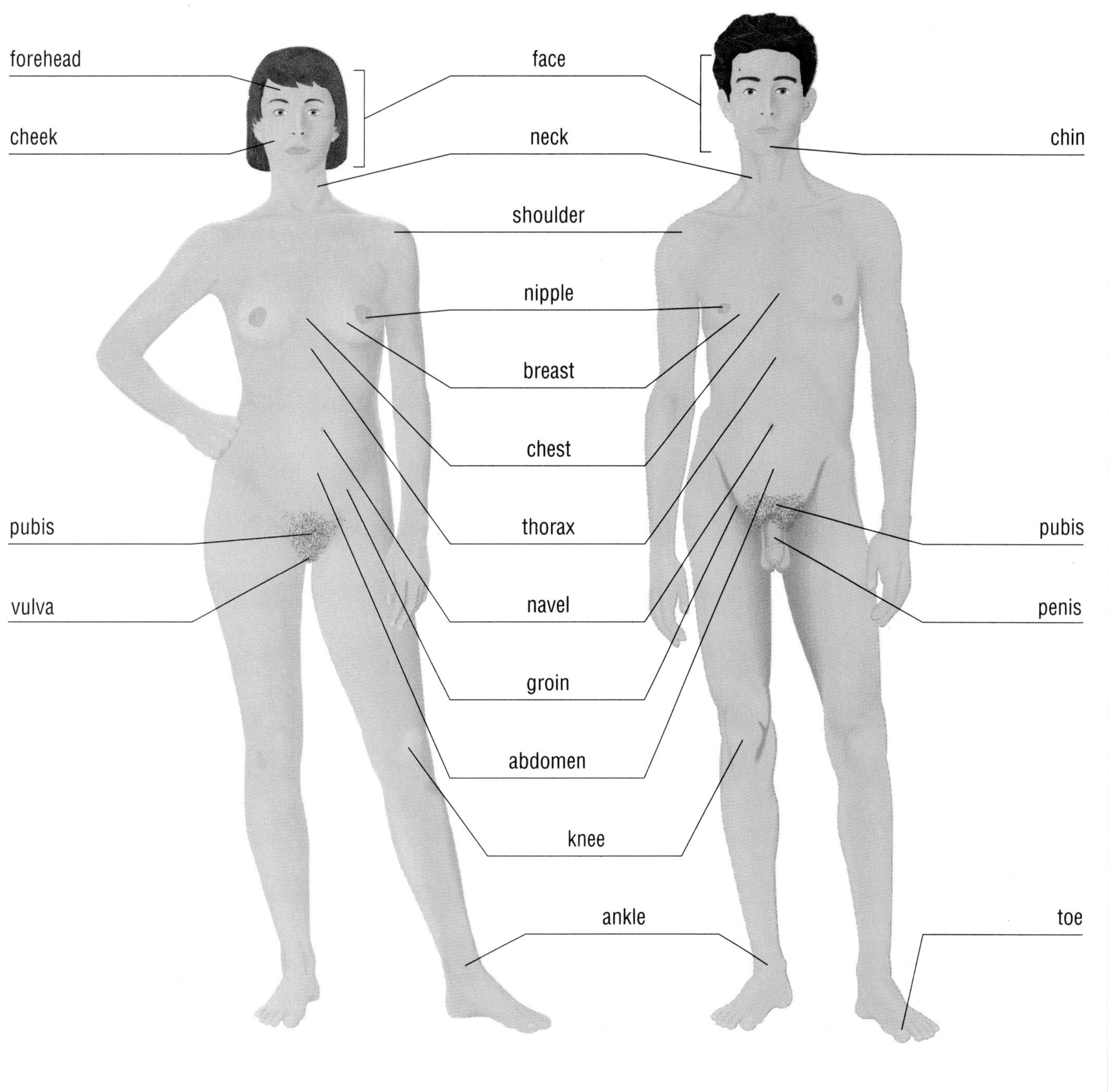

forehead

face

cheek

neck

chin

shoulder

nipple

breast

chest

thorax

pubis

pubis

vulva

penis

navel

groin

abdomen

knee

ankle

toe

body, rear view

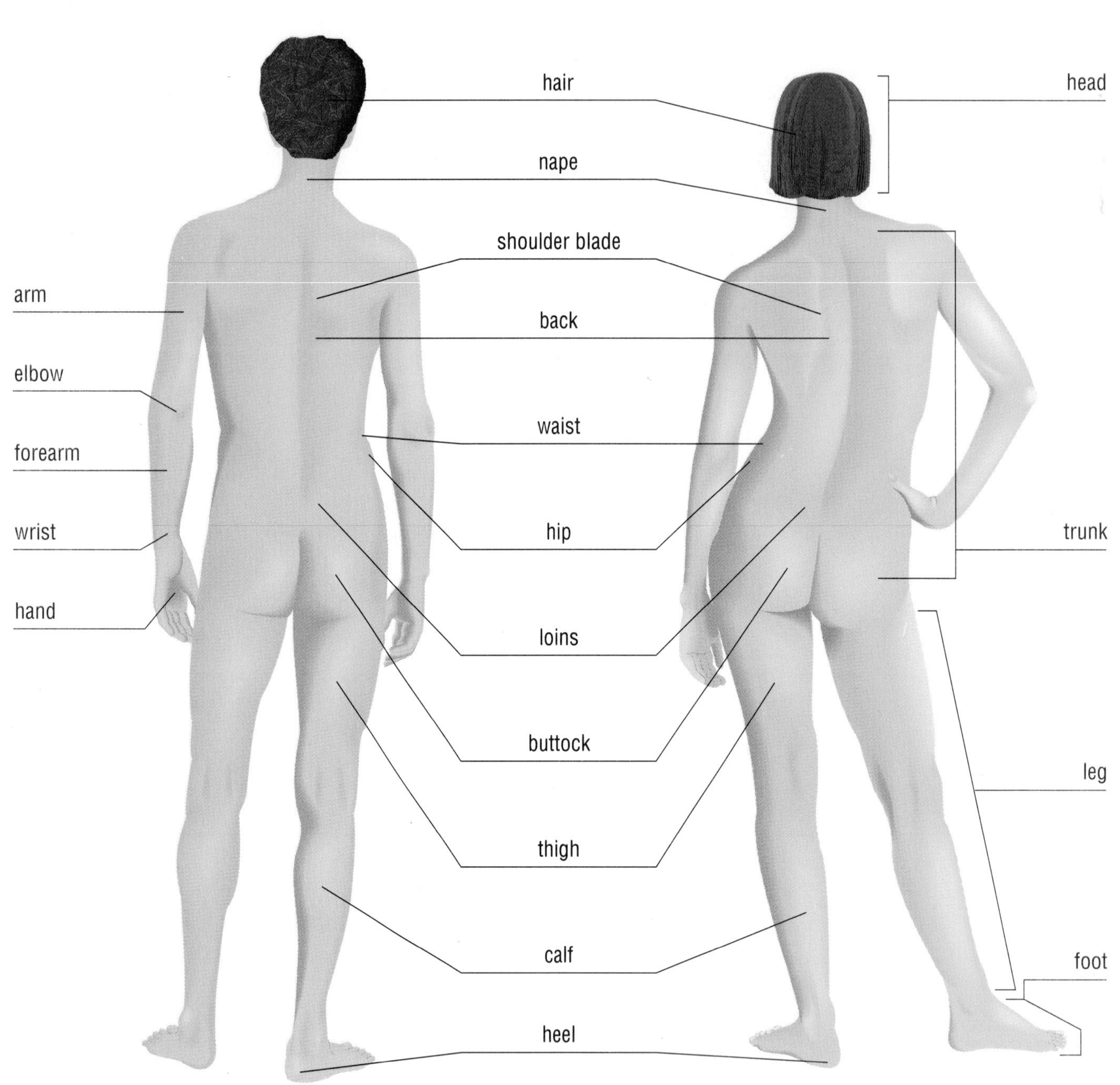

hair

nape

head

shoulder blade

back

arm

elbow

forearm

waist

wrist

hip

hand

trunk

loins

buttock

leg

thigh

calf

foot

heel

skeleton

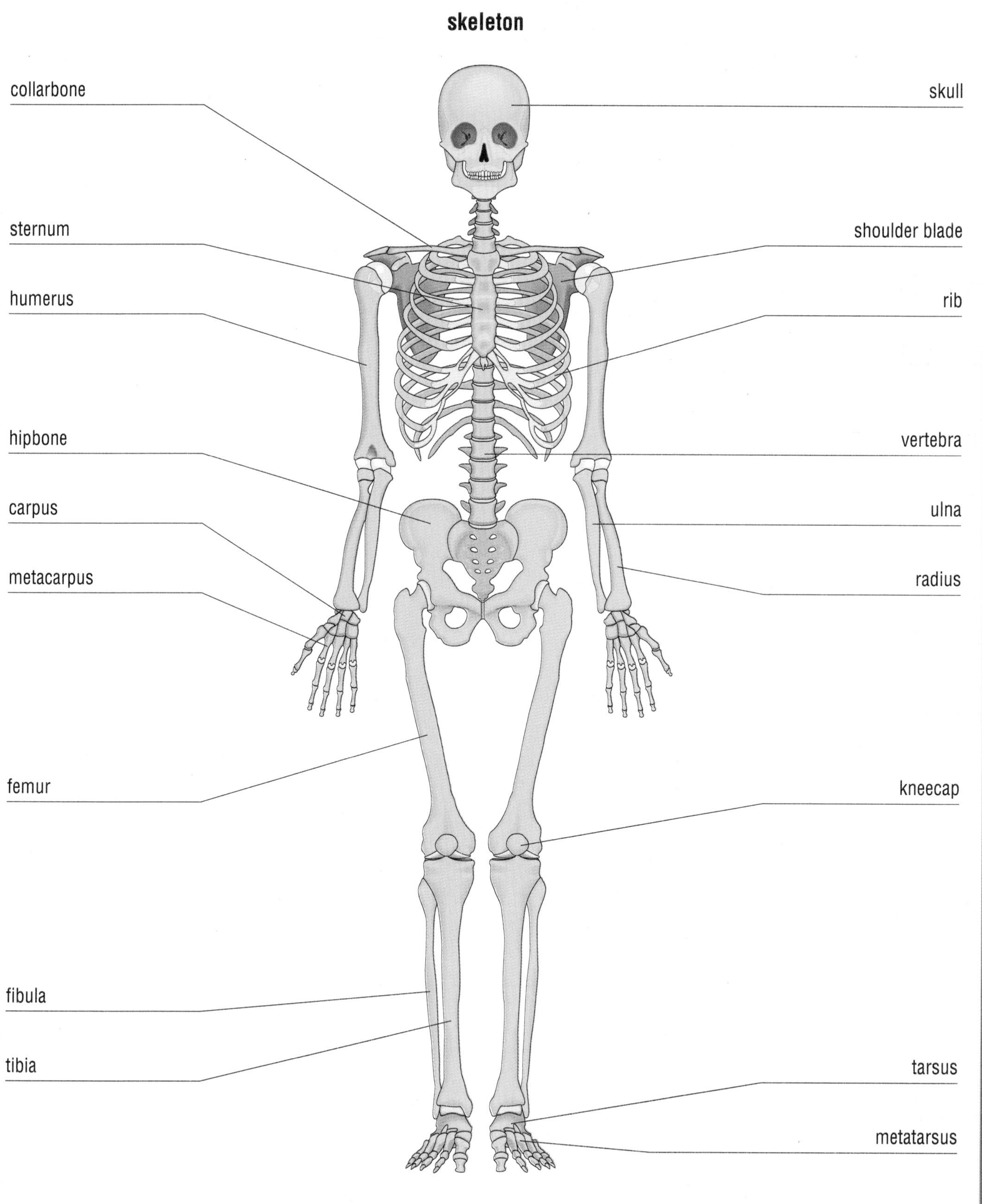

collarbone

sternum

humerus

hipbone

carpus

metacarpus

femur

fibula

tibia

skull

shoulder blade

rib

vertebra

ulna

radius

kneecap

tarsus

metatarsus

HUMAN BODY

human denture

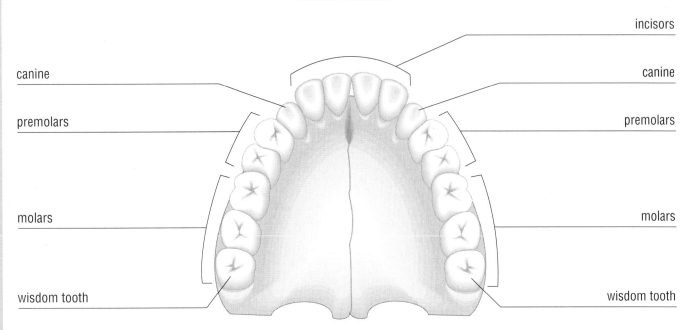

incisors

canine

canine

premolars

premolars

molars

molars

wisdom tooth

wisdom tooth

mouth: the organ of taste

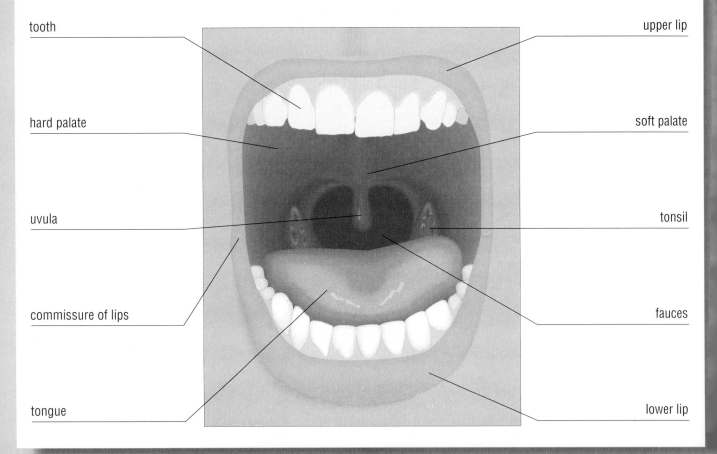

tooth

upper lip

hard palate

soft palate

uvula

tonsil

commissure of lips

fauces

tongue

lower lip

eye: the organ of sight

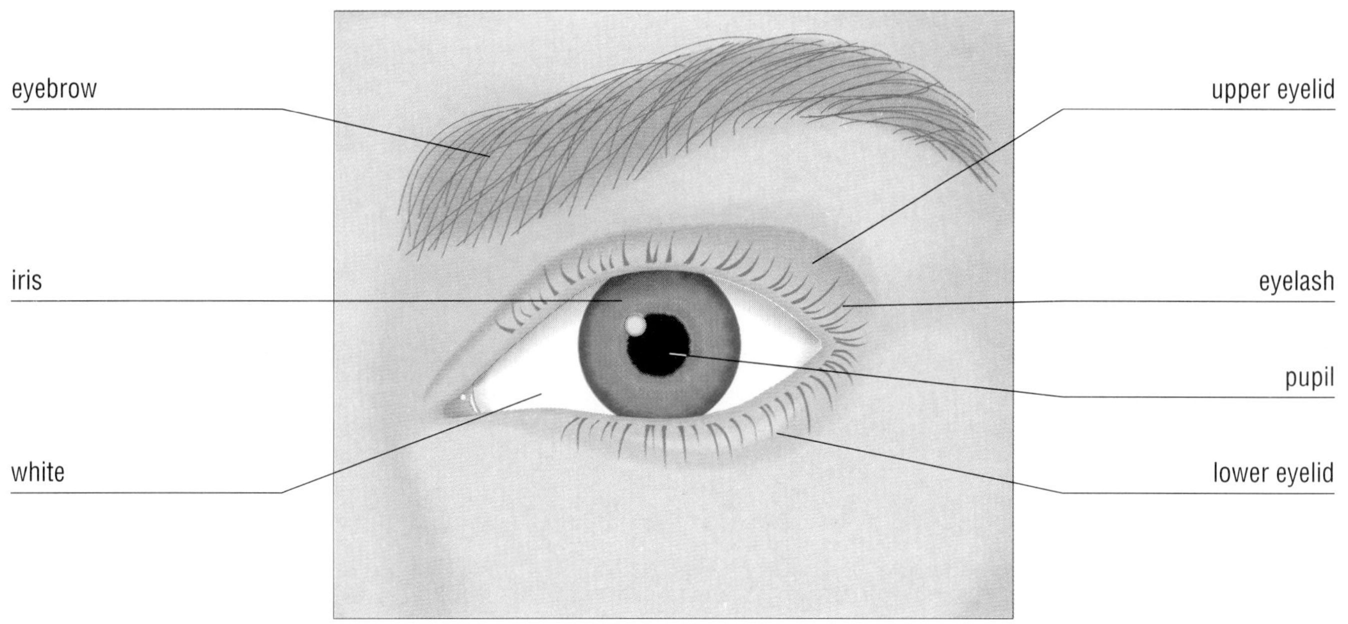

eyebrow

upper eyelid

iris

eyelash

pupil

white

lower eyelid

ear: the organ of hearing

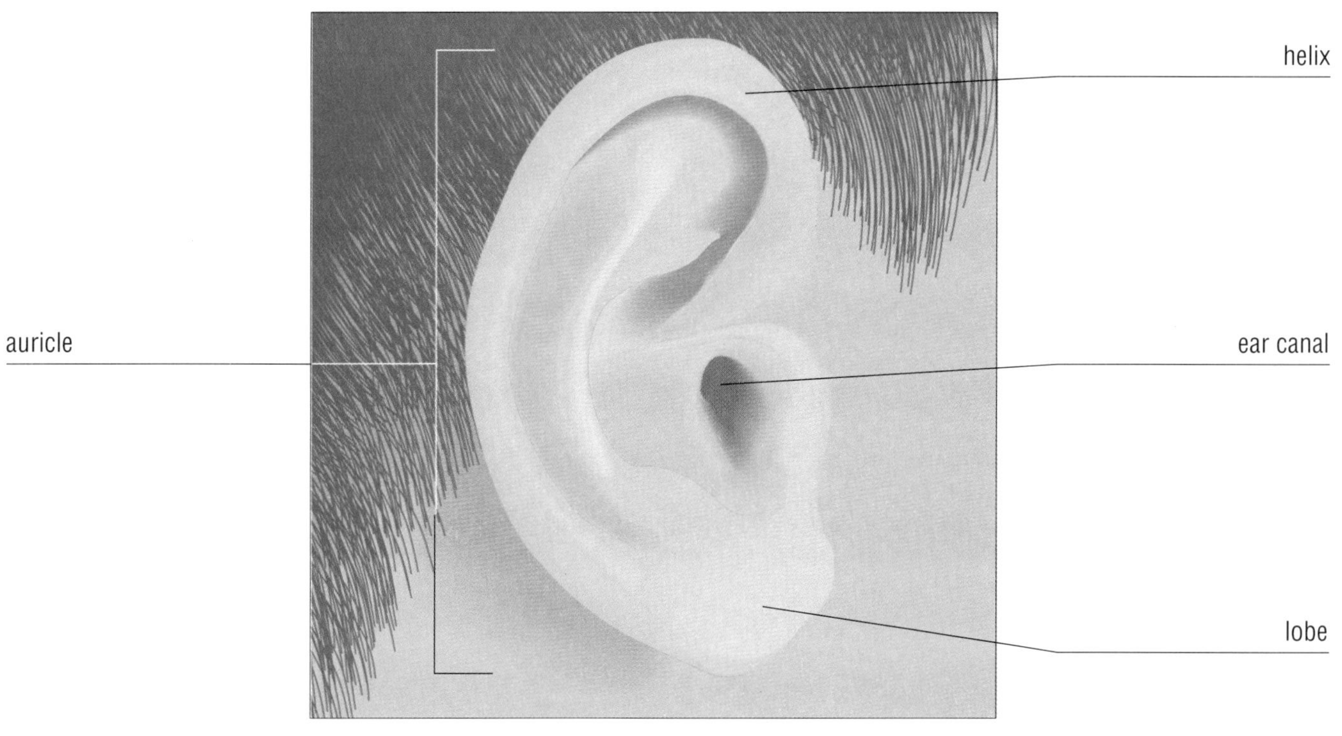

helix

auricle

ear canal

lobe

HUMAN BODY

nose: the organ of smell

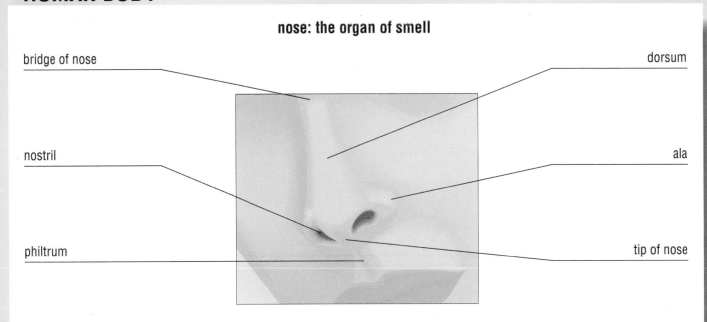

bridge of nose

dorsum

nostril

ala

philtrum

tip of nose

hand: the organ of touch

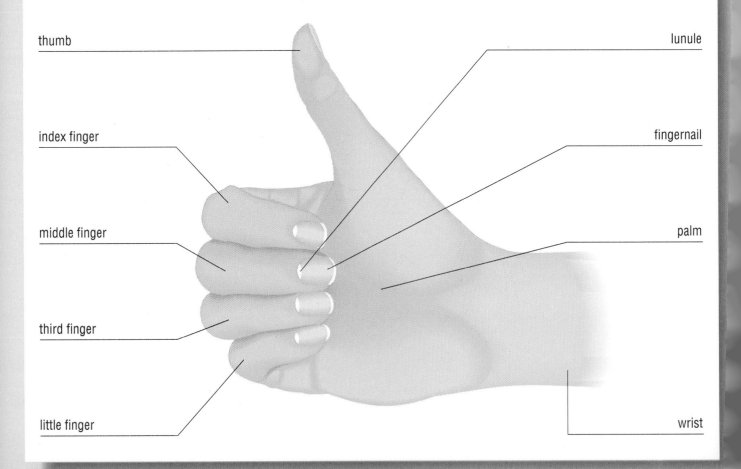

thumb

lunule

index finger

fingernail

middle finger

palm

third finger

little finger

wrist

bread

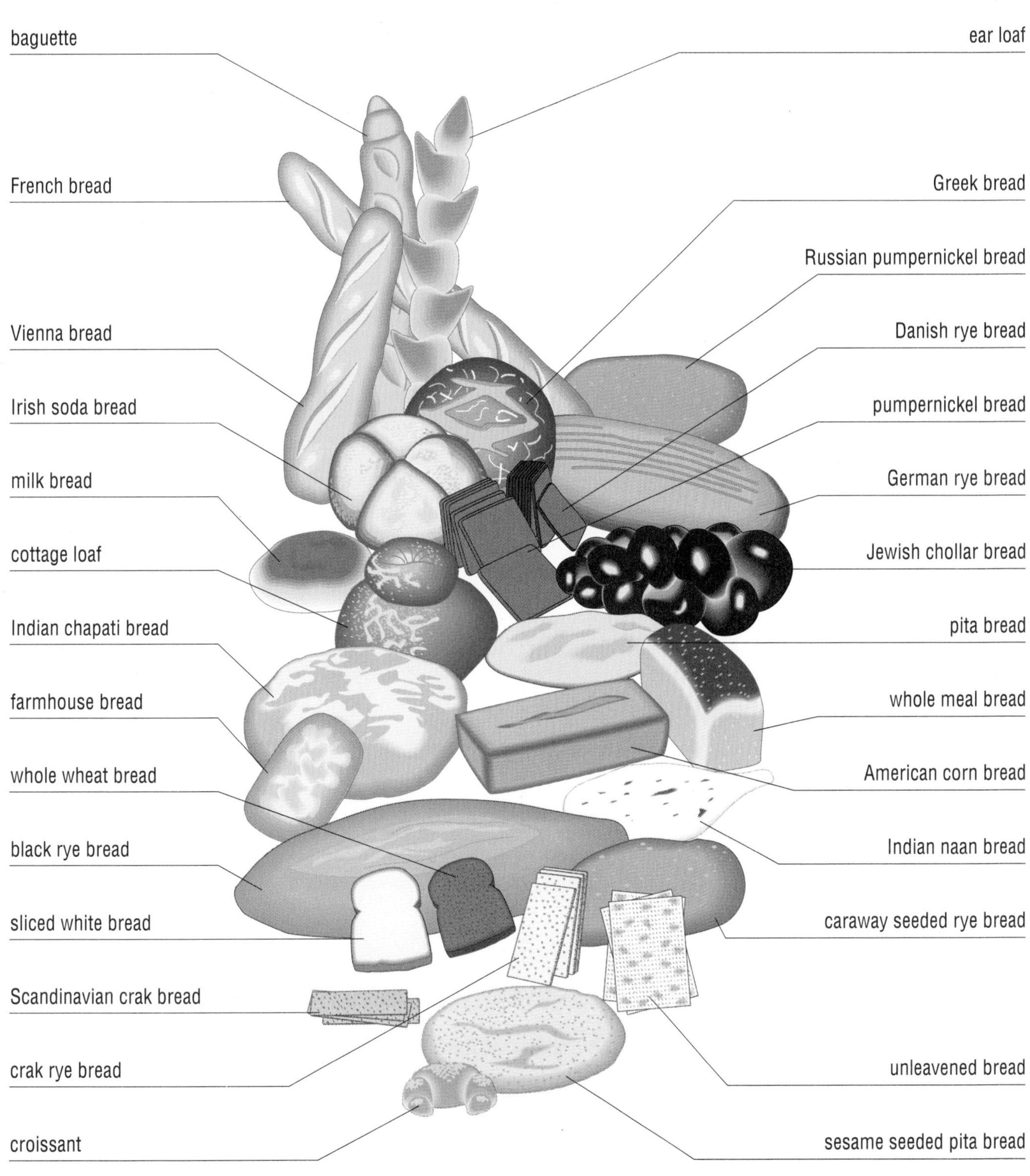

baguette

ear loaf

French bread

Greek bread

Russian pumpernickel bread

Vienna bread

Danish rye bread

Irish soda bread

pumpernickel bread

milk bread

German rye bread

cottage loaf

Jewish chollar bread

Indian chapati bread

pita bread

farmhouse bread

whole meal bread

whole wheat bread

American corn bread

black rye bread

Indian naan bread

sliced white bread

caraway seeded rye bread

Scandinavian crak bread

crak rye bread

unleavened bread

croissant

sesame seeded pita bread

leaf vegetables

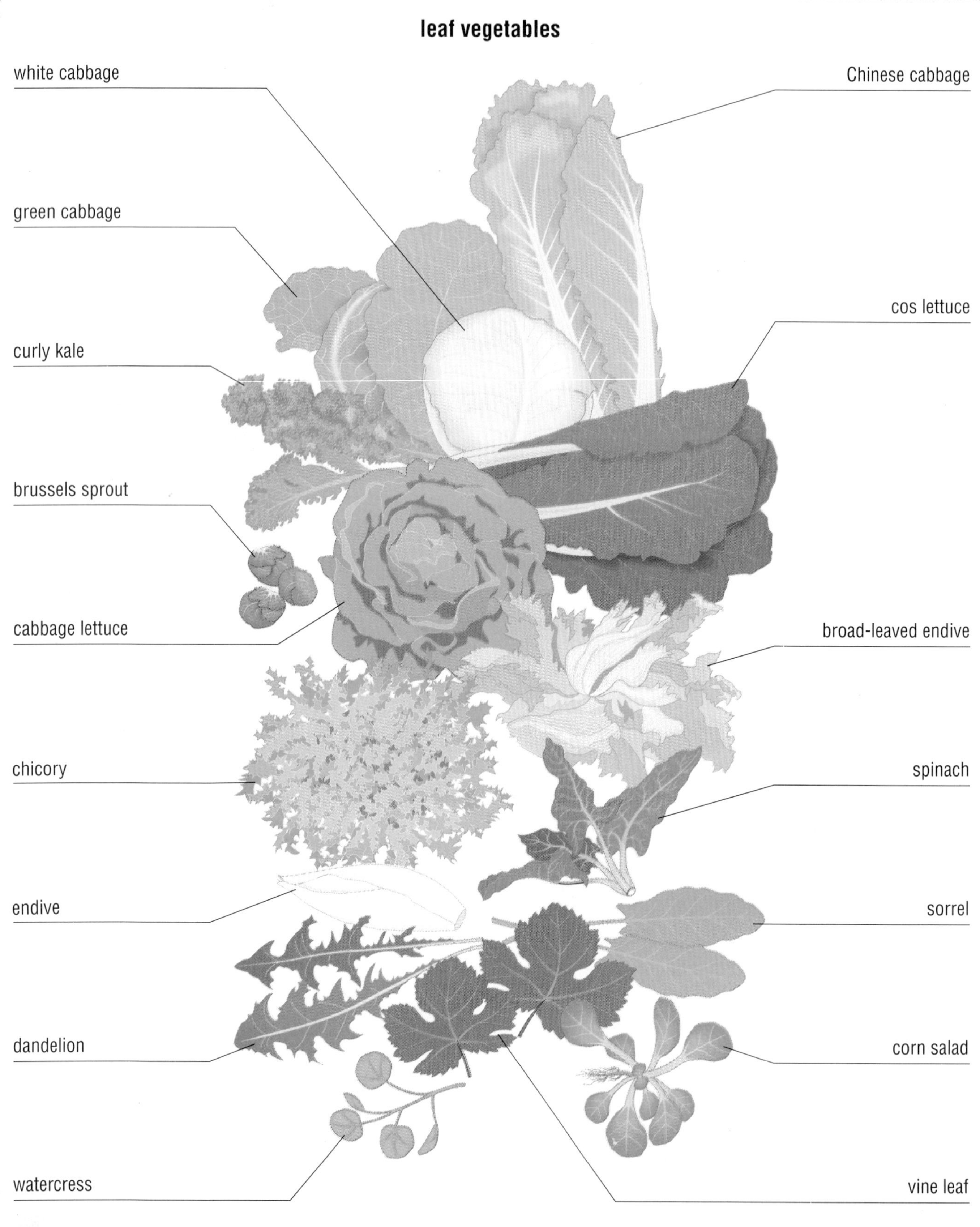

white cabbage

green cabbage

curly kale

brussels sprout

cabbage lettuce

chicory

endive

dandelion

watercress

Chinese cabbage

cos lettuce

broad-leaved endive

spinach

sorrel

corn salad

vine leaf

stalk vegetables

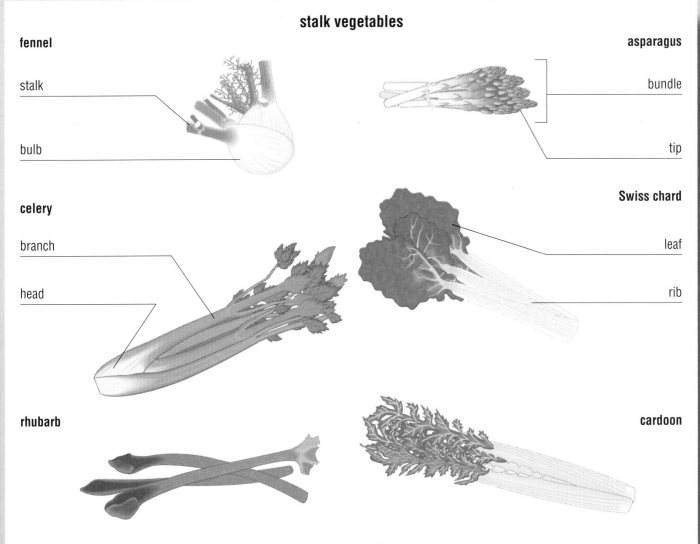

fennel

stalk

bulb

asparagus

bundle

tip

celery

branch

head

Swiss chard

leaf

rib

rhubarb

cardoon

seed vegetables

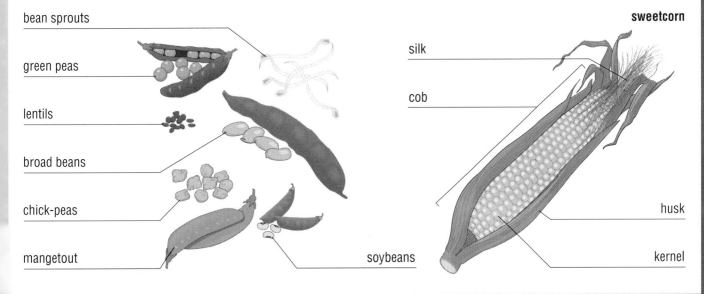

bean sprouts

green peas

lentils

broad beans

chick-peas

mangetout

soybeans

sweetcorn

silk

cob

husk

kernel

tuber vegetables

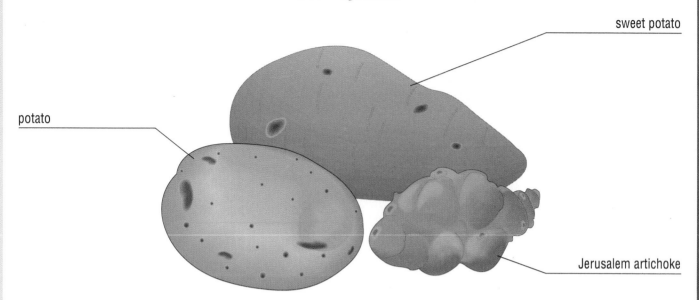

sweet potato

potato

Jerusalem artichoke

root vegetables

kohlrabi

turnip

celeriac

horseradish

beetroot

parsnip

swede

black salsify

radish

carrot

salsify

inflorescent vegetables

cauliflower

broccoli

artichoke

bulb vegetables

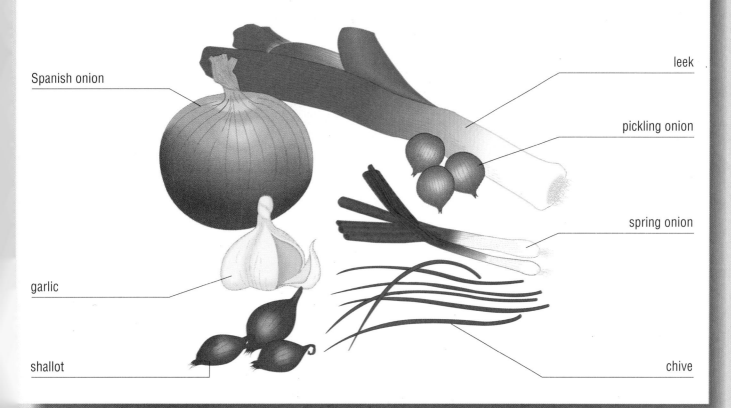

Spanish onion

leek

pickling onion

spring onion

garlic

shallot

chive

fruit vegetables

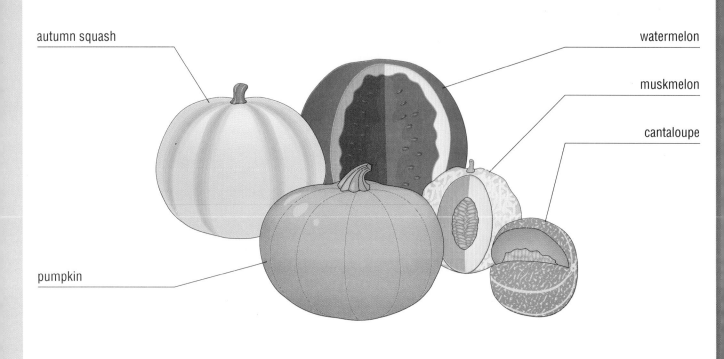

autumn squash

watermelon

muskmelon

cantaloupe

pumpkin

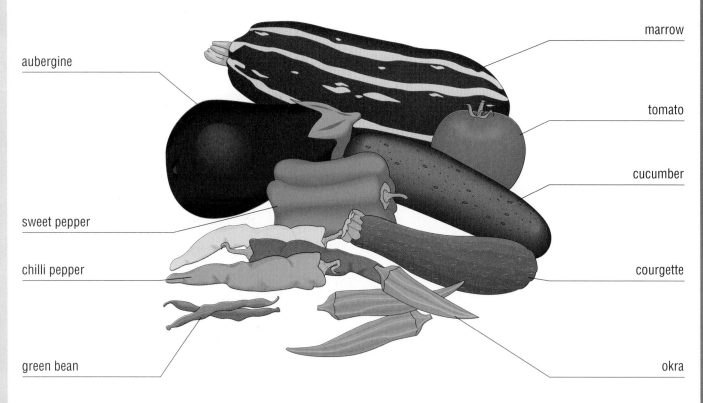

aubergine

marrow

tomato

cucumber

sweet pepper

chilli pepper

courgette

green bean

okra

pome fruits

apple

pear

quince

Japanese plum

stone fruits

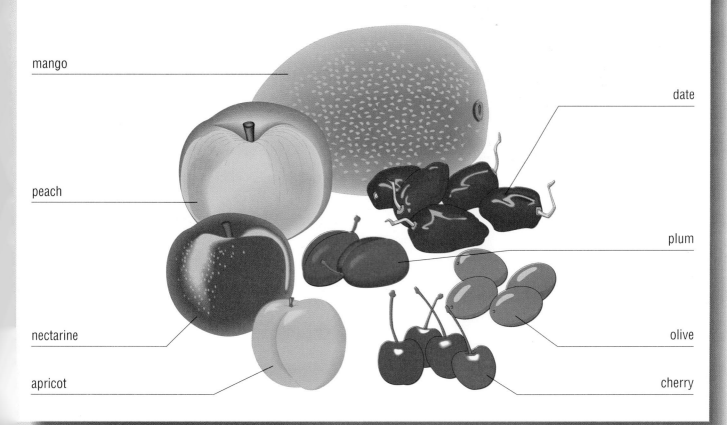

mango

date

peach

plum

nectarine

olive

apricot

cherry

berries

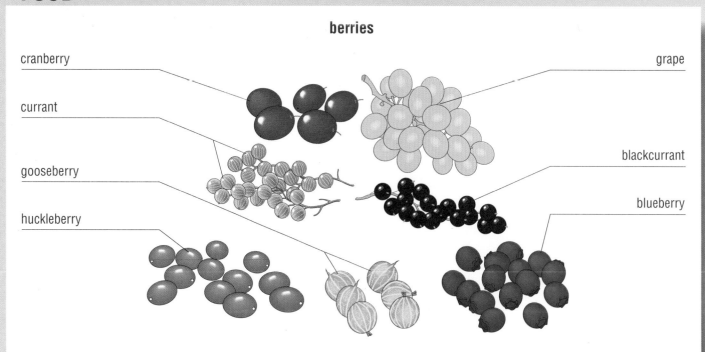

cranberry

currant

gooseberry

huckleberry

grape

blackcurrant

blueberry

citrus fruits

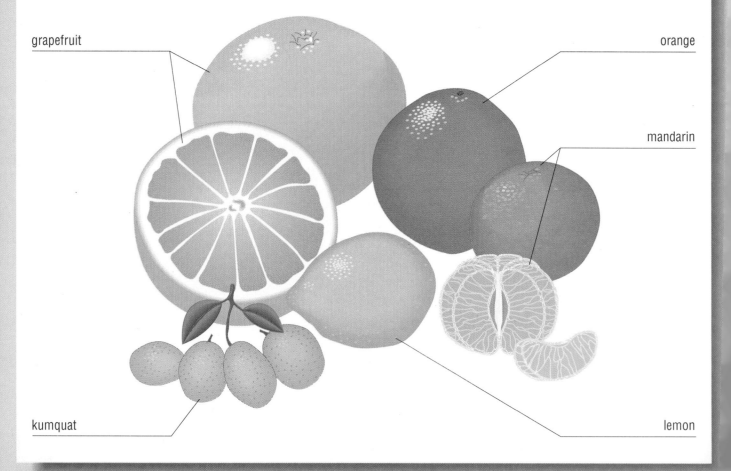

grapefruit

kumquat

orange

mandarin

lemon

tropical fruits

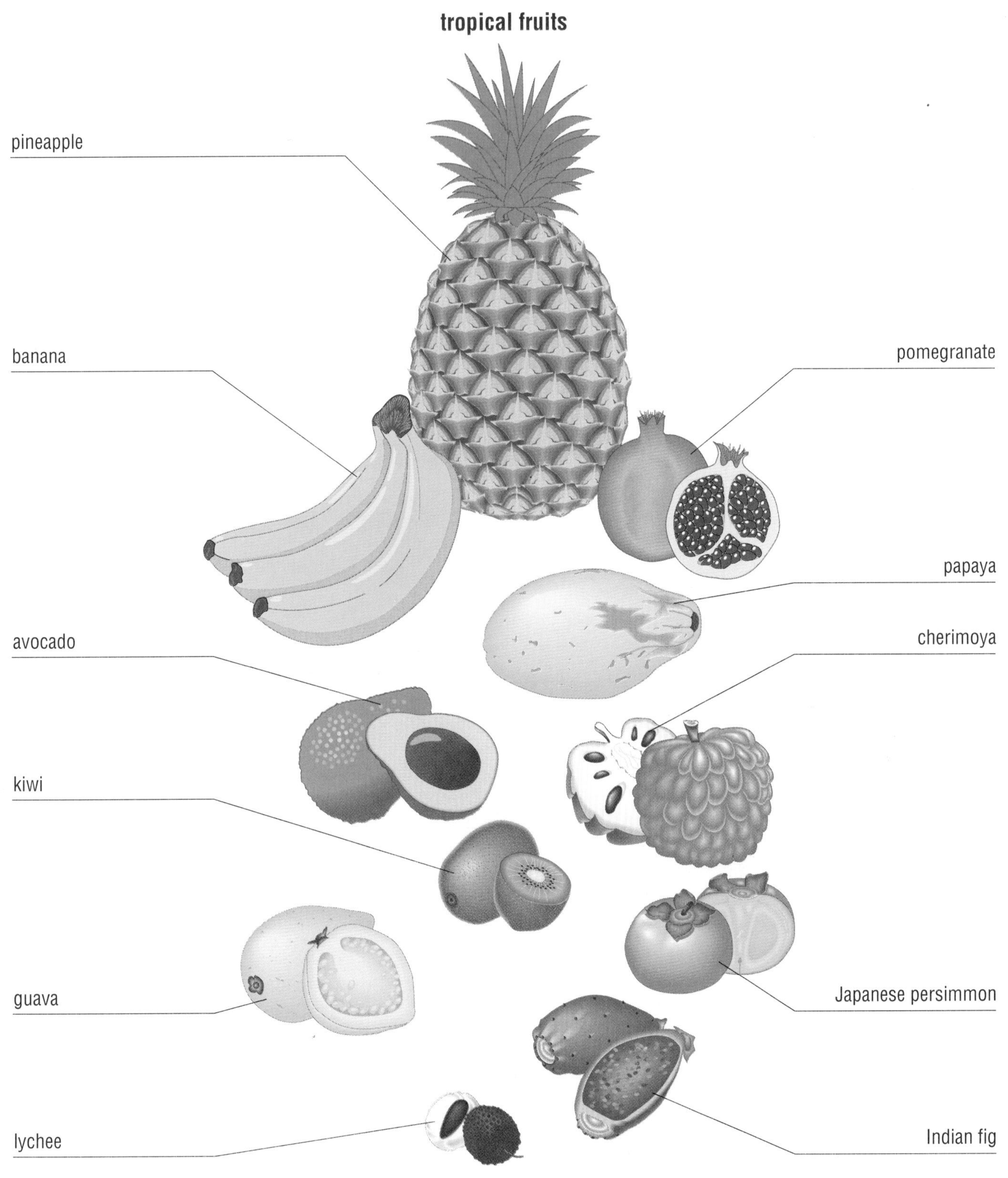

pineapple

banana

pomegranate

papaya

avocado

cherimoya

kiwi

guava

Japanese persimmon

lychee

Indian fig

nuts

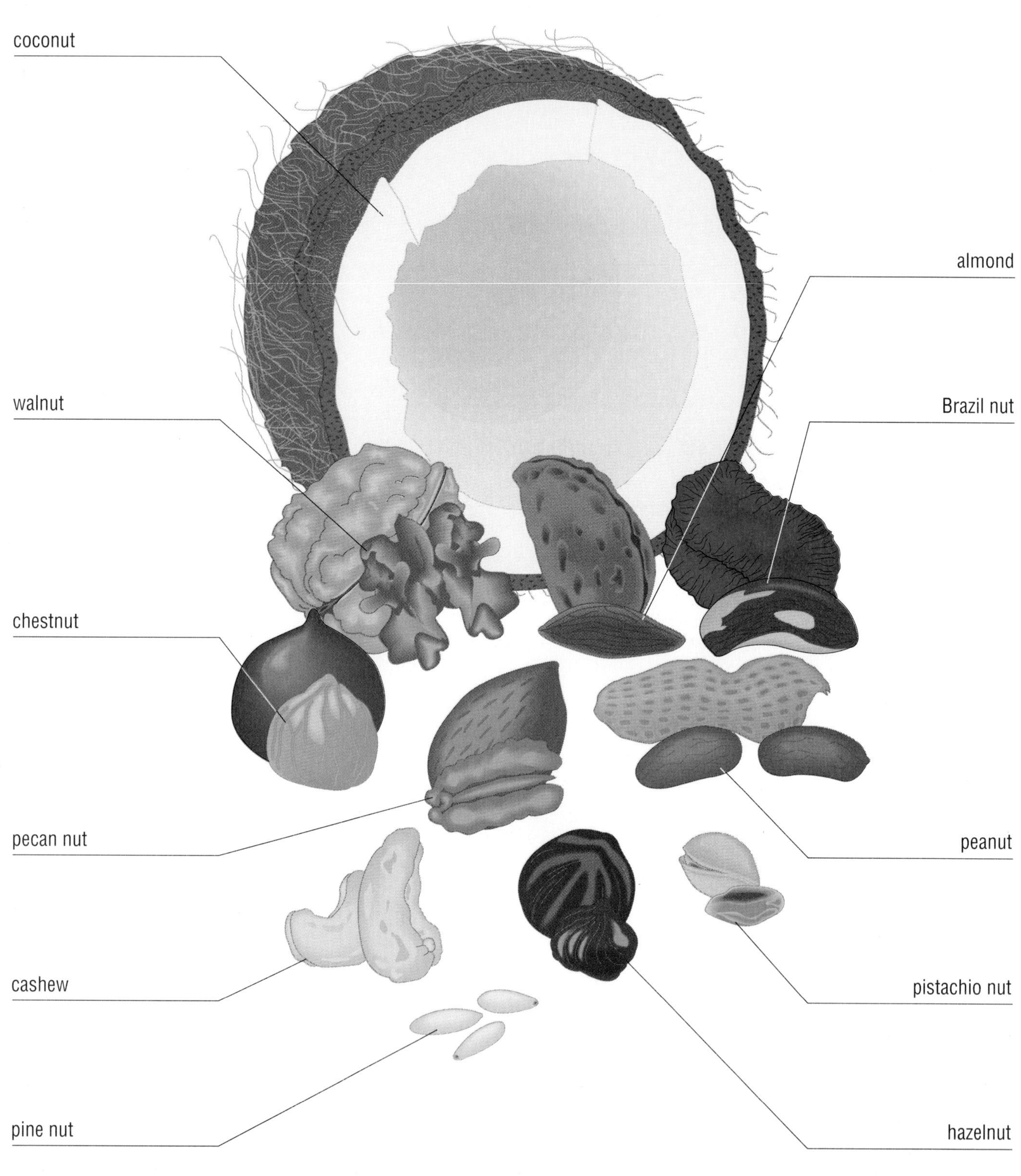

coconut

almond

walnut

Brazil nut

chestnut

pecan nut

peanut

cashew

pistachio nut

pine nut

hazelnut

cheeses

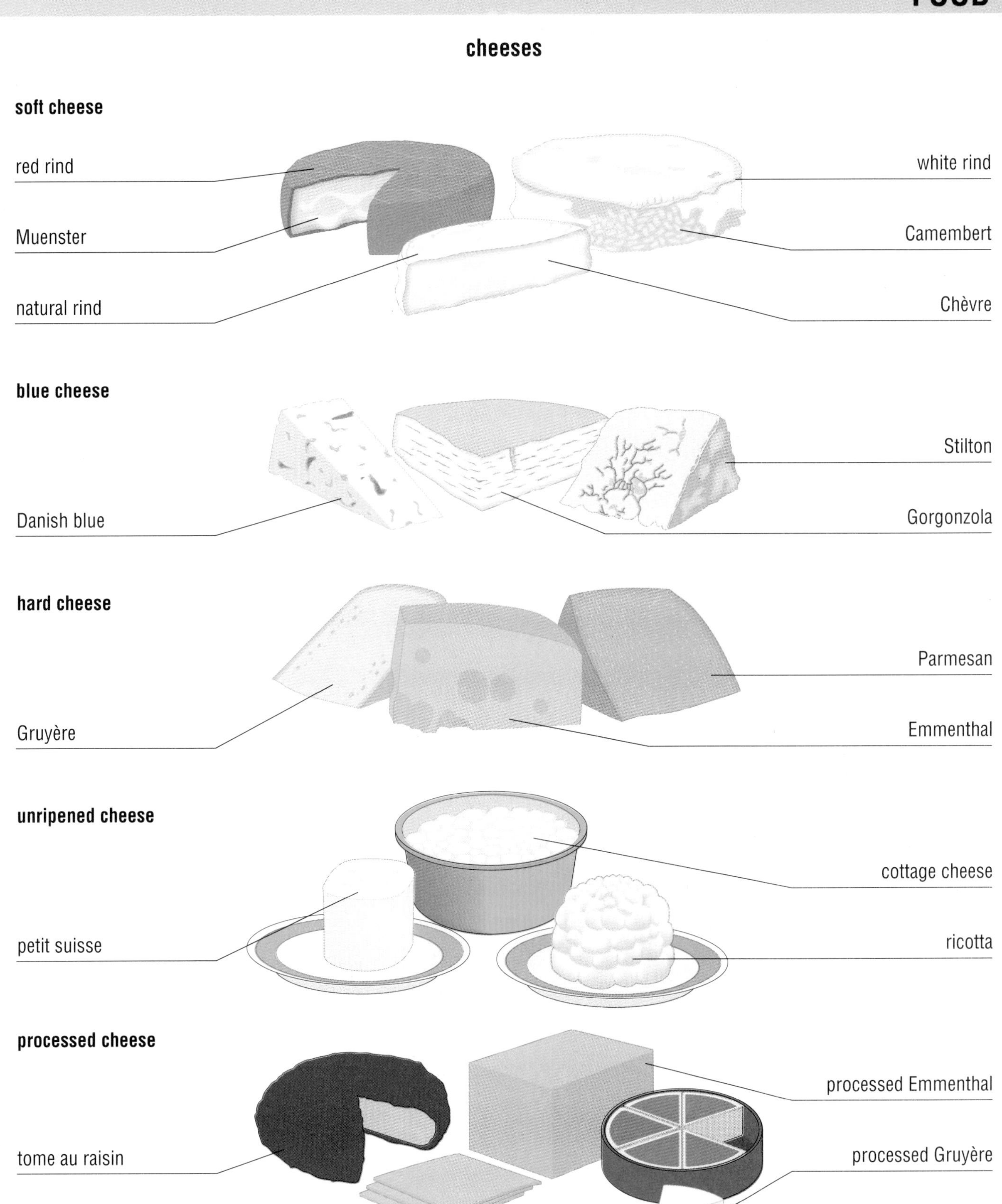

soft cheese

red rind

Muenster

natural rind

white rind

Camembert

Chèvre

blue cheese

Danish blue

Stilton

Gorgonzola

hard cheese

Gruyère

Parmesan

Emmenthal

unripened cheese

petit suisse

cottage cheese

ricotta

processed cheese

tome au raisin

processed Emmenthal

processed Gruyère

desserts

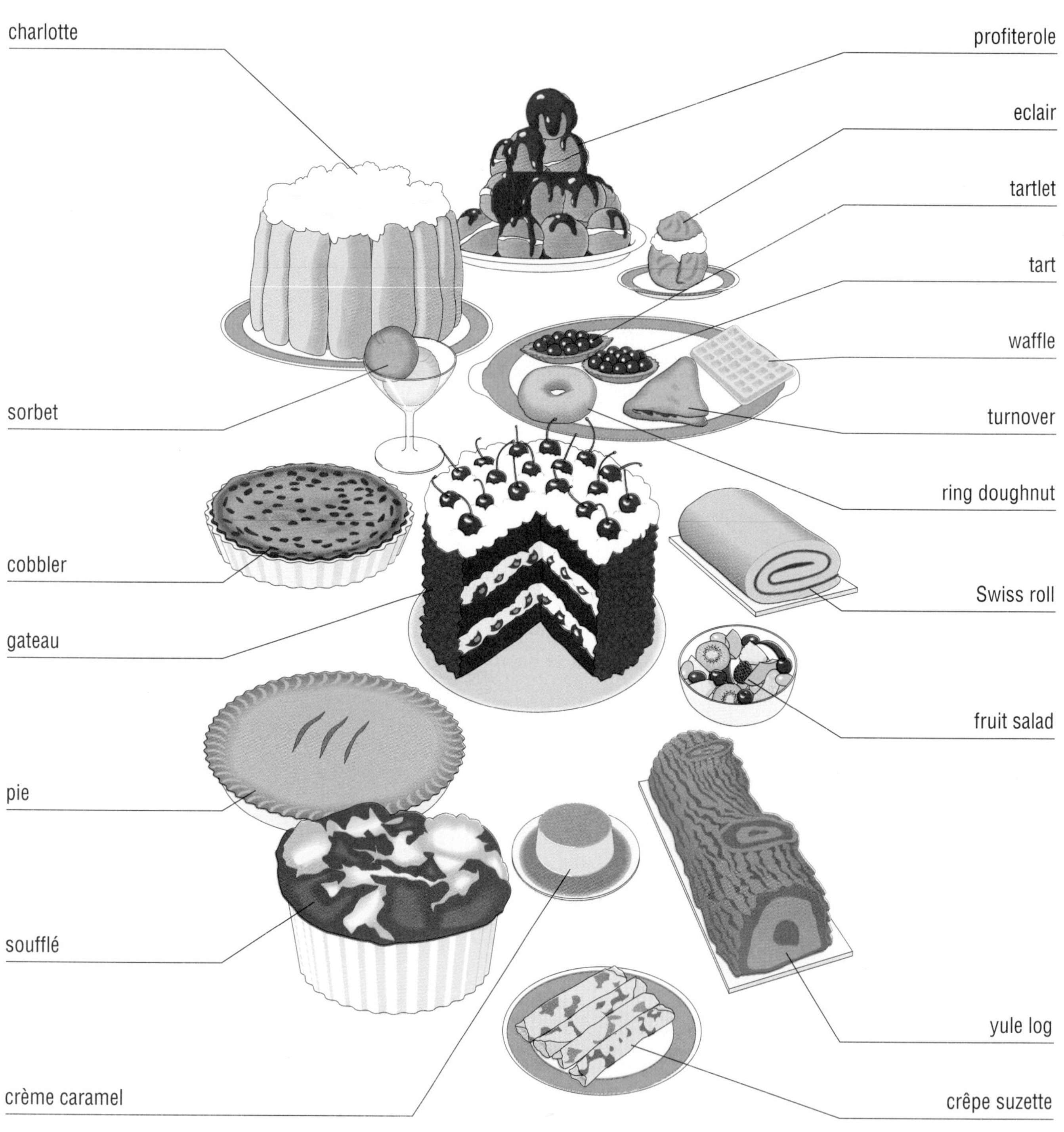

charlotte

profiterole

eclair

tartlet

tart

waffle

sorbet

turnover

cobbler

ring doughnut

gateau

Swiss roll

pie

fruit salad

soufflé

yule log

crème caramel

crêpe suzette

farm buildings

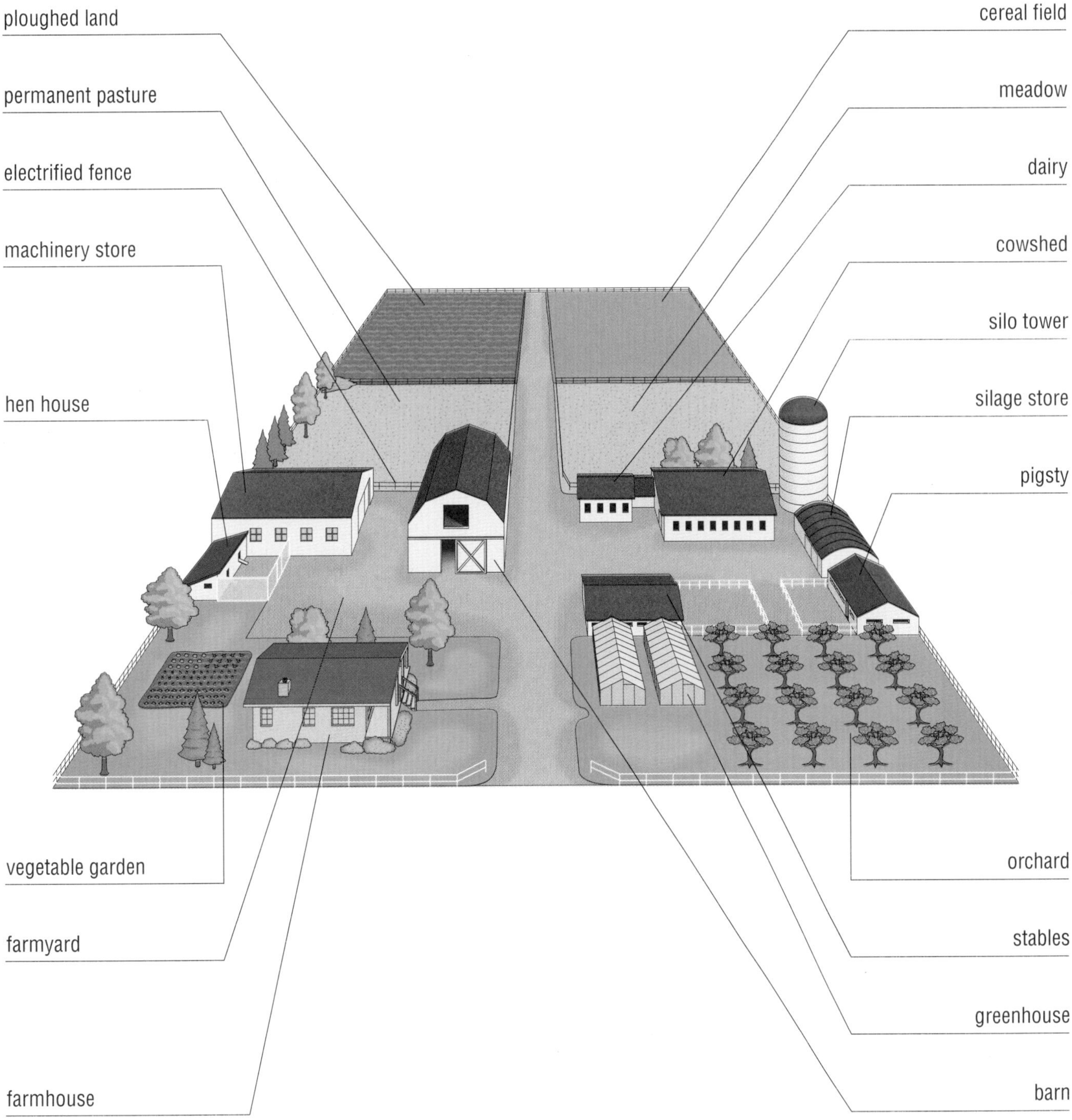
ploughed land
permanent pasture
electrified fence
machinery store
hen house
vegetable garden
farmyard
farmhouse
cereal field
meadow
dairy
cowshed
silo tower
silage store
pigsty
orchard
stables
greenhouse
barn

FARMING

farm animals

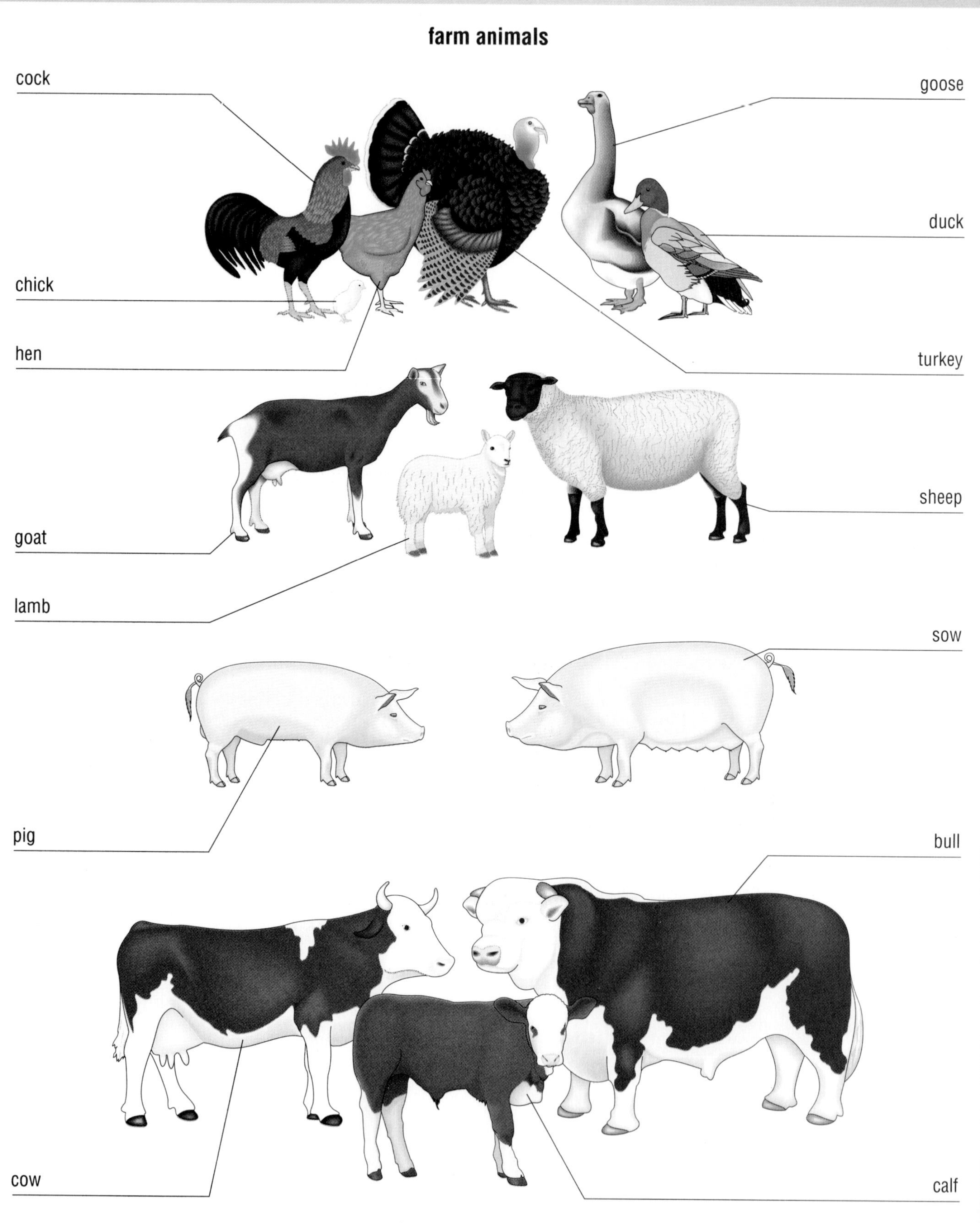

cock

goose

chick

duck

hen

turkey

goat

sheep

lamb

sow

pig

bull

cow

calf

garden

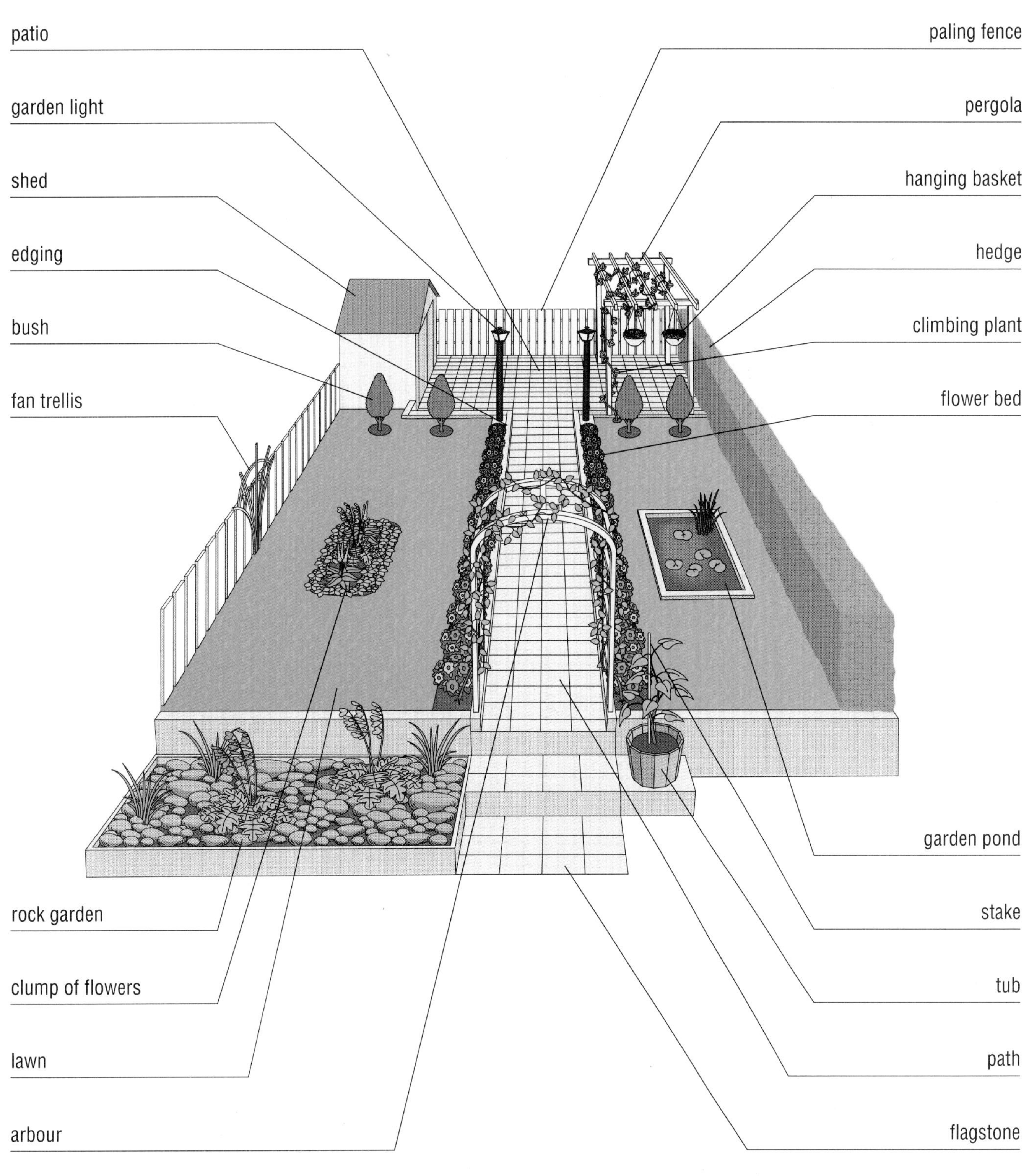

patio

garden light

shed

edging

bush

fan trellis

rock garden

clump of flowers

lawn

arbour

paling fence

pergola

hanging basket

hedge

climbing plant

flower bed

garden pond

stake

tub

path

flagstone

GARDENING

tools and equipment

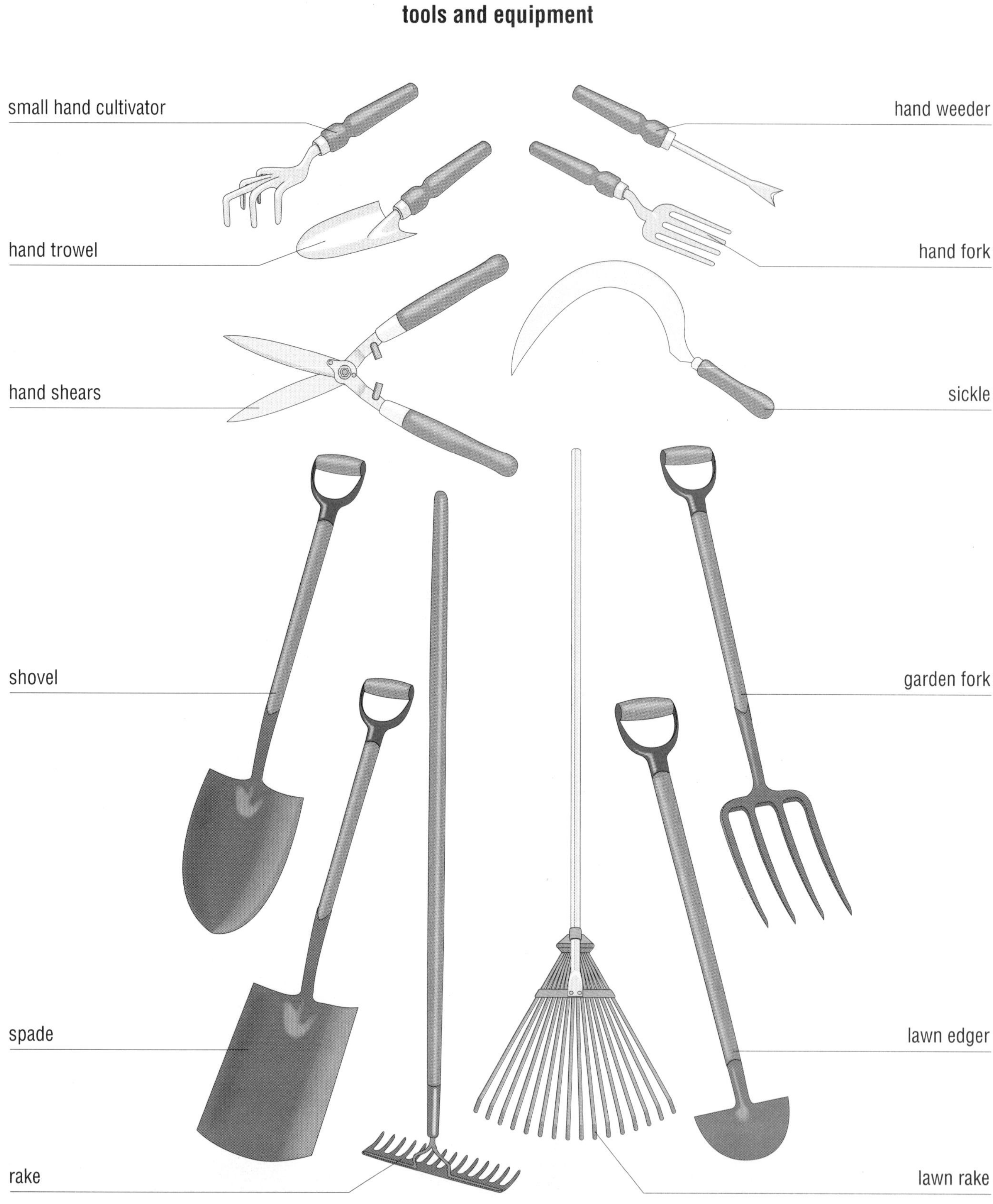

small hand cultivator

hand weeder

hand trowel

hand fork

hand shears

sickle

shovel

garden fork

spade

lawn edger

rake

lawn rake

tools and equipment

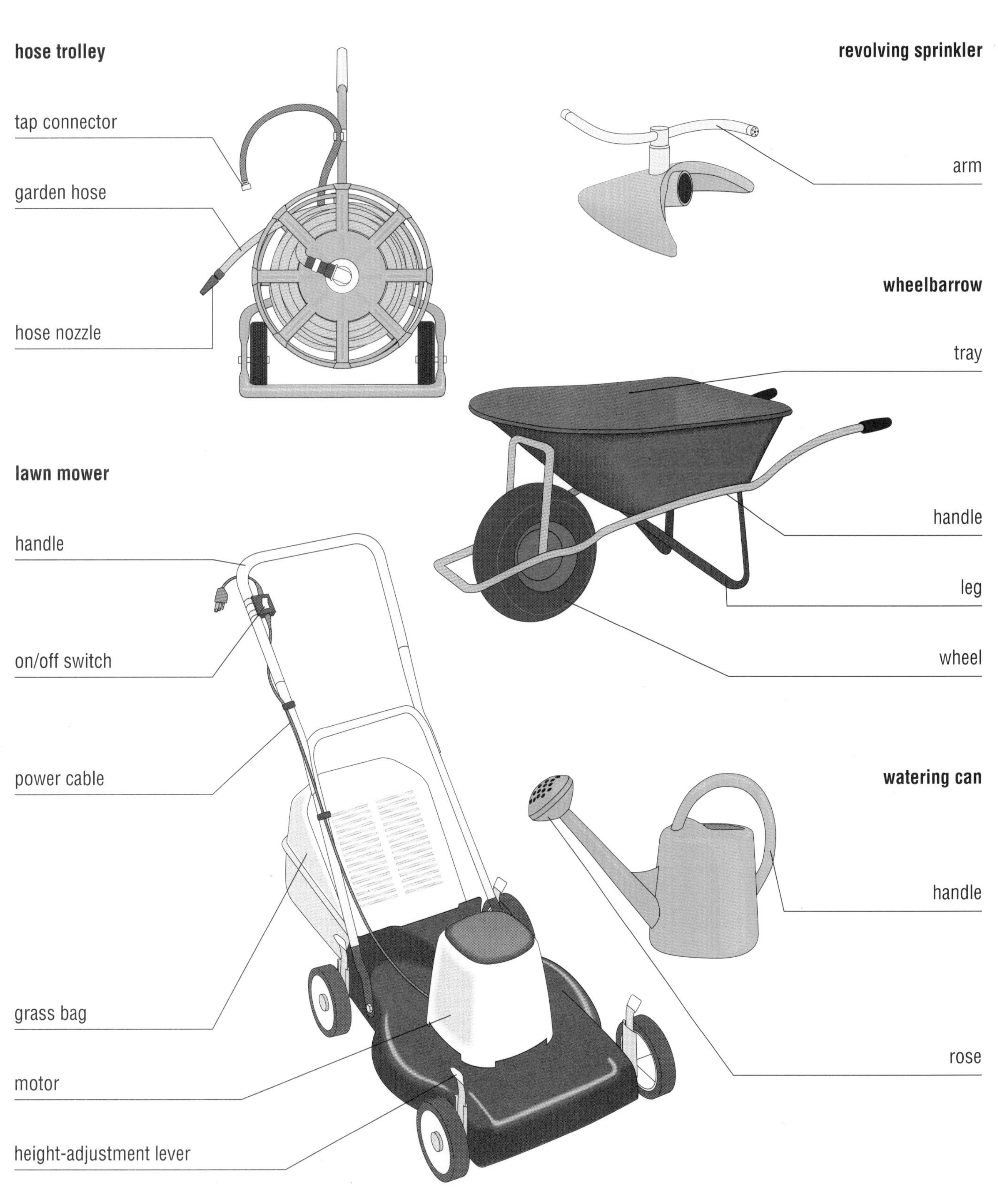

hose trolley

tap connector

garden hose

hose nozzle

lawn mower

handle

on/off switch

power cable

grass bag

motor

height-adjustment lever

revolving sprinkler

arm

wheelbarrow

tray

handle

leg

wheel

watering can

handle

rose

ARCHITECTURE

traditional houses

yurt

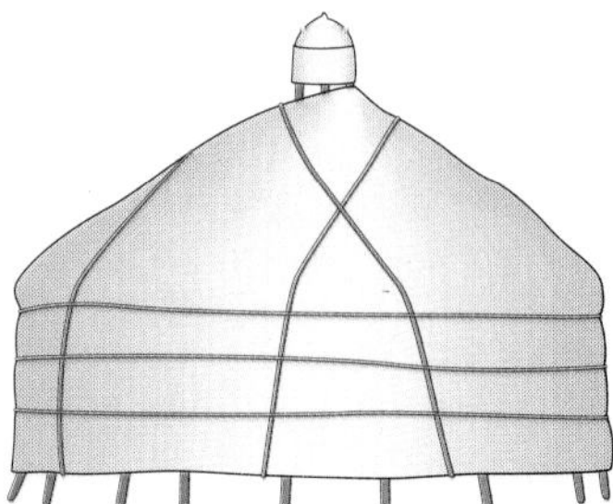

hut

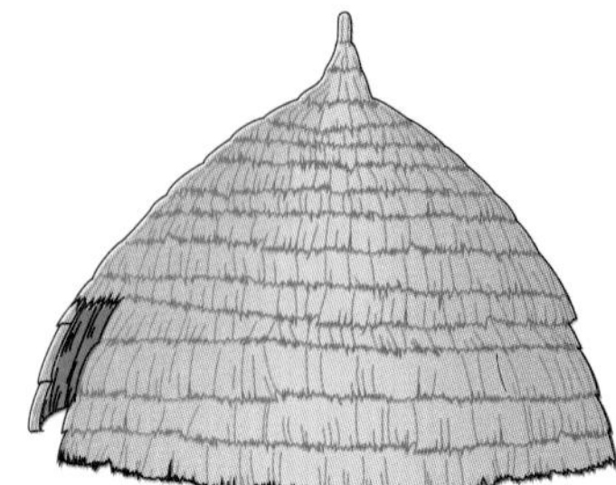

igloo

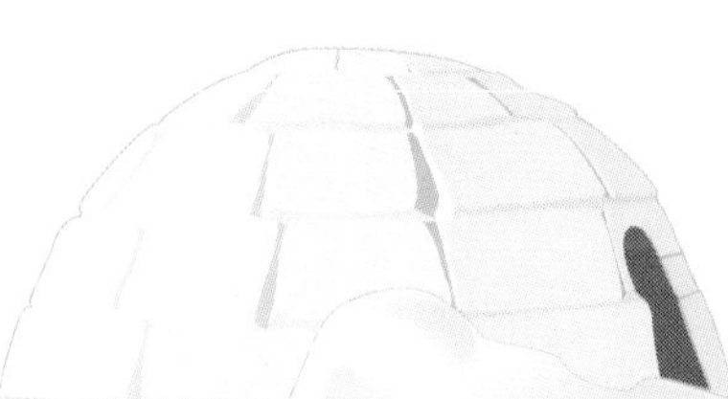

isba

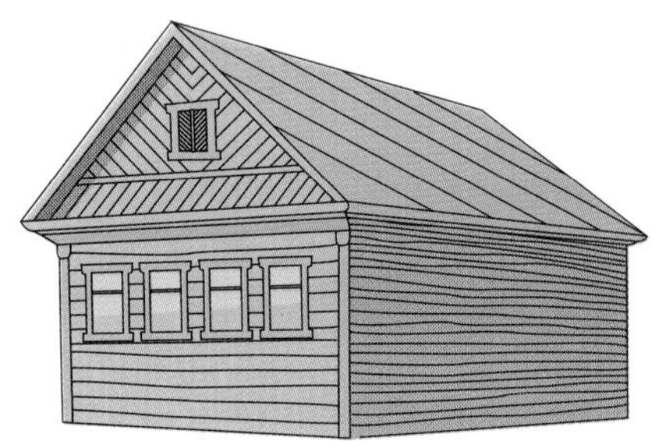

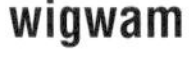

wigwam

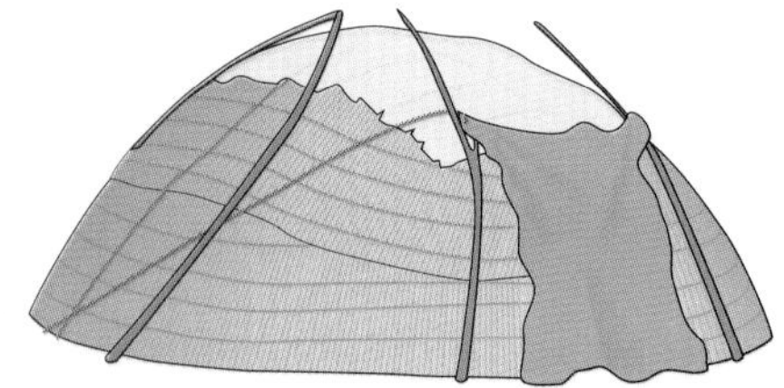

grass hut

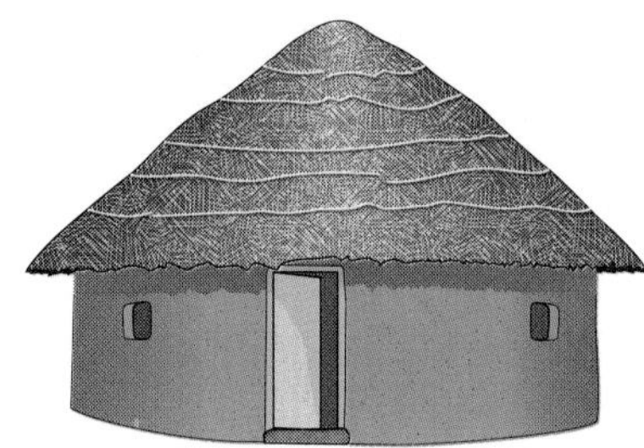

tepee

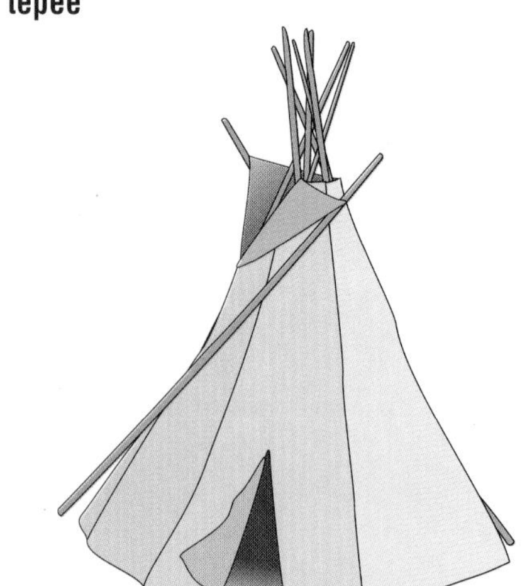

house on stilts

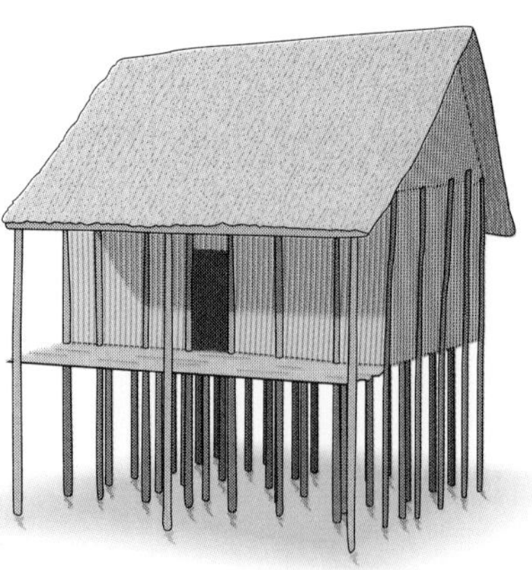

castle

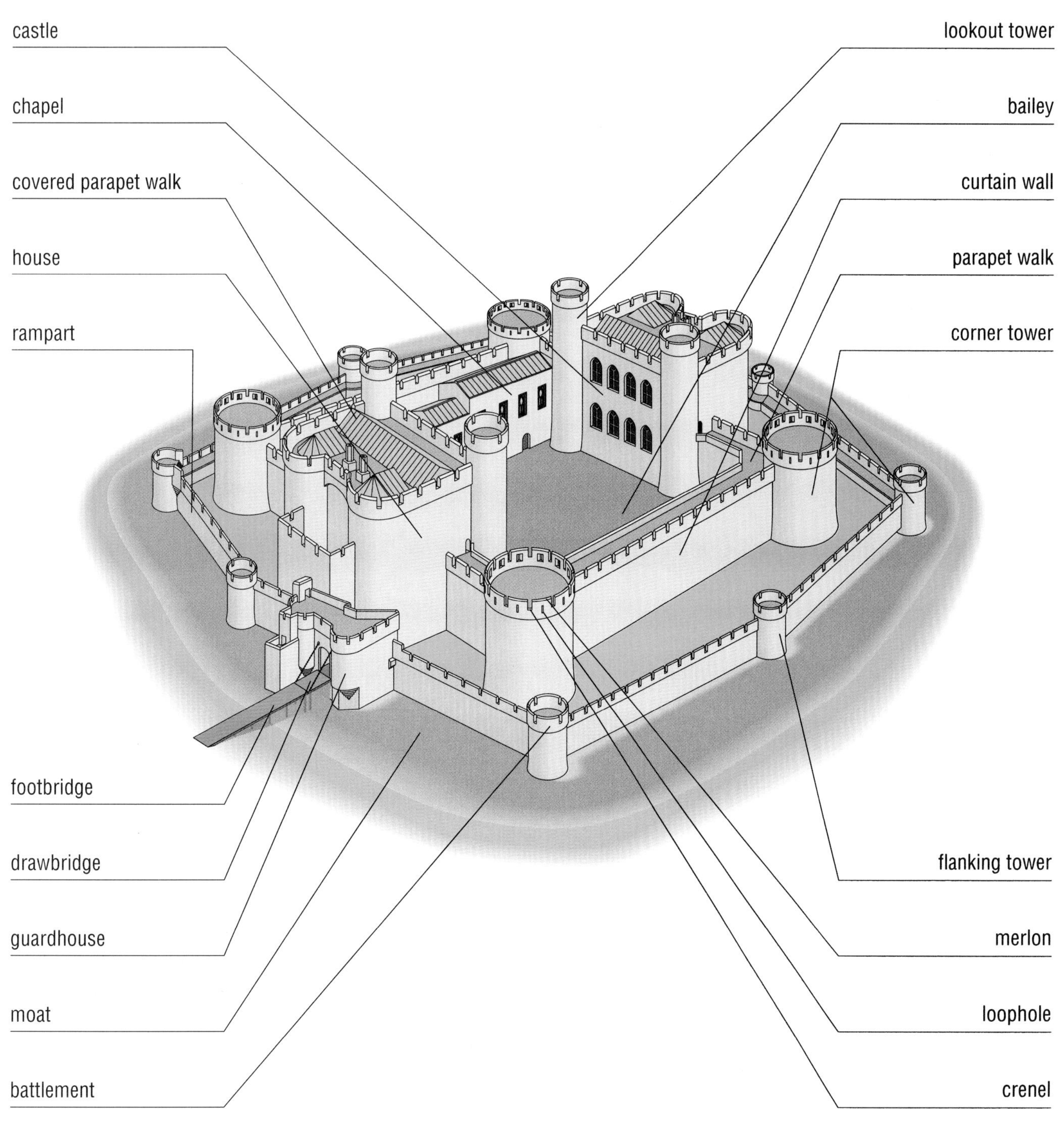

castle

chapel

covered parapet walk

house

rampart

footbridge

drawbridge

guardhouse

moat

battlement

lookout tower

bailey

curtain wall

parapet walk

corner tower

flanking tower

merlon

loophole

crenel

HOUSE

exterior of a house

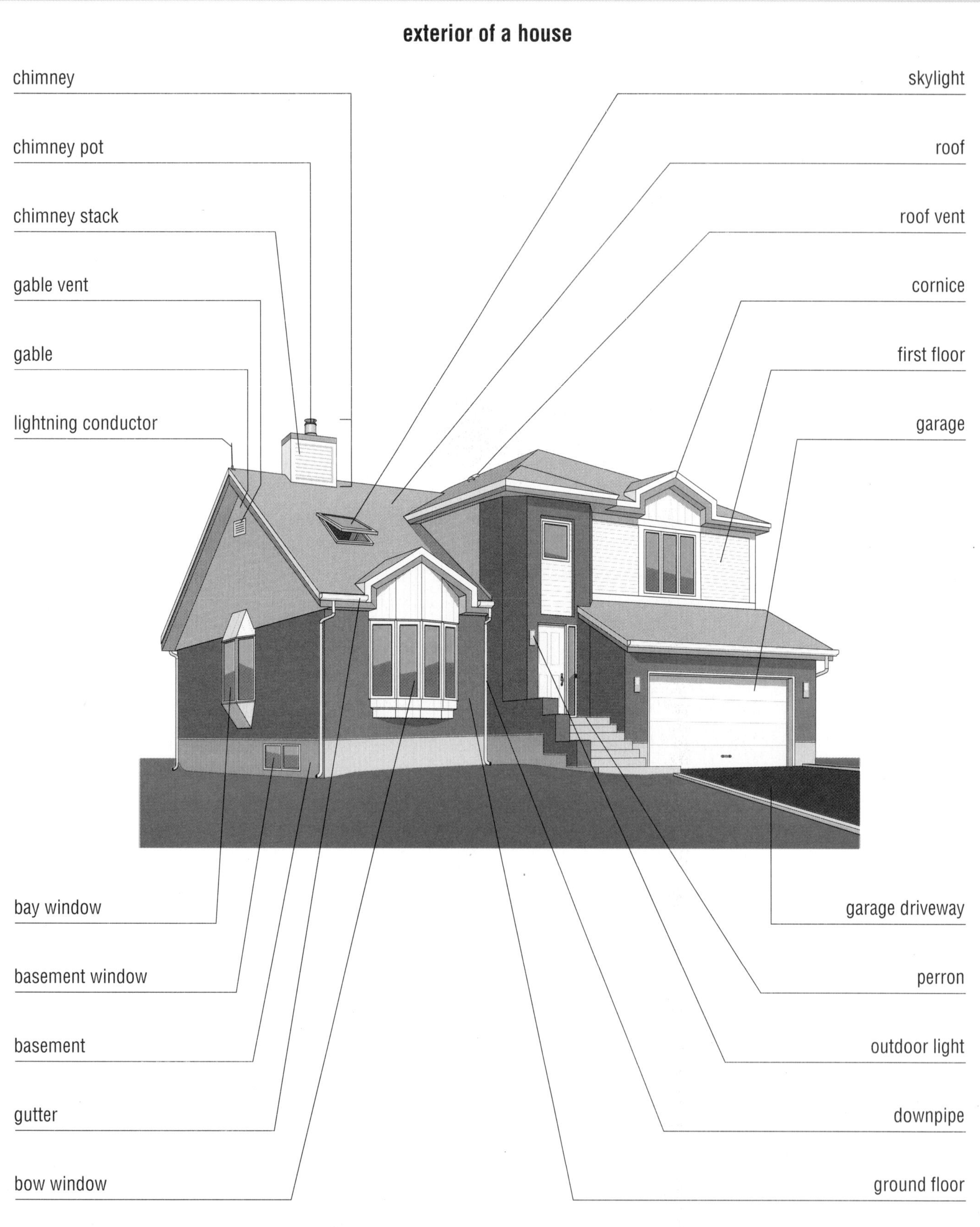

chimney

chimney pot

chimney stack

gable vent

gable

lightning conductor

skylight

roof

roof vent

cornice

first floor

garage

bay window

basement window

basement

gutter

bow window

garage driveway

perron

outdoor light

downpipe

ground floor

exterior door

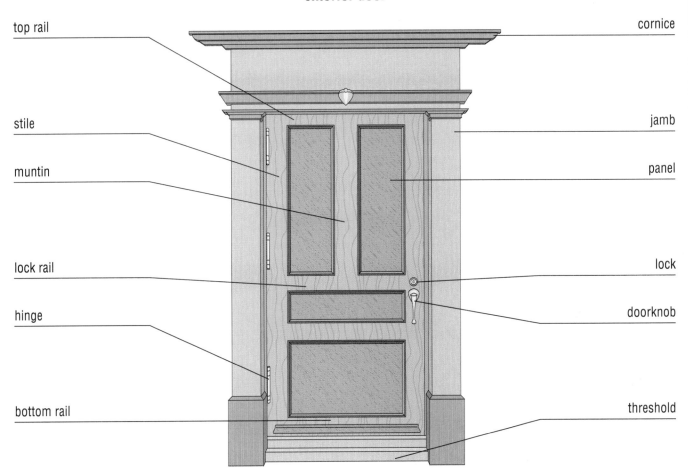

top rail

cornice

stile

jamb

muntin

panel

lock rail

lock

hinge

doorknob

bottom rail

threshold

window

muntin

jamb

pane

sash-frame

shutter

stile

hook

louvre shutter

weatherboard

window sill

stairs

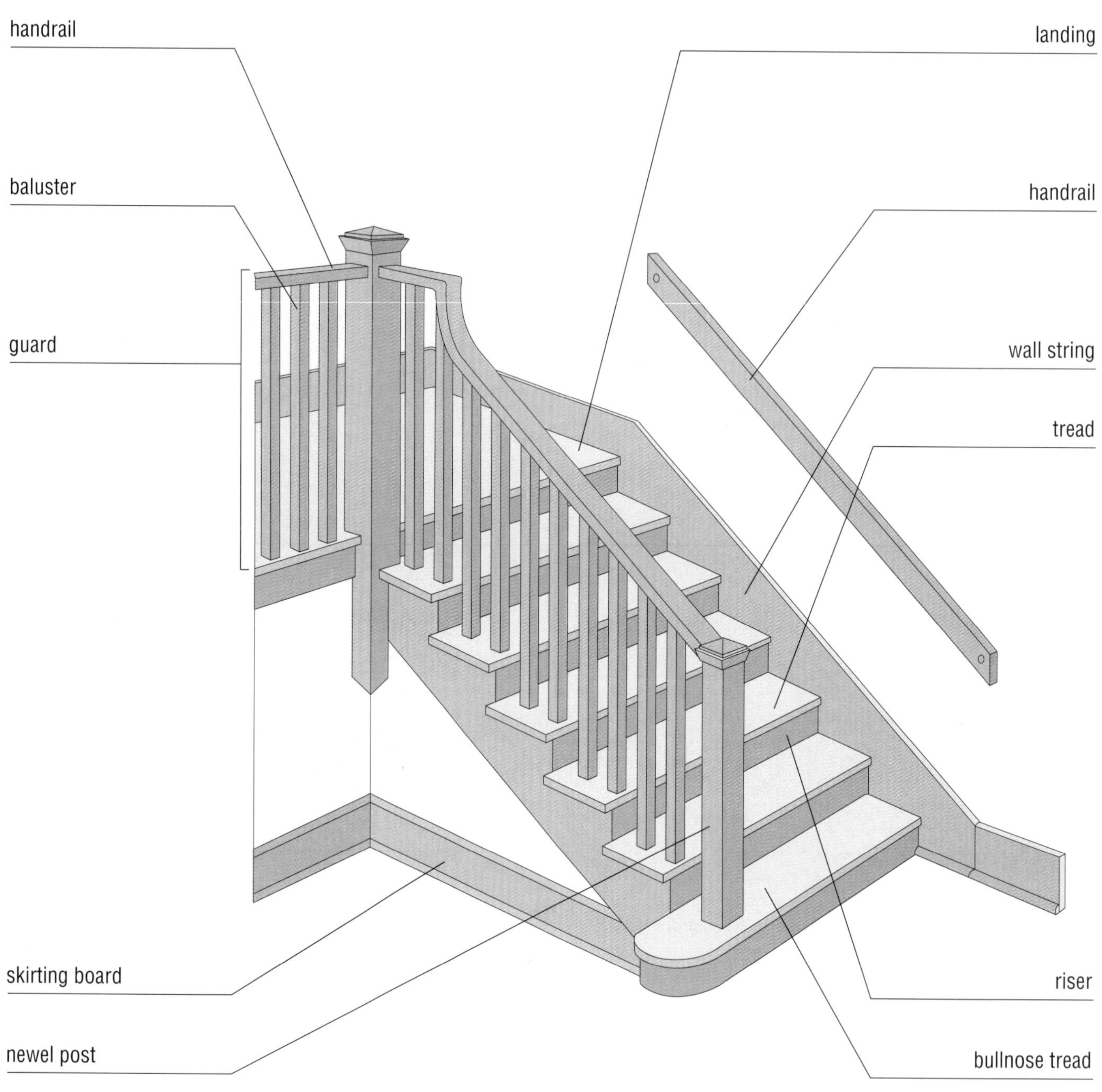

handrail

baluster

guard

landing

handrail

wall string

tread

skirting board

newel post

riser

bullnose tread

bathroom

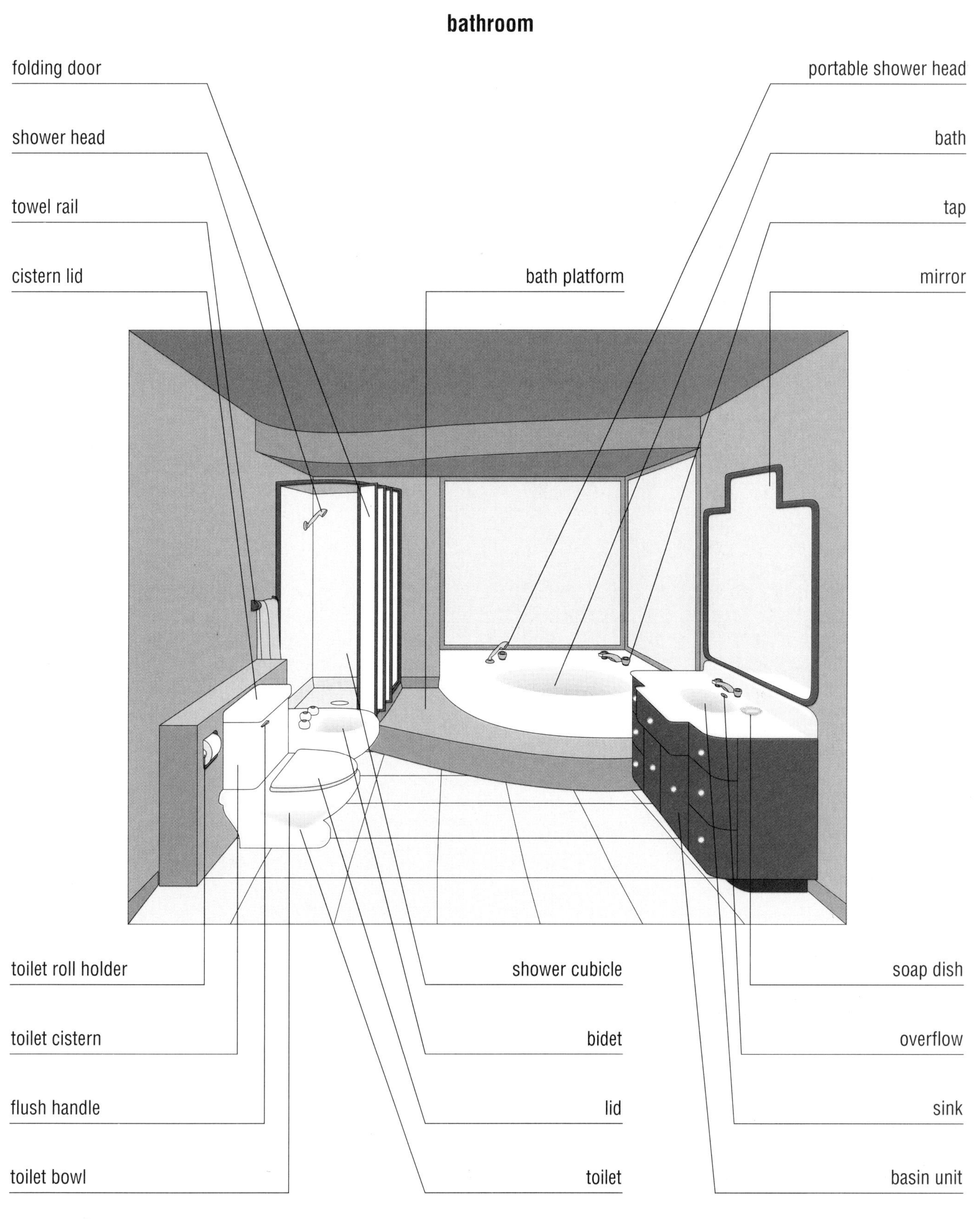

folding door

shower head

towel rail

cistern lid

bath platform

portable shower head

bath

tap

mirror

toilet roll holder

toilet cistern

flush handle

toilet bowl

shower cubicle

bidet

lid

toilet

soap dish

overflow

sink

basin unit

dining chair

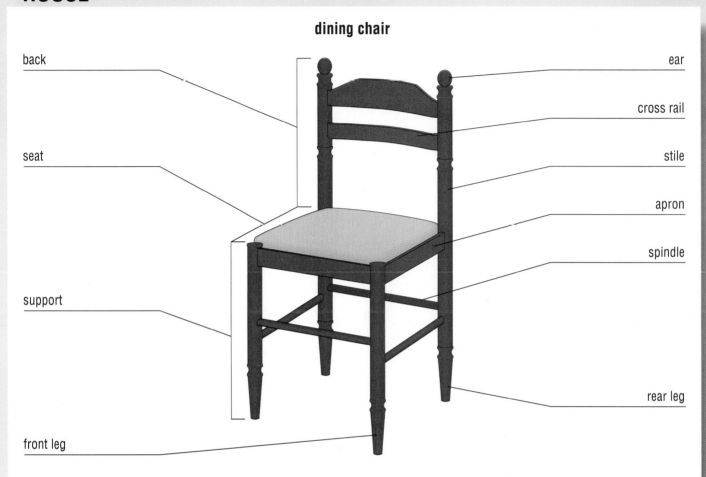

back

ear

cross rail

seat

stile

apron

spindle

support

rear leg

front leg

gateleg table

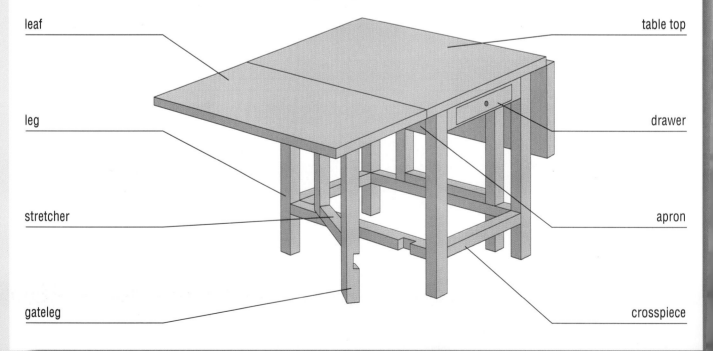

leaf

table top

leg

drawer

stretcher

apron

gateleg

crosspiece

formal chair

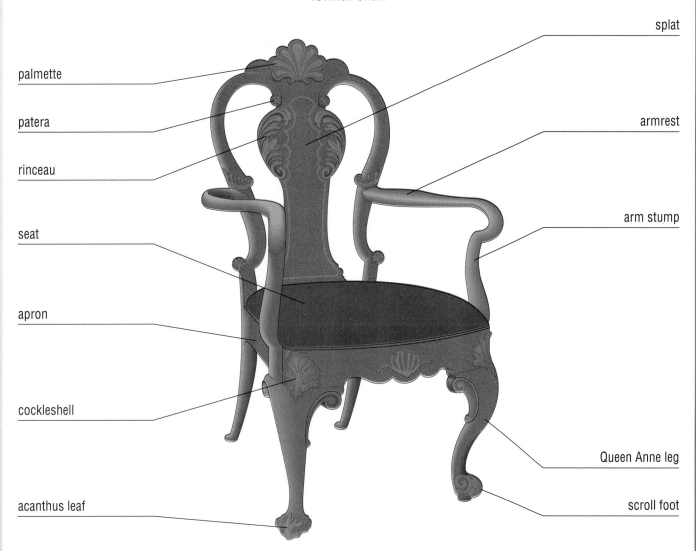

splat

palmette

patera

armrest

rinceau

arm stump

seat

apron

cockleshell

Queen Anne leg

scroll foot

acanthus leaf

armchair

sofa

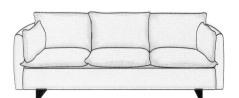

two-seater settee

bed

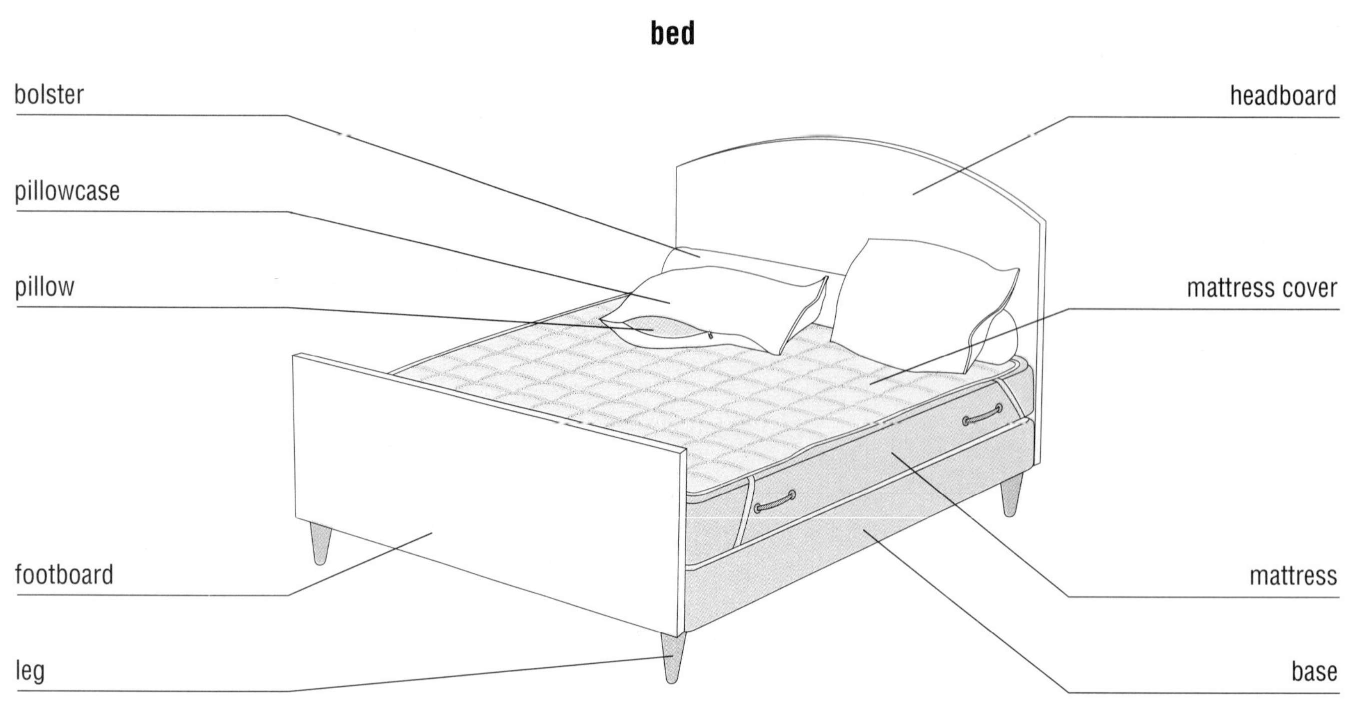

bolster

pillowcase

pillow

footboard

leg

headboard

mattress cover

mattress

base

linen

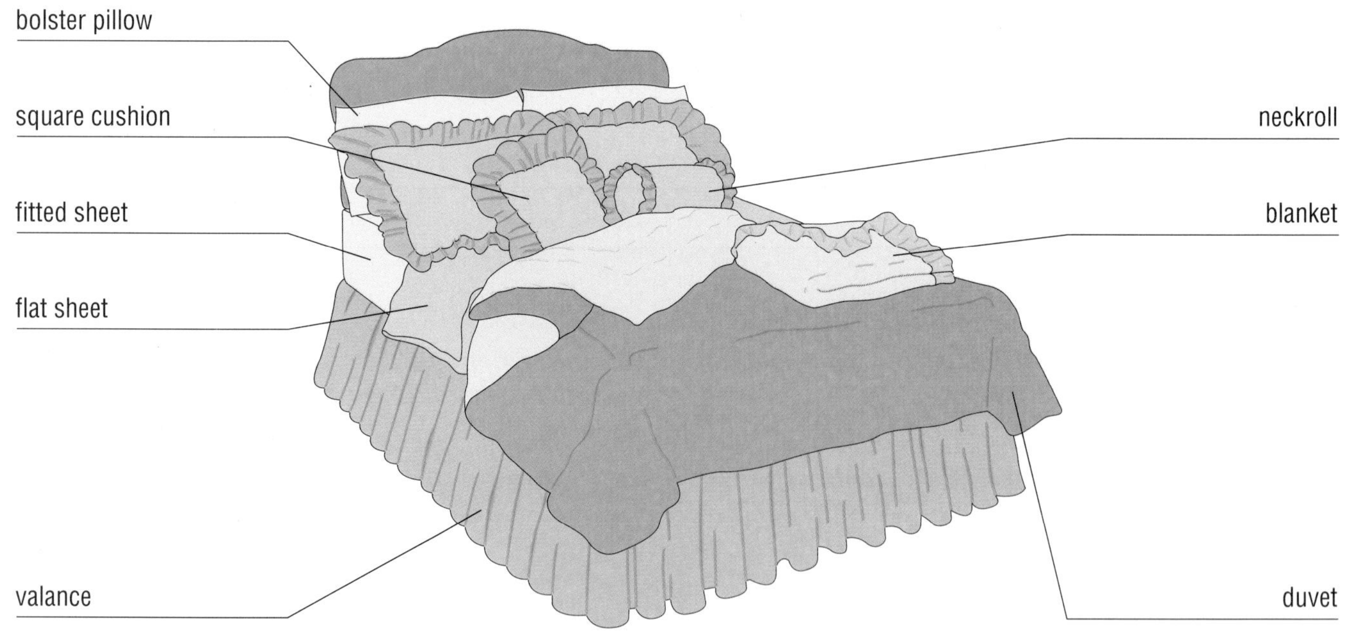

bolster pillow

square cushion

fitted sheet

flat sheet

valance

neckroll

blanket

duvet

lights

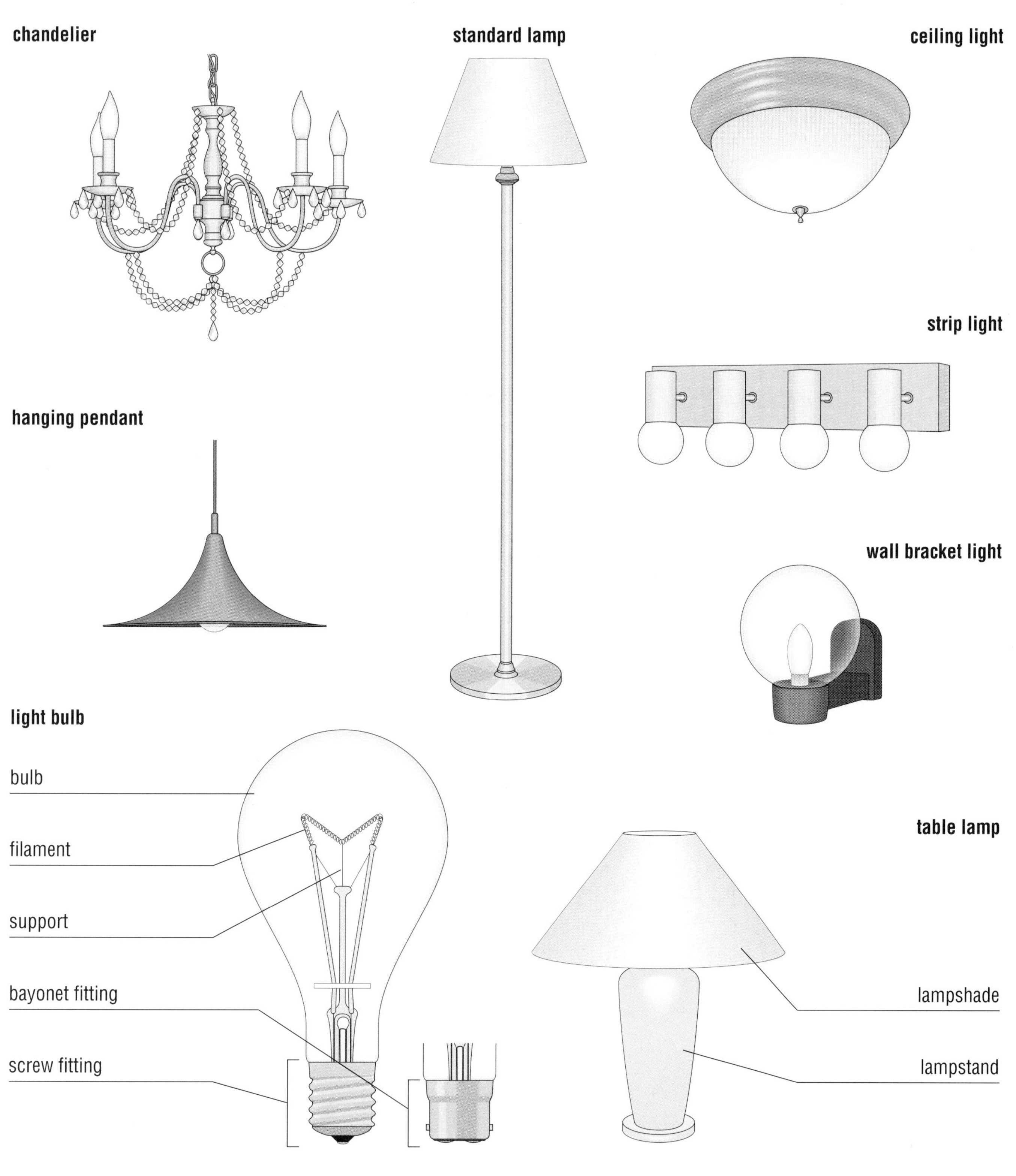

chandelier

standard lamp

ceiling light

strip light

hanging pendant

wall bracket light

light bulb

bulb

filament

support

bayonet fitting

screw fitting

table lamp

lampshade

lampstand

crockery

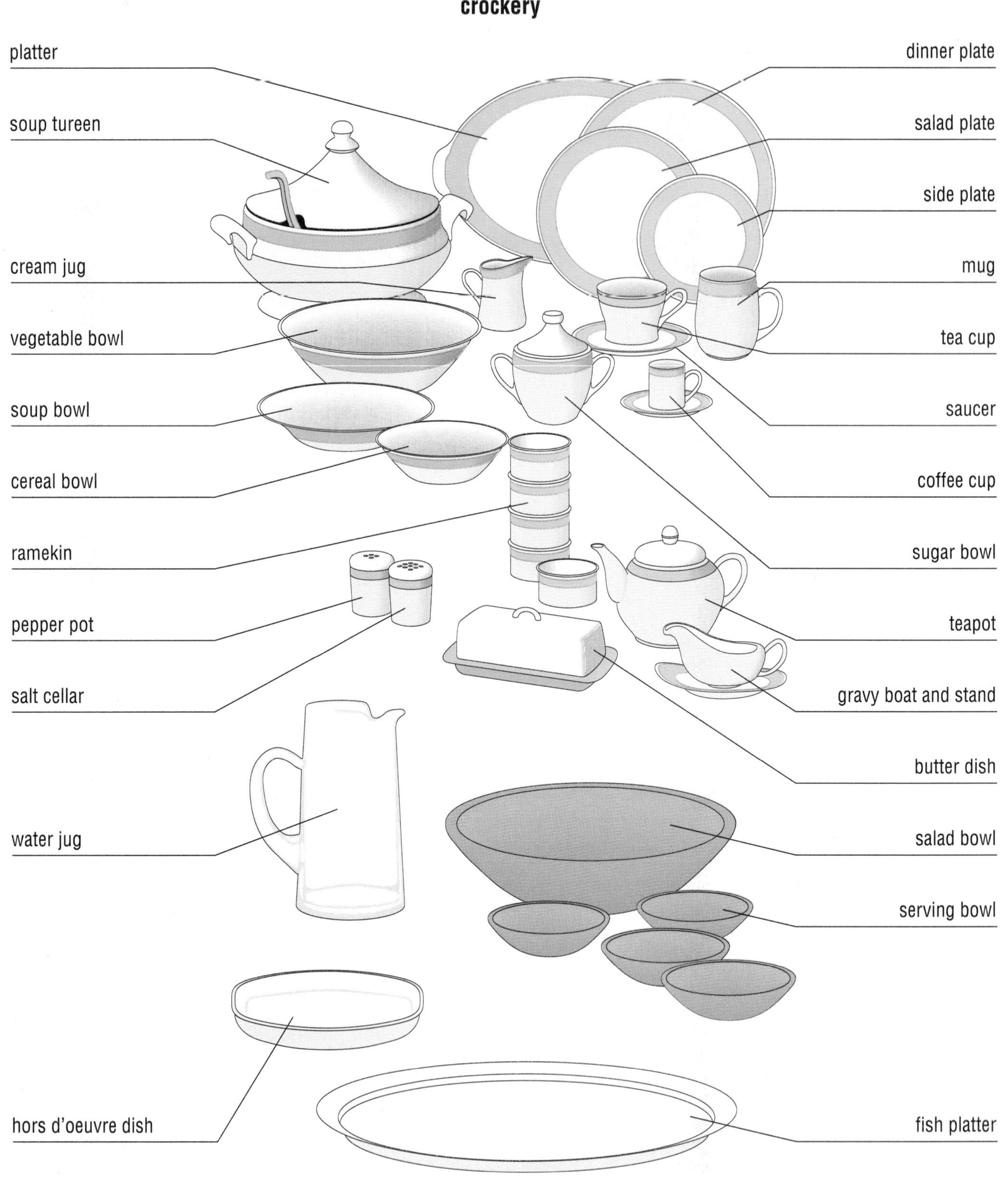

platter

soup tureen

cream jug

vegetable bowl

soup bowl

cereal bowl

ramekin

pepper pot

salt cellar

water jug

hors d'oeuvre dish

dinner plate

salad plate

side plate

mug

tea cup

saucer

coffee cup

sugar bowl

teapot

gravy boat and stand

butter dish

salad bowl

serving bowl

fish platter

cutlery

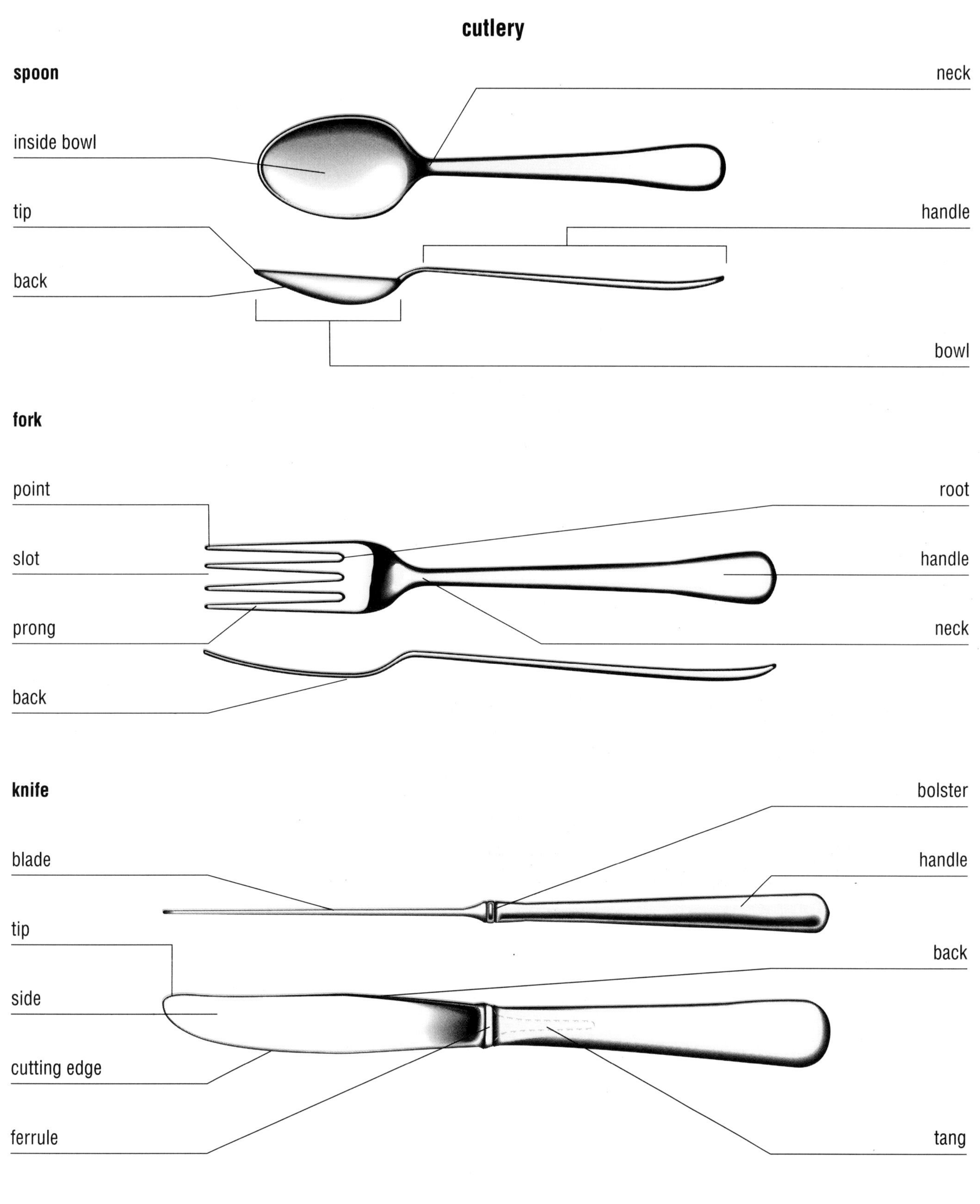

spoon

neck

inside bowl

tip

handle

back

bowl

fork

point

root

slot

handle

prong

neck

back

knife

bolster

blade

handle

tip

back

side

cutting edge

ferrule

tang

kitchen utensils

set of utensils

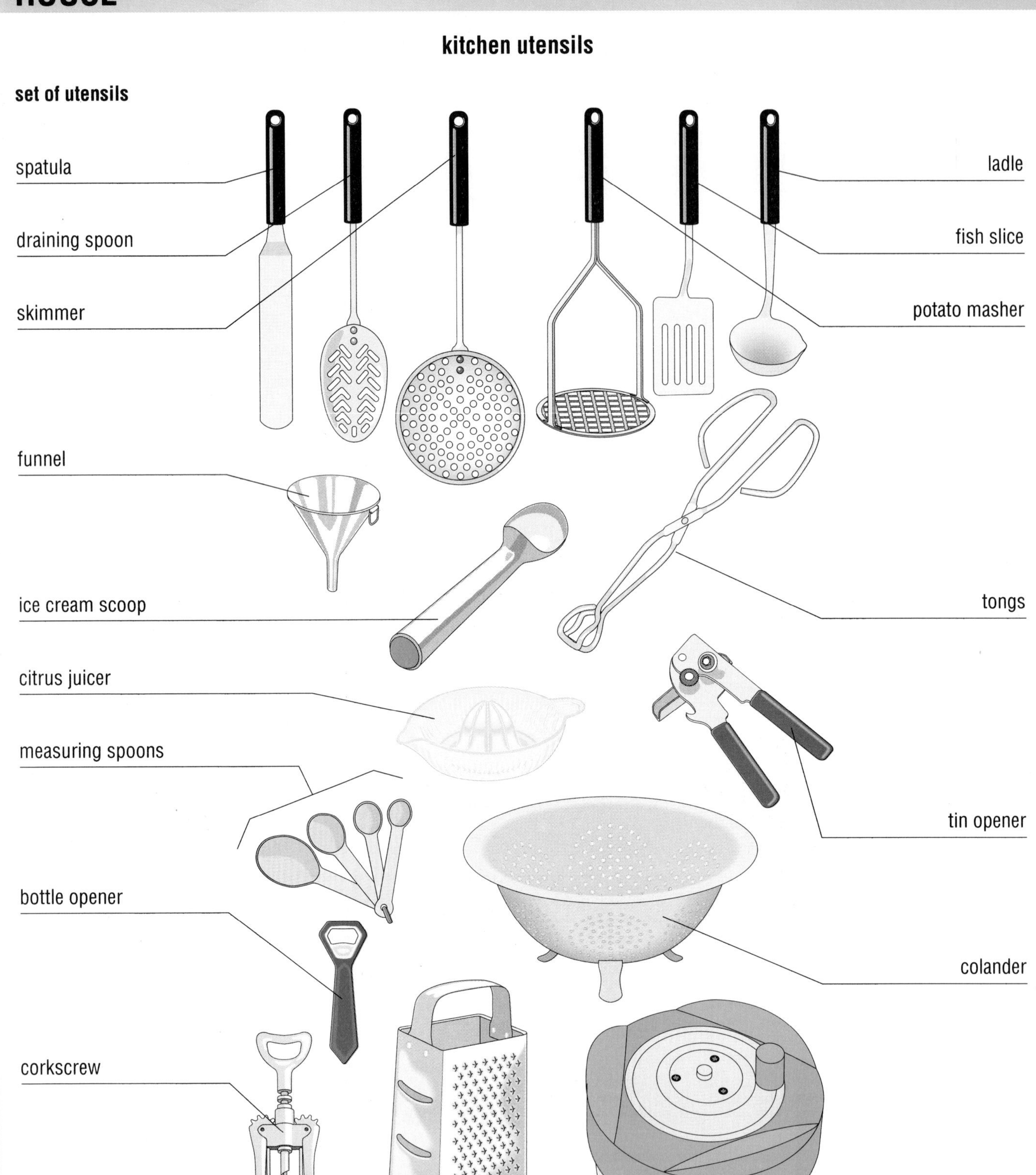

spatula

draining spoon

skimmer

funnel

ice cream scoop

citrus juicer

measuring spoons

bottle opener

corkscrew

grater

ladle

fish slice

potato masher

tongs

tin opener

colander

salad spinner

cooking utensils

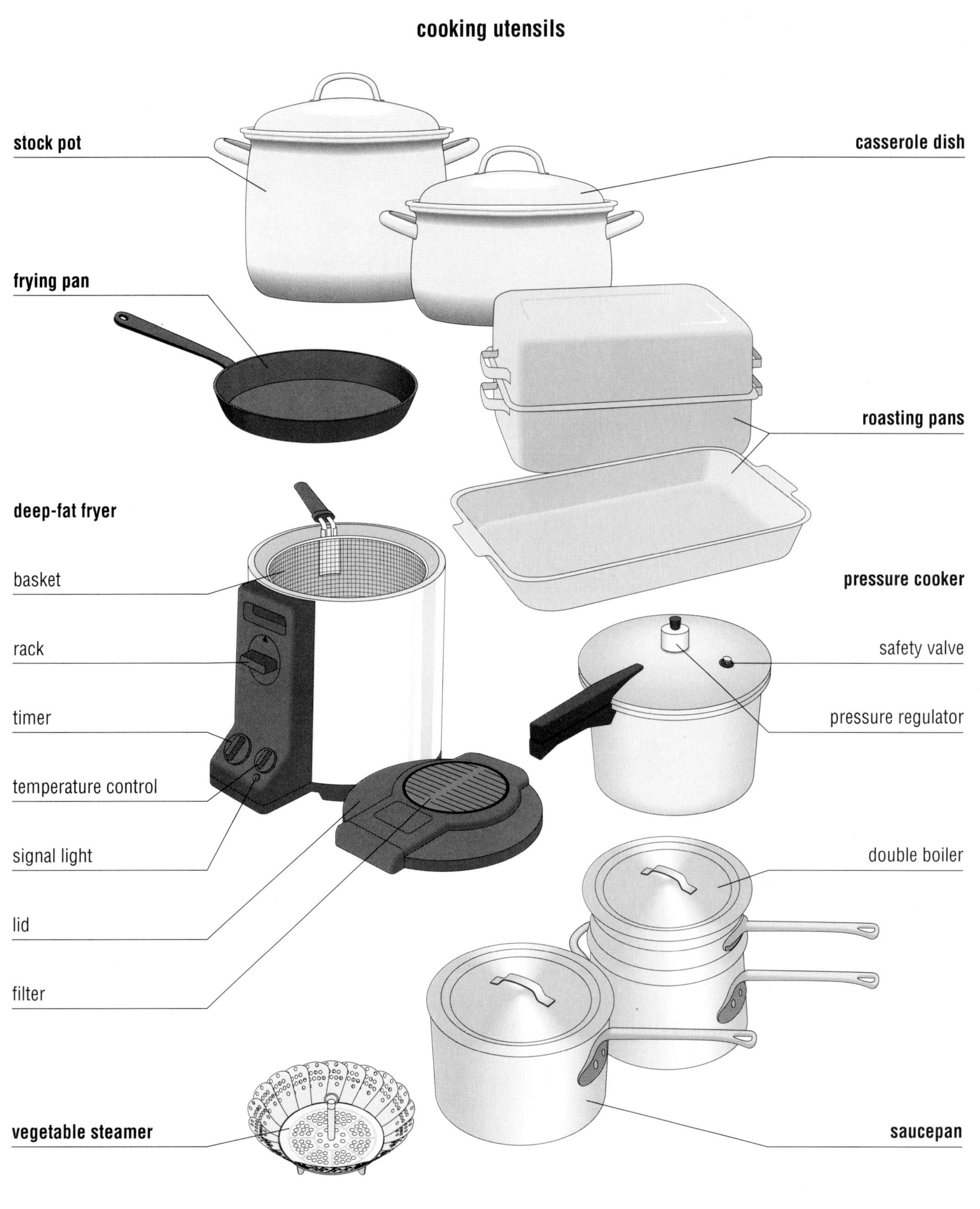

stock pot

casserole dish

frying pan

roasting pans

deep-fat fryer

basket

pressure cooker

rack

safety valve

timer

pressure regulator

temperature control

signal light

lid

double boiler

filter

vegetable steamer

saucepan

domestic appliances

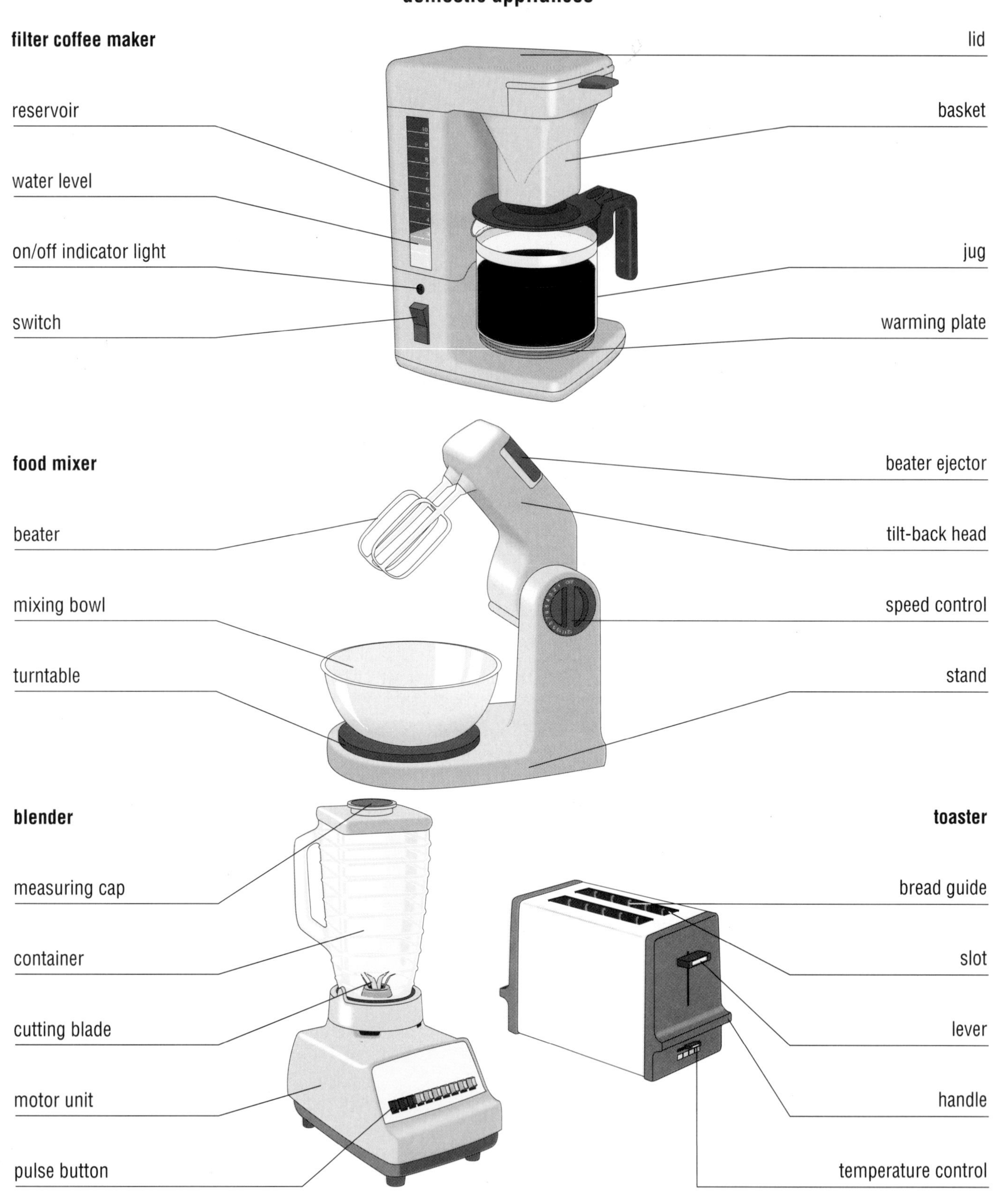

filter coffee maker

reservoir

water level

on/off indicator light

switch

lid

basket

jug

warming plate

food mixer

beater

mixing bowl

turntable

beater ejector

tilt-back head

speed control

stand

blender

measuring cap

container

cutting blade

motor unit

pulse button

toaster

bread guide

slot

lever

handle

temperature control

electric cooker

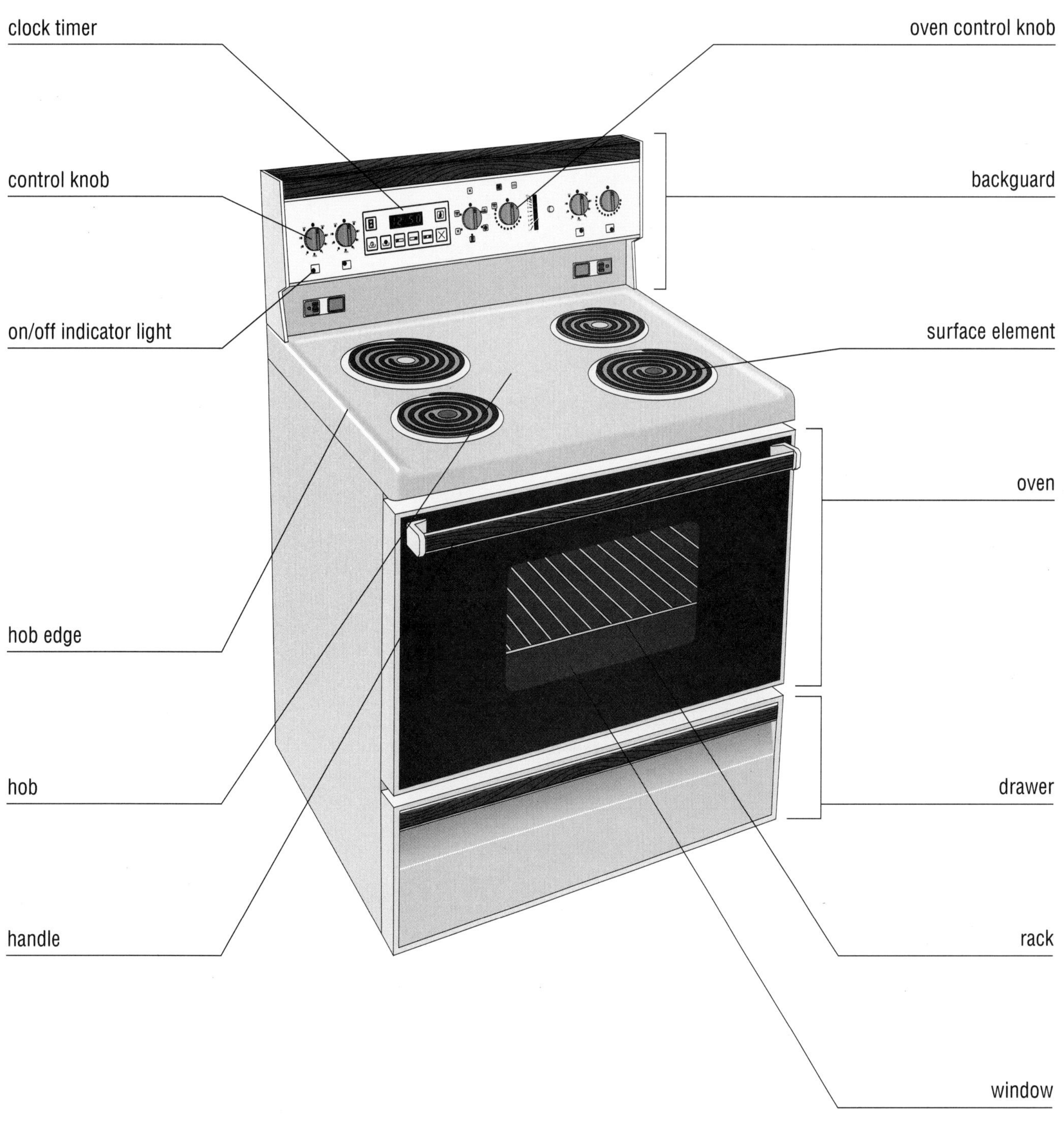

clock timer

oven control knob

control knob

backguard

on/off indicator light

surface element

oven

hob edge

hob

drawer

handle

rack

window

fridge-freezer

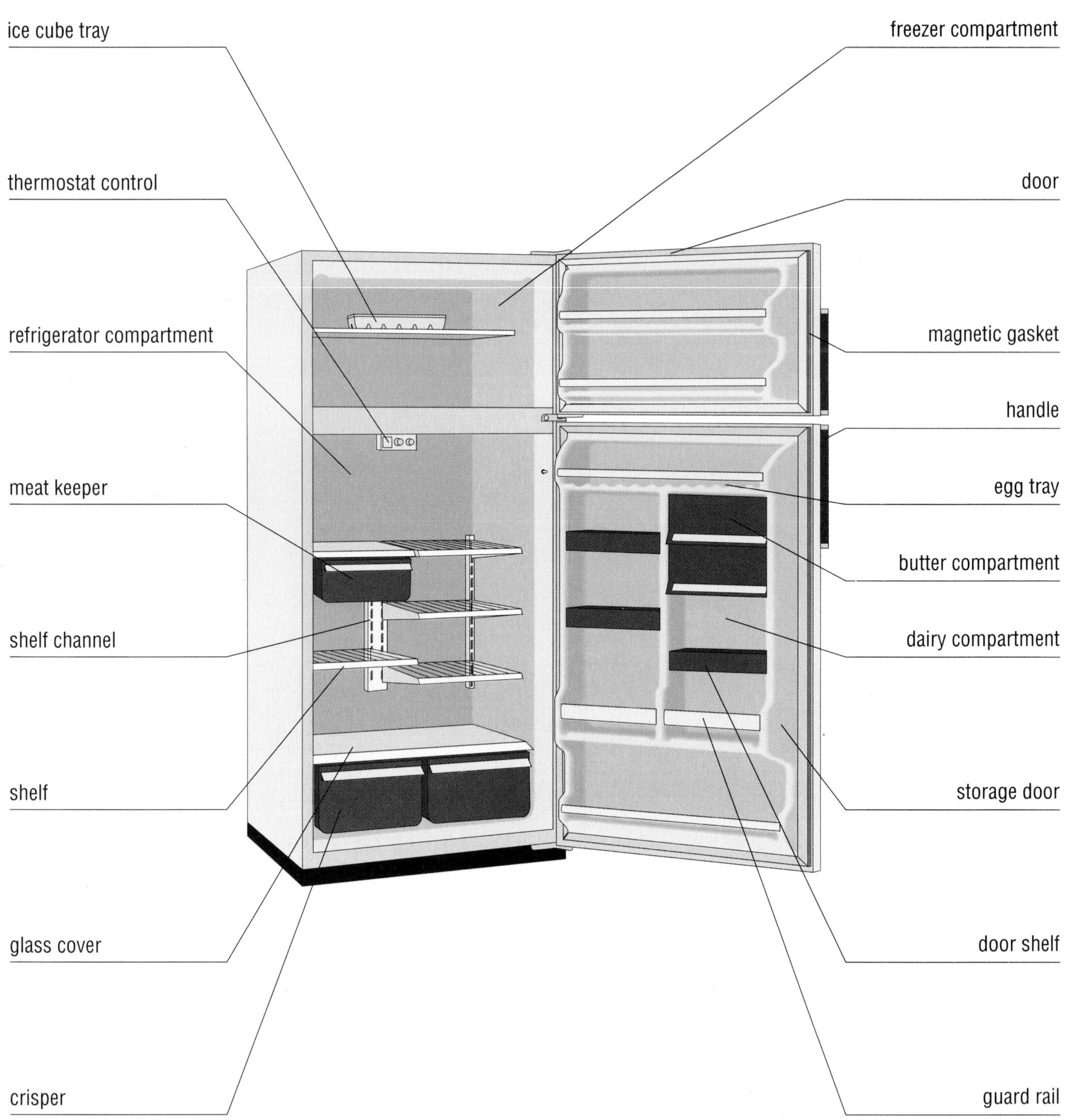

ice cube tray

thermostat control

refrigerator compartment

meat keeper

shelf channel

shelf

glass cover

crisper

freezer compartment

door

magnetic gasket

handle

egg tray

butter compartment

dairy compartment

storage door

door shelf

guard rail

plane surfaces

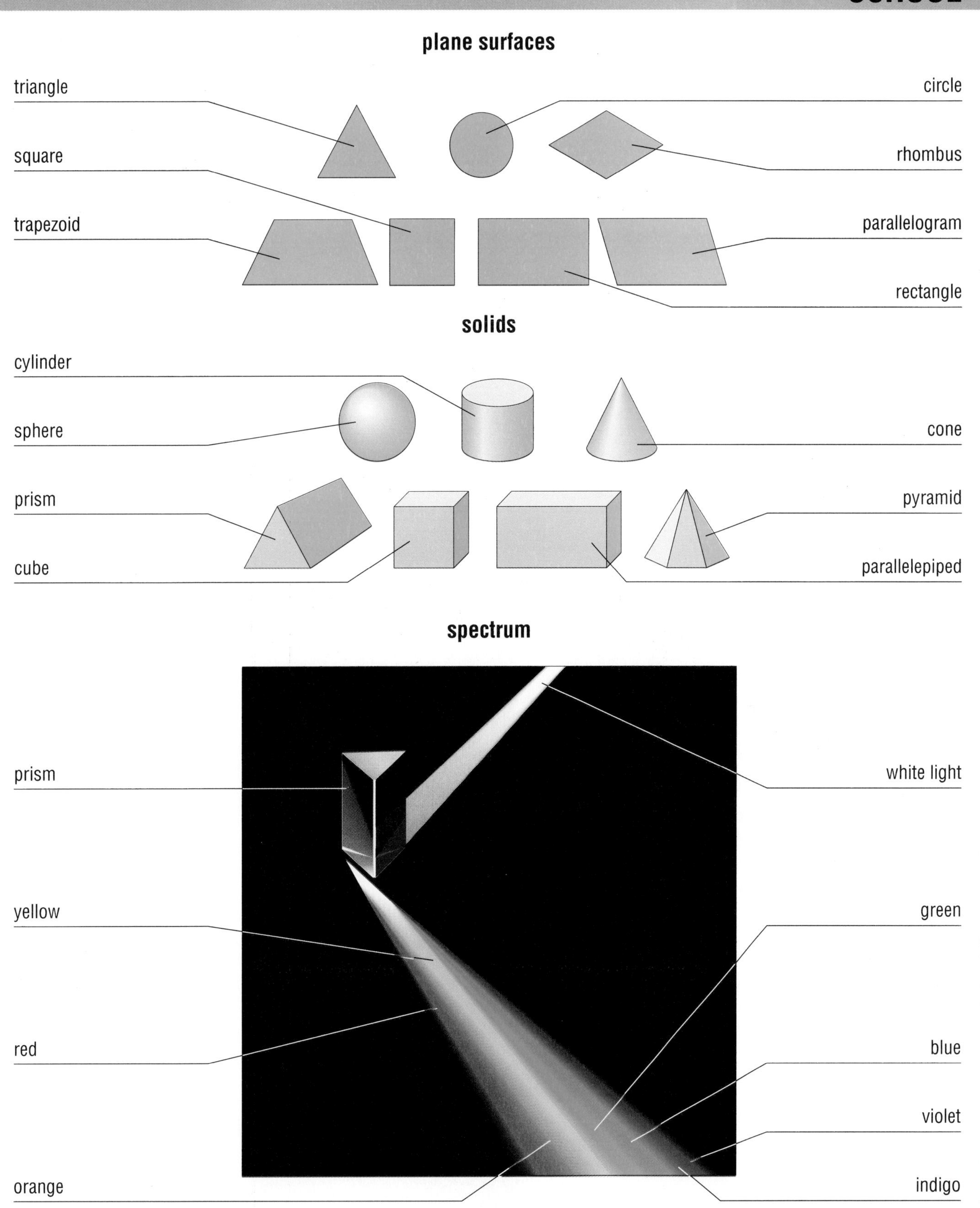

triangle

circle

square

rhombus

trapezoid

parallelogram

rectangle

solids

cylinder

sphere

cone

prism

pyramid

cube

parallelepiped

spectrum

prism

white light

yellow

green

red

blue

violet

orange

indigo

SCHOOL

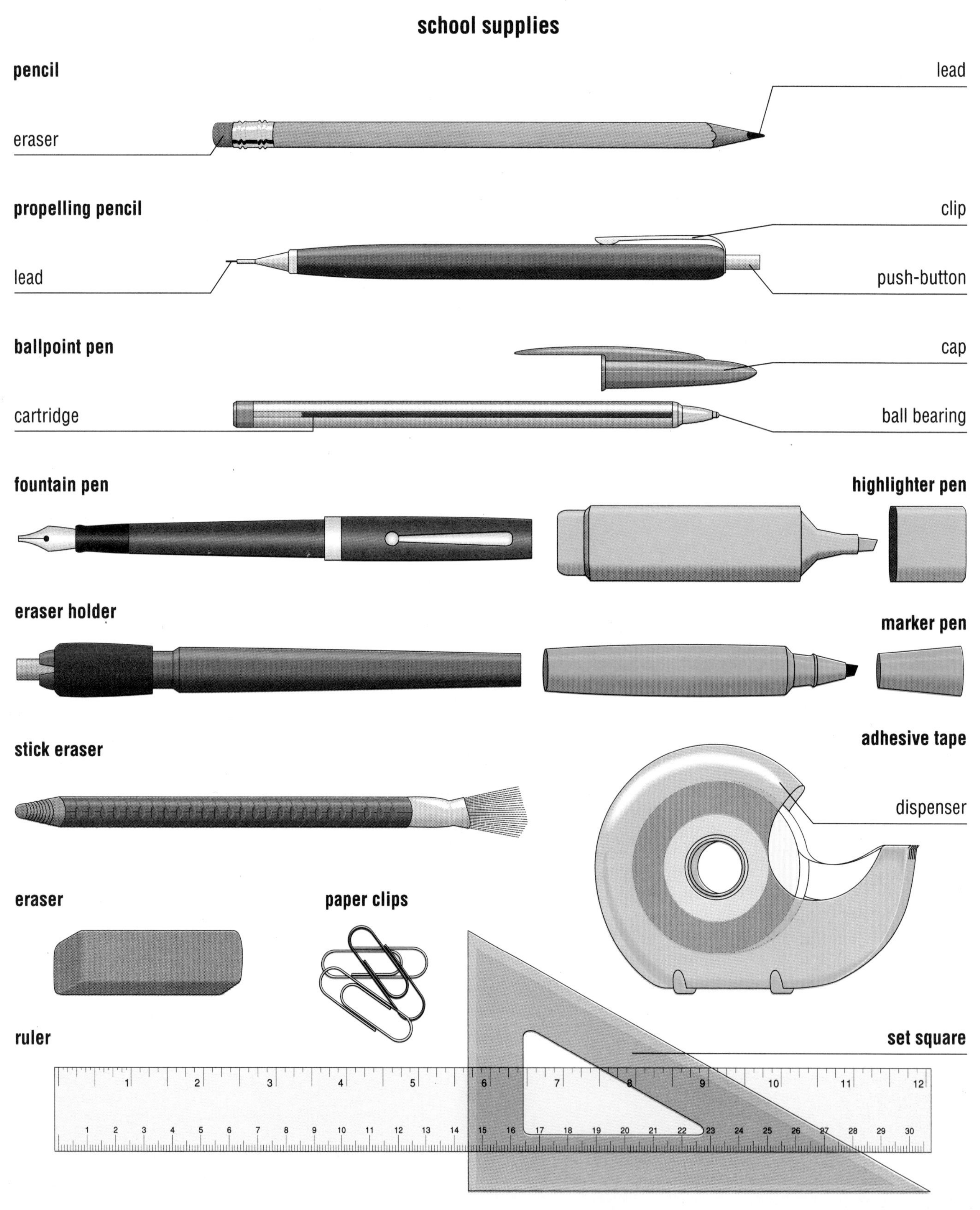

school supplies

pencil

lead

eraser

propelling pencil

clip

lead

push-button

ballpoint pen

cap

cartridge

ball bearing

fountain pen

highlighter pen

eraser holder

marker pen

stick eraser

adhesive tape

dispenser

eraser

paper clips

ruler

set square

school supplies

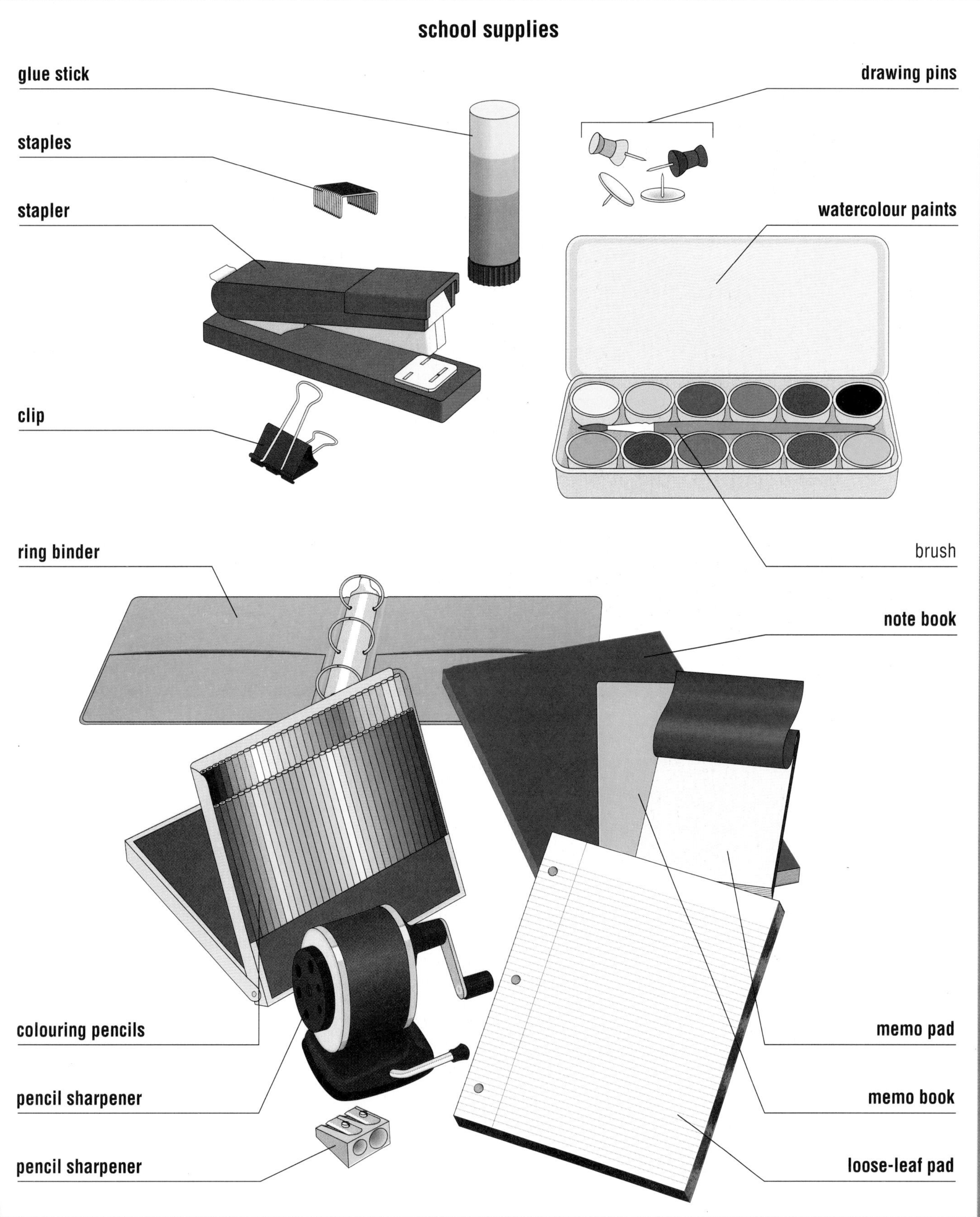

glue stick

staples

stapler

clip

ring binder

colouring pencils

pencil sharpener

pencil sharpener

drawing pins

watercolour paints

brush

note book

memo pad

memo book

loose-leaf pad

SCHOOL

microcomputer

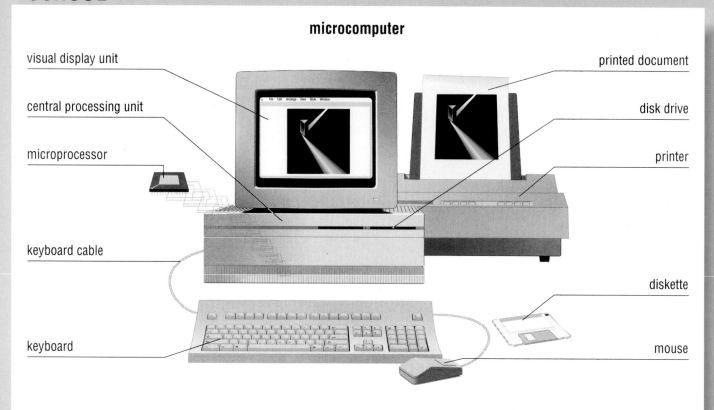

visual display unit

central processing unit

microprocessor

keyboard cable

keyboard

printed document

disk drive

printer

diskette

mouse

pocket calculator

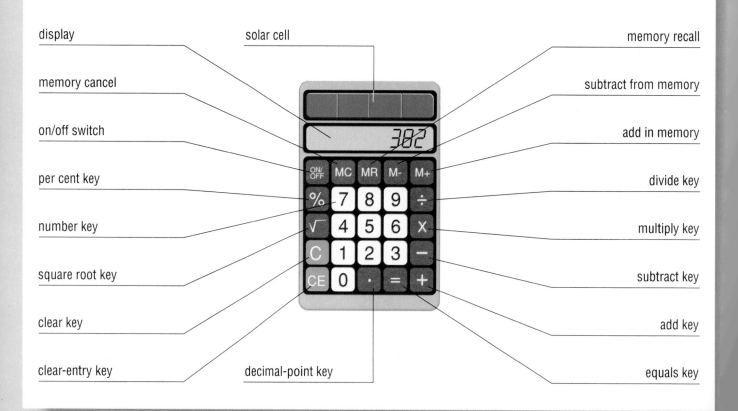

display

solar cell

memory recall

memory cancel

subtract from memory

on/off switch

add in memory

per cent key

divide key

number key

multiply key

square root key

subtract key

clear key

add key

clear-entry key

decimal-point key

equals key

carpentry

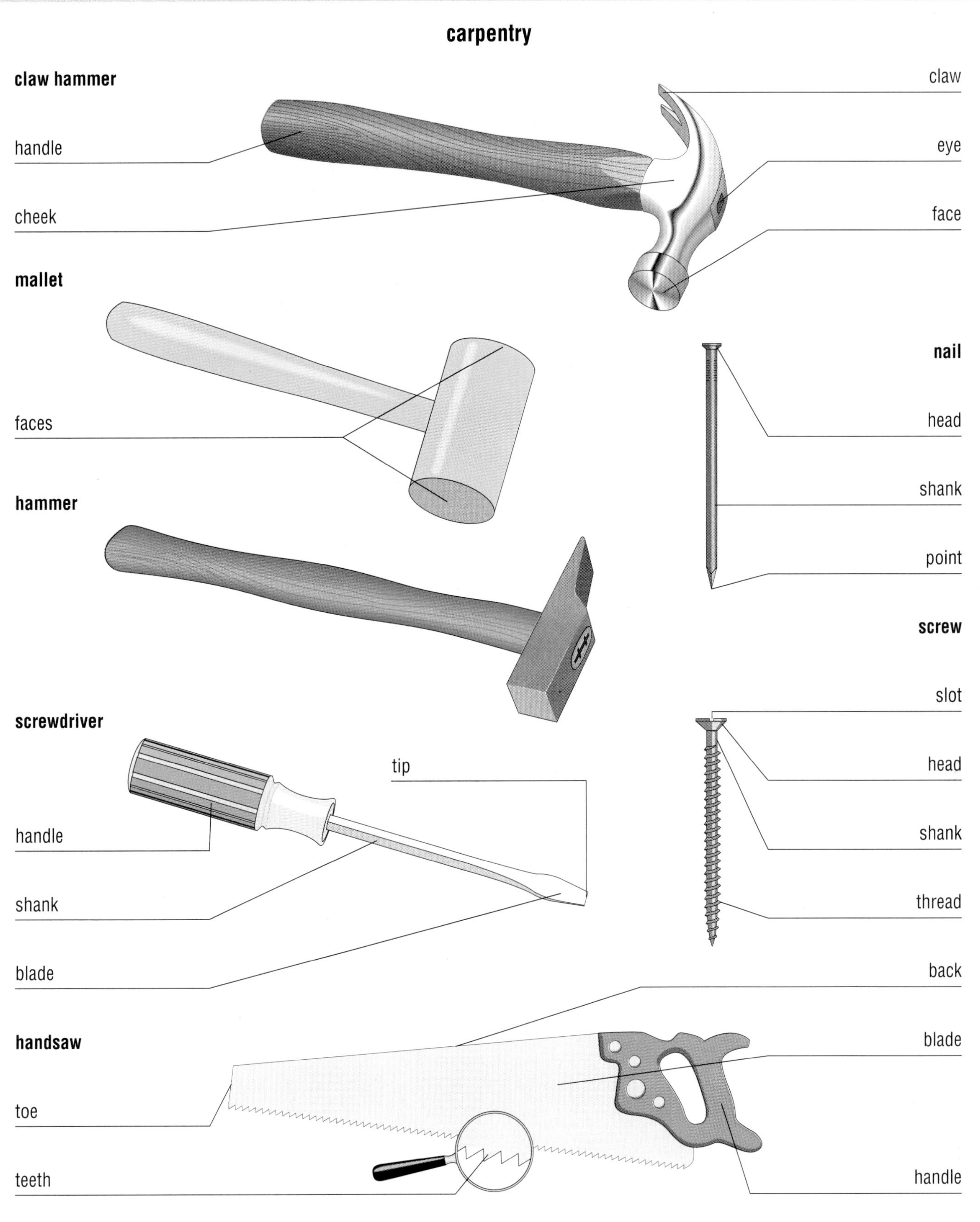

claw hammer

handle

cheek

claw

eye

face

mallet

faces

nail

head

shank

point

hammer

screw

slot

head

shank

thread

screwdriver

handle

tip

shank

blade

back

handsaw

blade

toe

teeth

handle

DO-IT-YOURSELF

tools

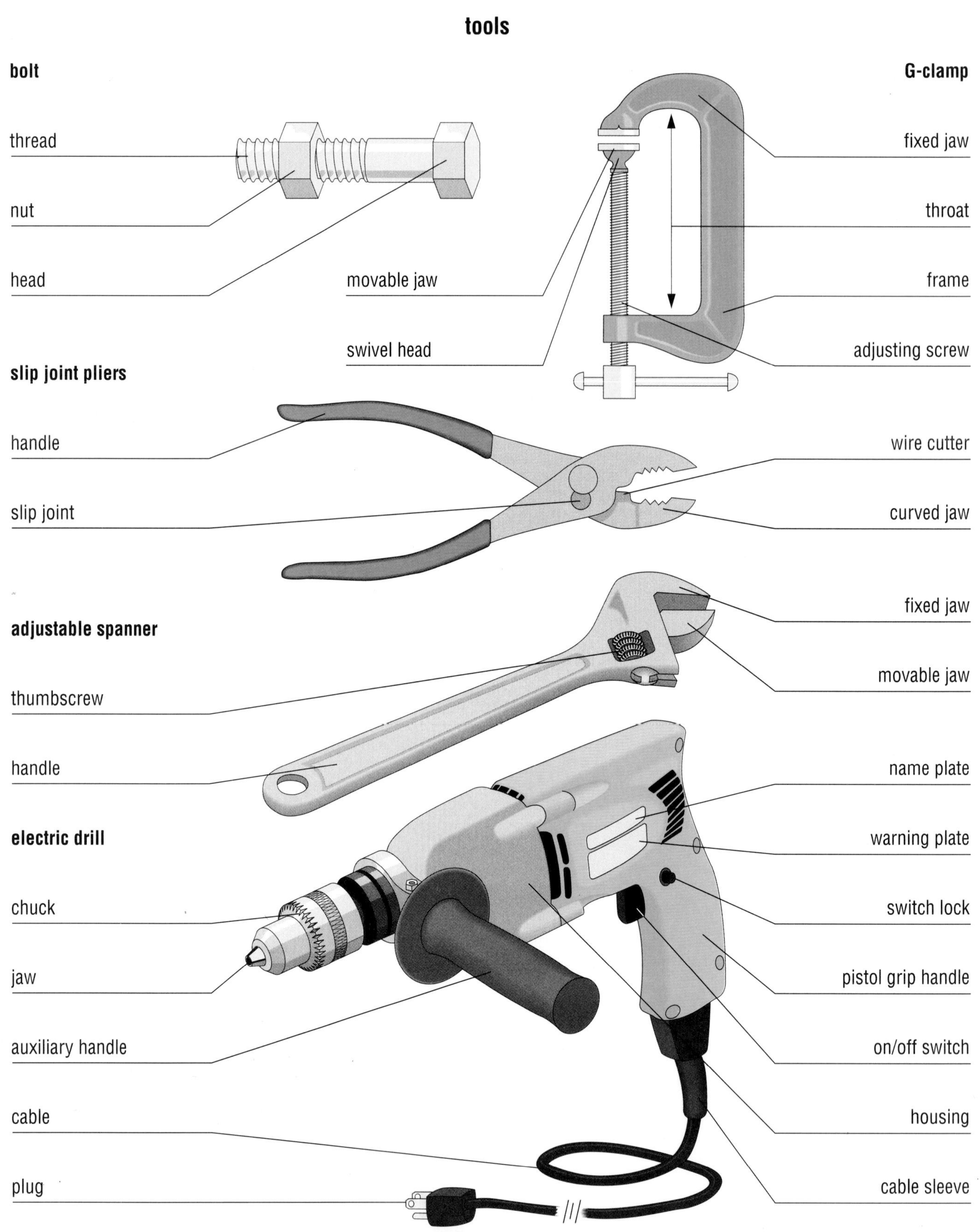

bolt

thread

nut

head

movable jaw

swivel head

G-clamp

fixed jaw

throat

frame

adjusting screw

slip joint pliers

handle

slip joint

wire cutter

curved jaw

adjustable spanner

thumbscrew

handle

fixed jaw

movable jaw

electric drill

chuck

jaw

auxiliary handle

cable

plug

name plate

warning plate

switch lock

pistol grip handle

on/off switch

housing

cable sleeve

painting upkeep

paint roller

roller frame

roller cover

paint tray

brush

handle

ferrule

bristles

scraper

removable blade

knurled bolt

handle

extension ladder

rung

side rail

pulley

locking device

hoisting rope

stepladder

tool tray

brace

step

platform ladder

safety rail

shelf

platform

step

anti-slip shoe

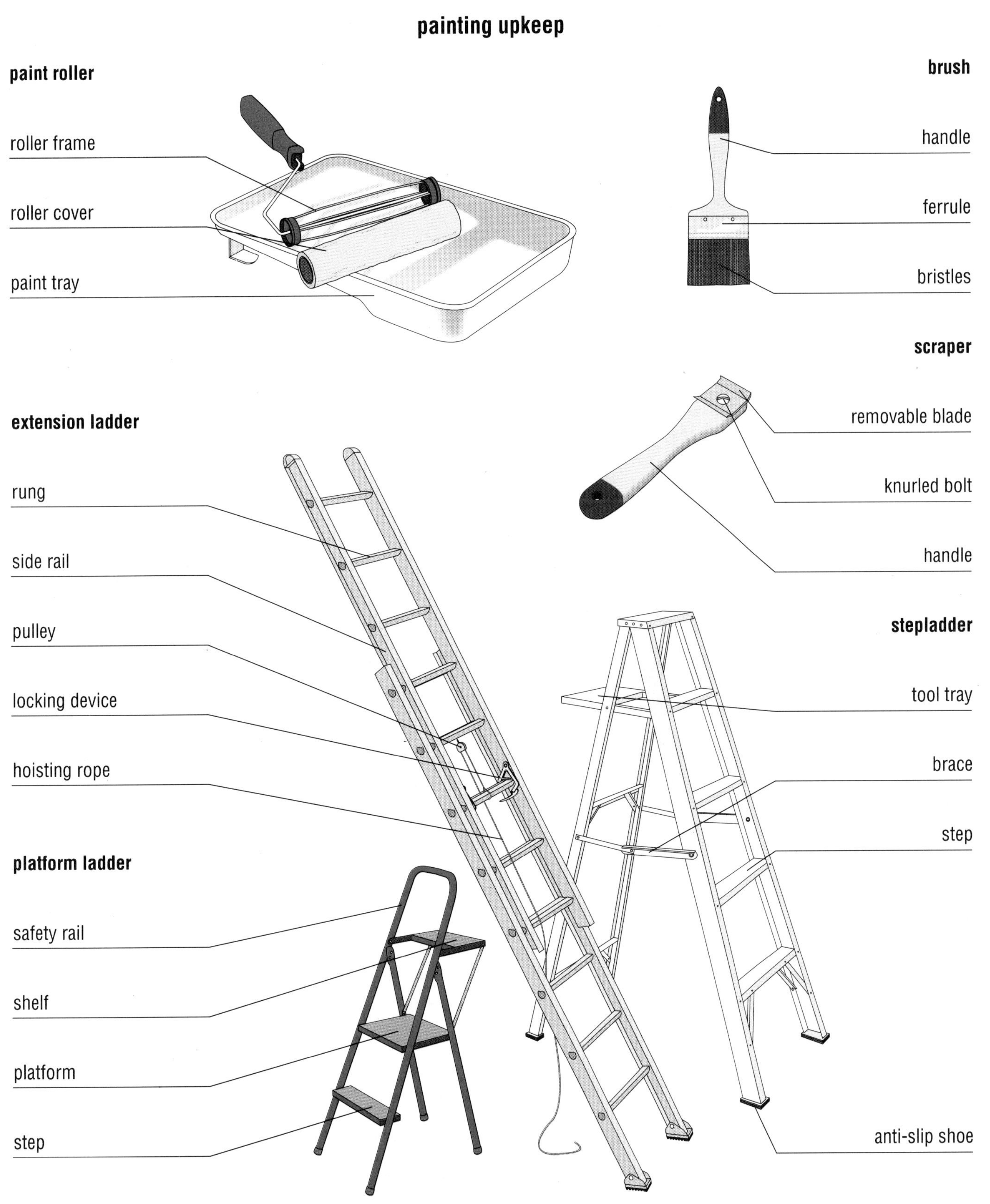

trainer

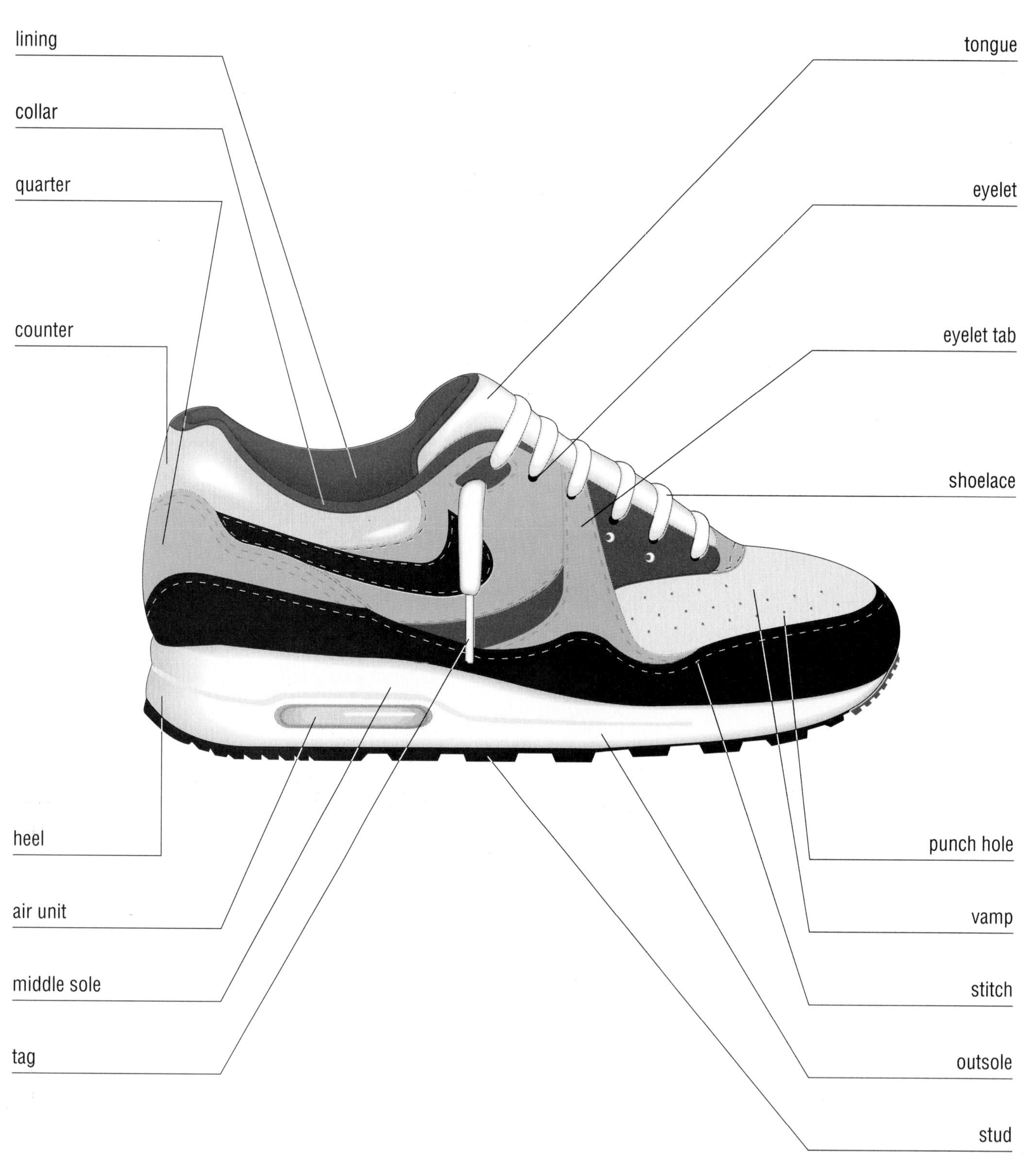

lining

collar

quarter

counter

heel

air unit

middle sole

tag

tongue

eyelet

eyelet tab

shoelace

punch hole

vamp

stitch

outsole

stud

men's clothing

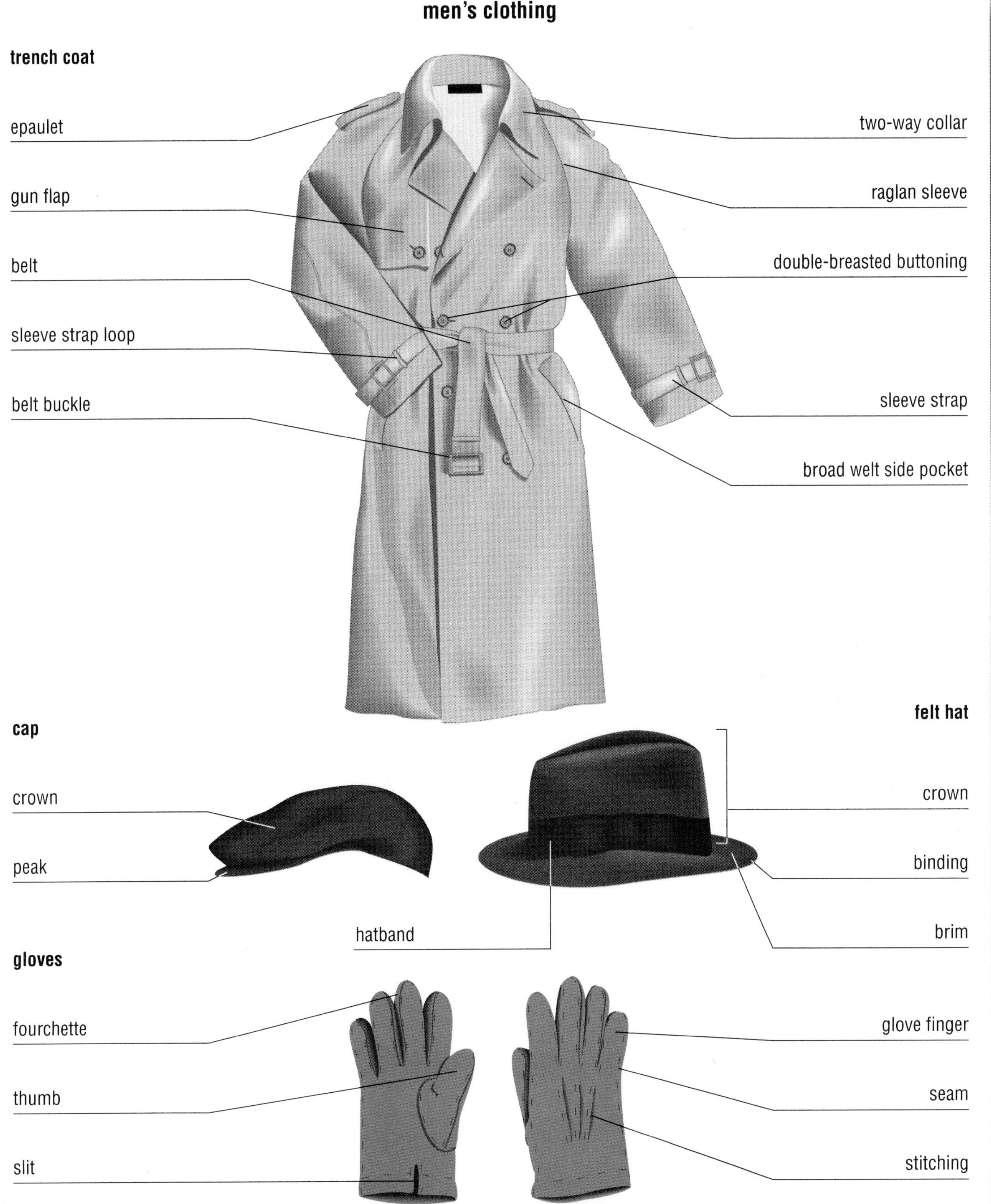

trench coat

epaulet

gun flap

belt

sleeve strap loop

belt buckle

two-way collar

raglan sleeve

double-breasted buttoning

sleeve strap

broad welt side pocket

cap

crown

peak

felt hat

crown

binding

brim

hatband

gloves

fourchette

thumb

slit

glove finger

seam

stitching

CLOTHING

single-breasted jacket

waistcoat

single-breasted jacket

tie

top collar

pocket handkerchief

notch

watch pocket

lapel

breast welt pocket

shirt

shirt cuff

flap pocket

shirt tail

trousers

casual jacket

waistband

front top pocket

waistband extension

belt loop

fly

crease

elastic waistband

snap fastener

turn-up

hand warmer pocket

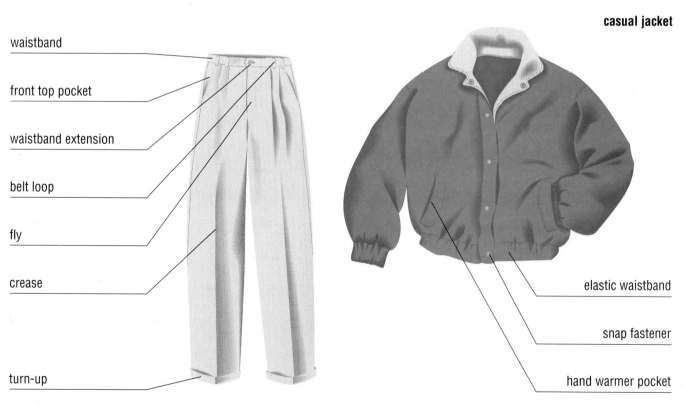

sweaters

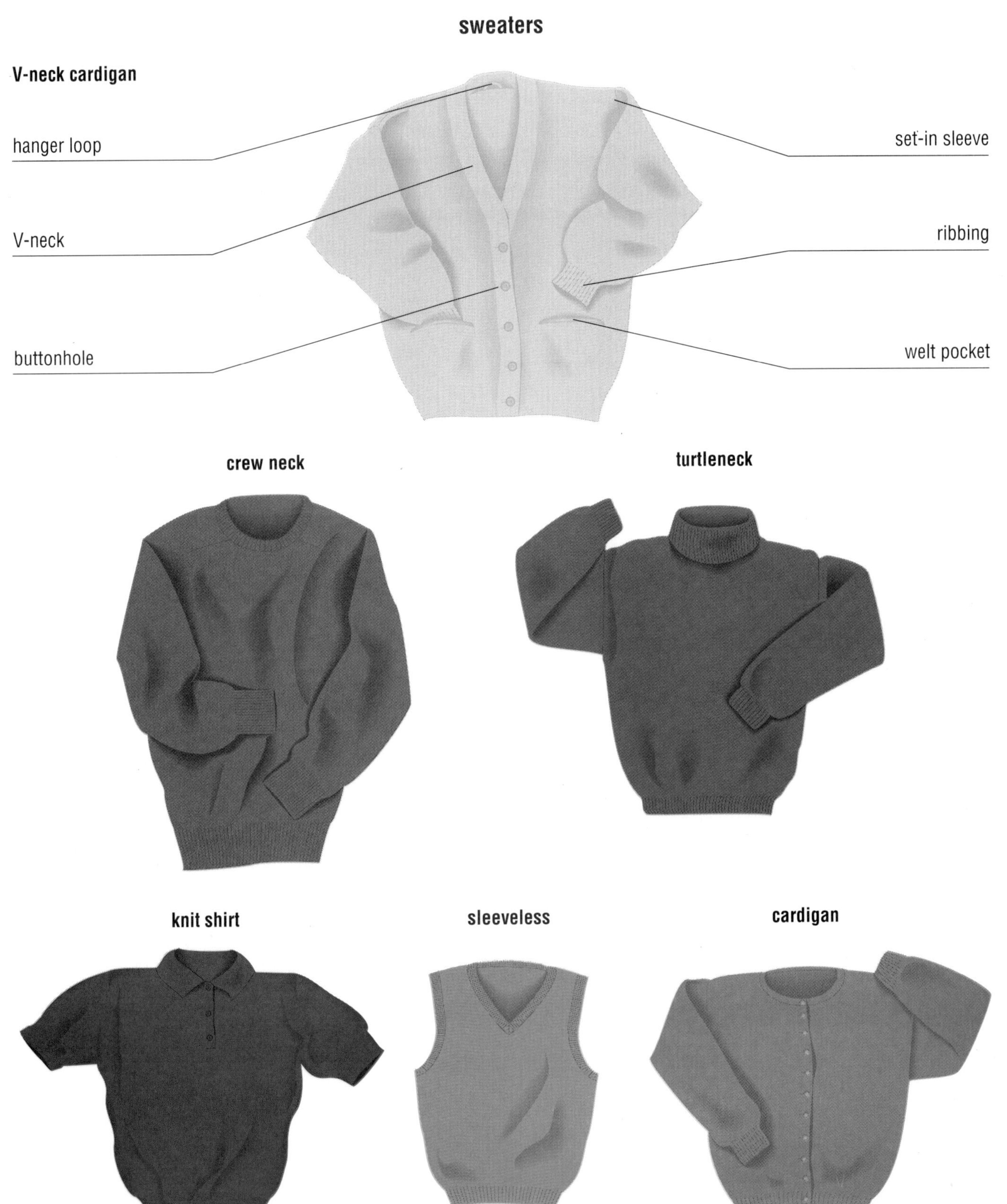

V-neck cardigan

hanger loop

set-in sleeve

V-neck

ribbing

buttonhole

welt pocket

crew neck

turtleneck

knit shirt

sleeveless

cardigan

CLOTHING

women's clothing

coats

jacket

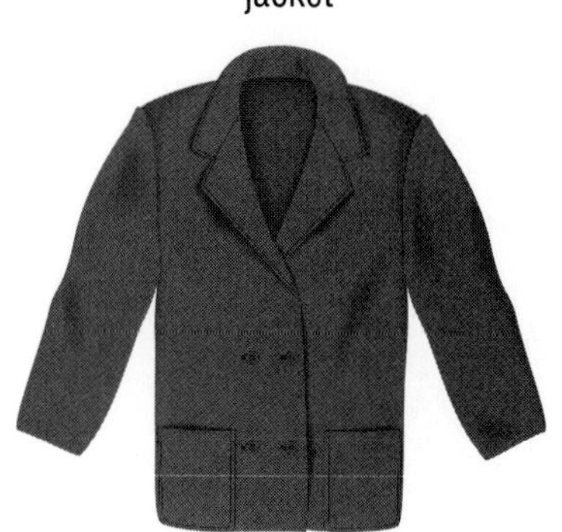

car coat

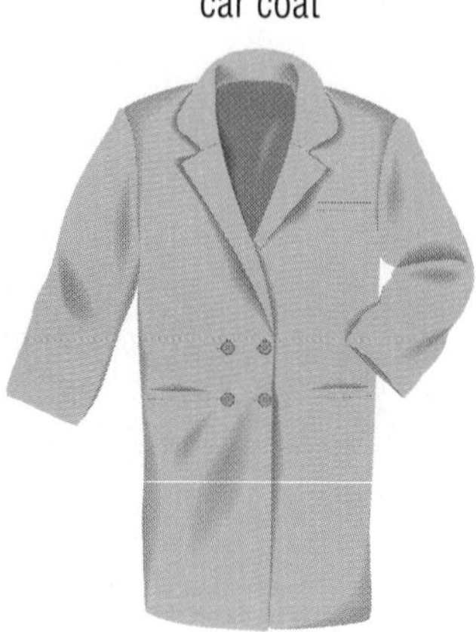

overcoat

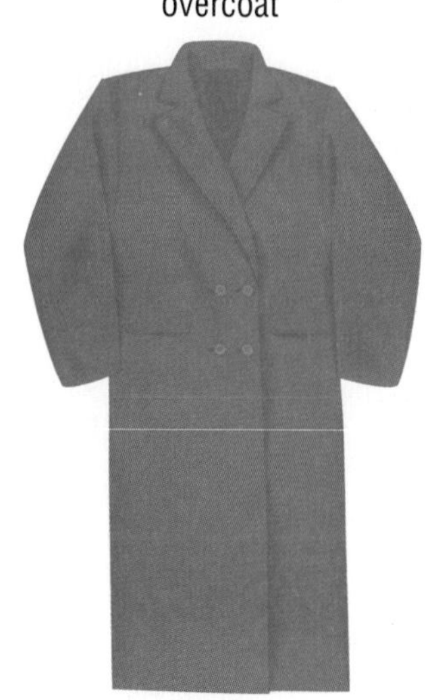

blouses

classic blouse

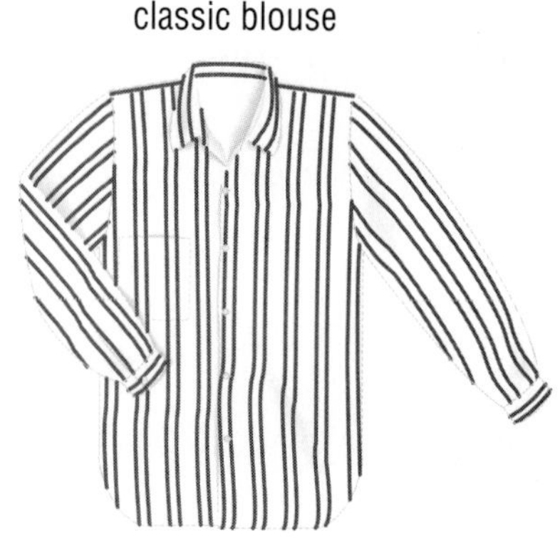

wrap-over top

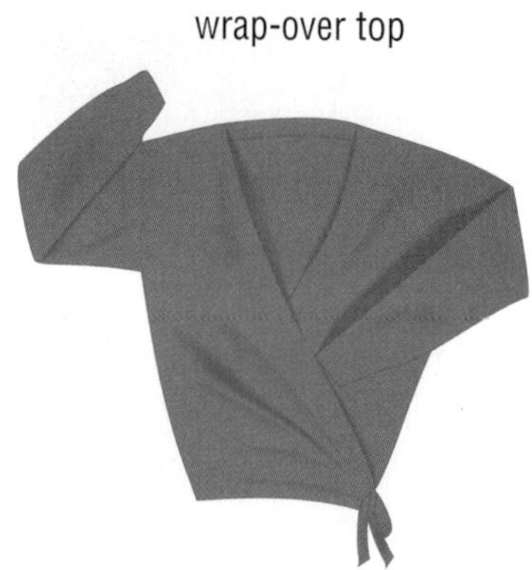

leotard

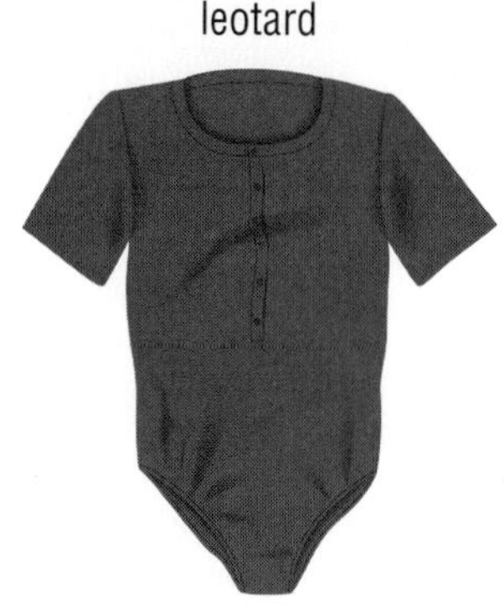

skirts

pleated skirt

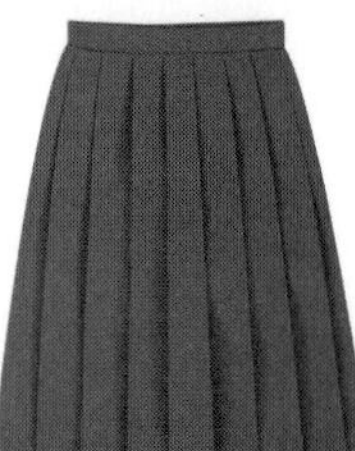

straight skirt

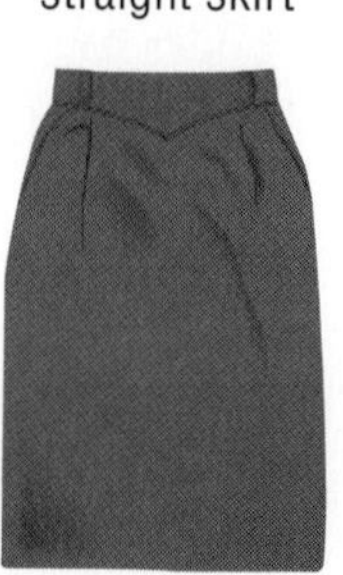

culottes

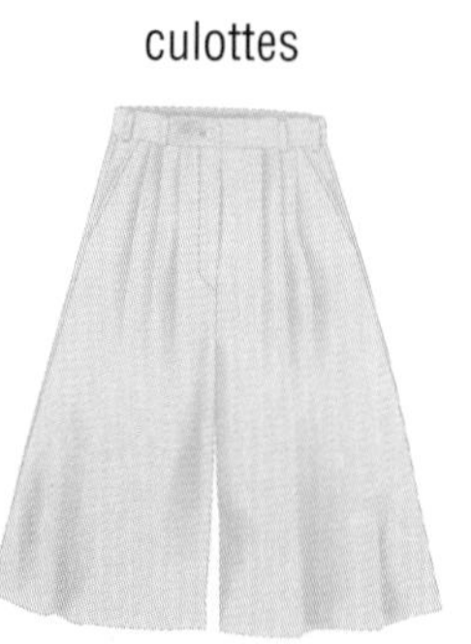

children's clothing

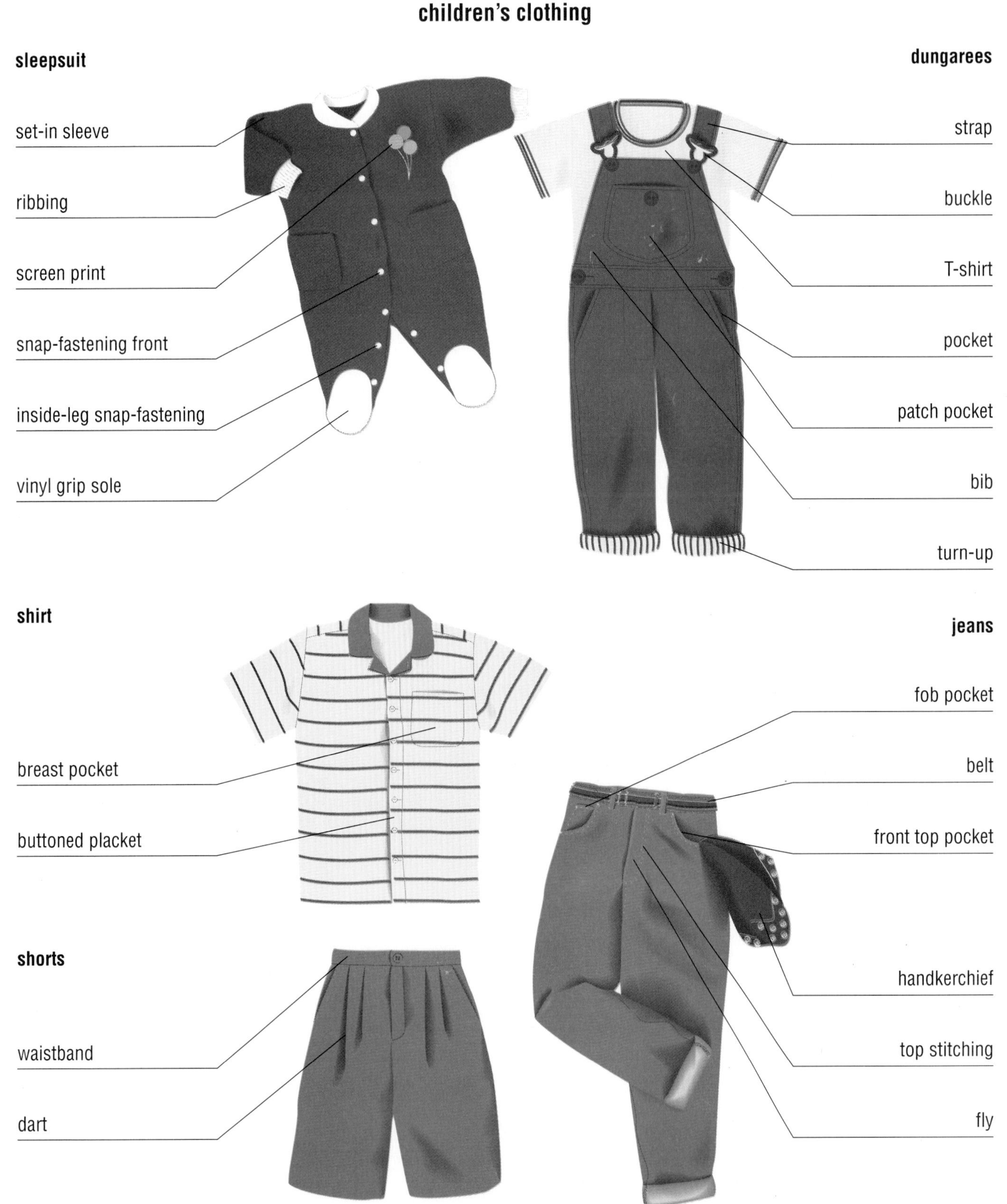

sleepsuit

set-in sleeve

ribbing

screen print

snap-fastening front

inside-leg snap-fastening

vinyl grip sole

dungarees

strap

buckle

T-shirt

pocket

patch pocket

bib

turn-up

shirt

breast pocket

buttoned placket

shorts

waistband

dart

jeans

fob pocket

belt

front top pocket

handkerchief

top stitching

fly

CLOTHING

personal articles

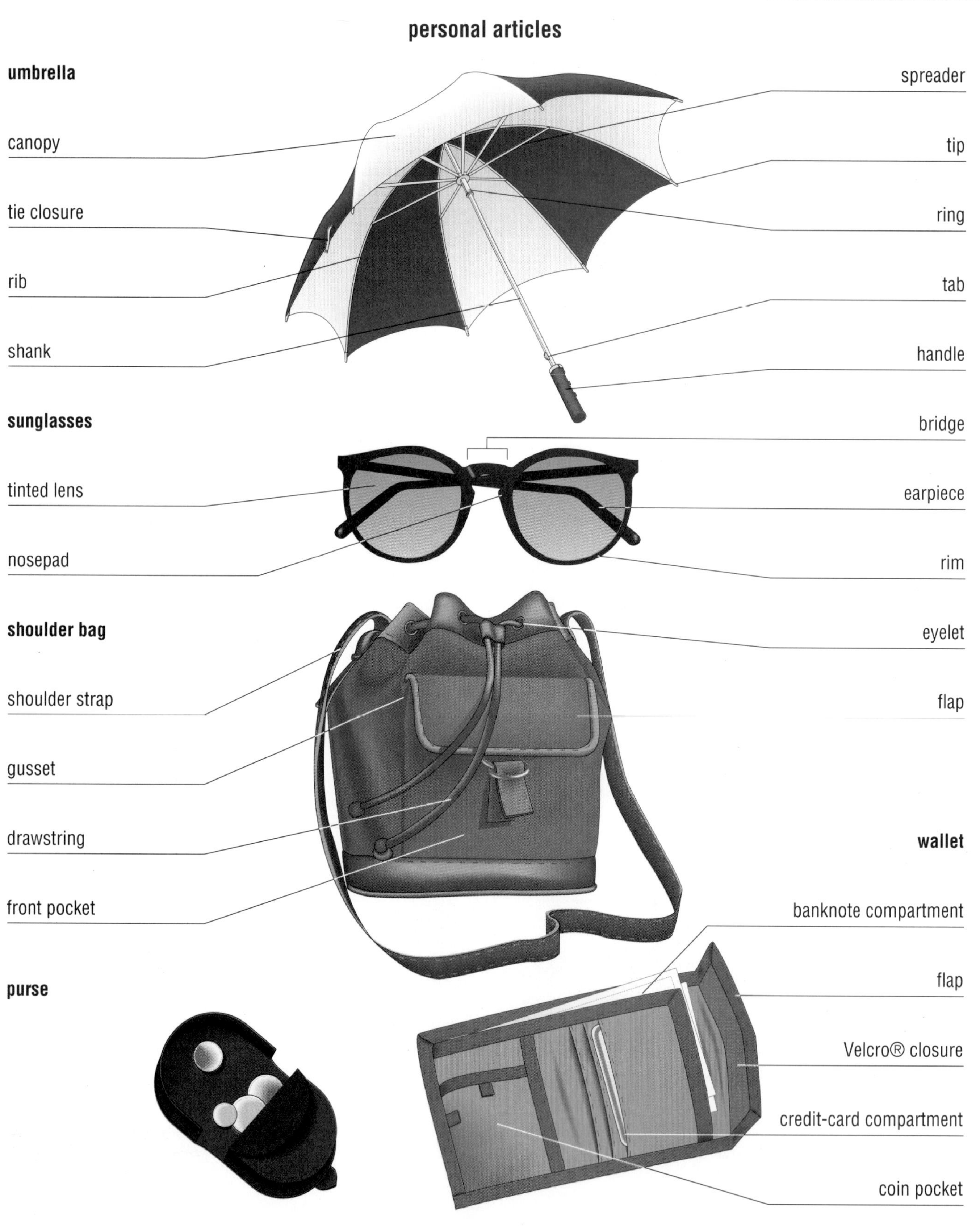

umbrella

canopy

tie closure

rib

shank

spreader

tip

ring

tab

handle

sunglasses

tinted lens

nosepad

bridge

earpiece

rim

shoulder bag

shoulder strap

gusset

drawstring

front pocket

eyelet

flap

wallet

banknote compartment

flap

Velcro® closure

credit-card compartment

coin pocket

purse

telephones

telephone answering system

handset

speaker

tone selector

speaker volume control

message delay selector

message length selector

handset cord

memory index

incoming message cassette

calls indicator

push buttons

on/off light

on/off switch

message playback button

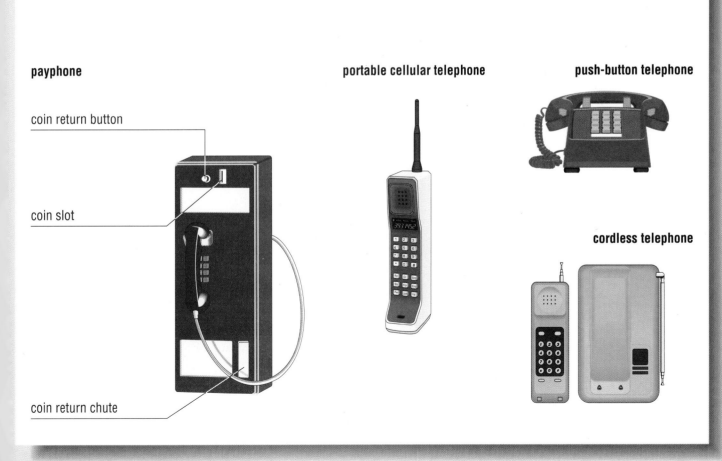

payphone

coin return button

coin slot

coin return chute

portable cellular telephone

push-button telephone

cordless telephone

Walkman®

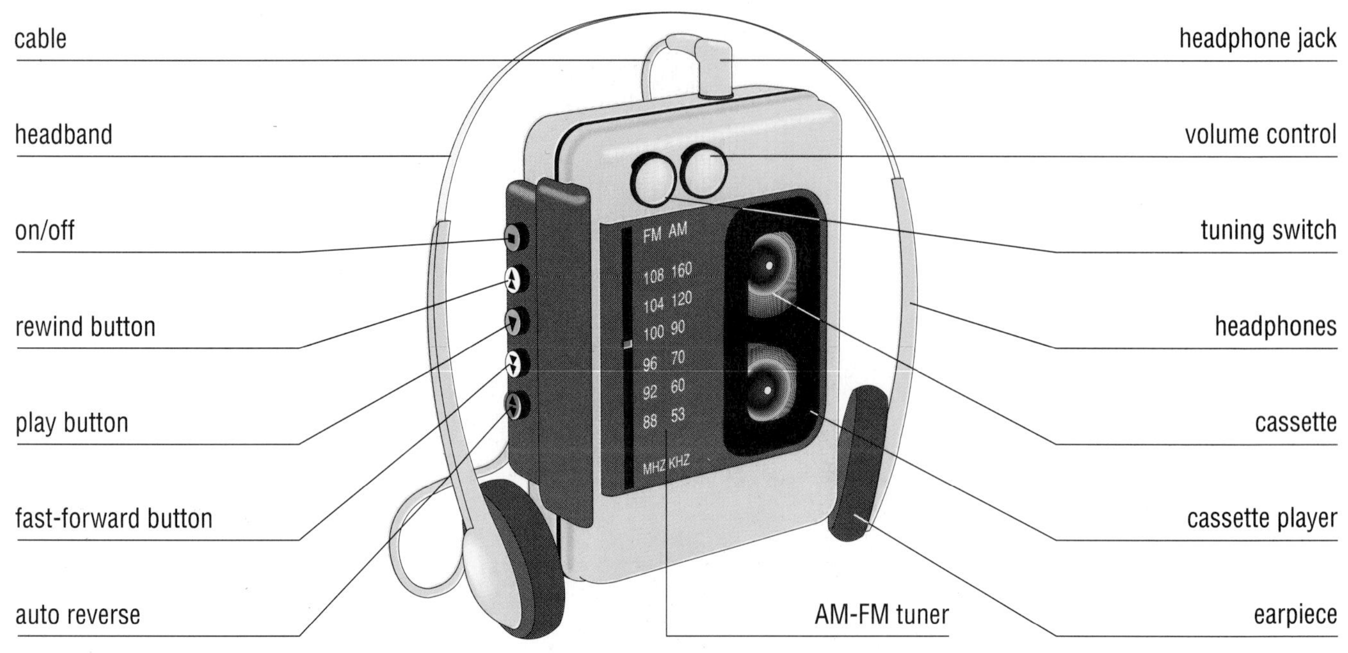

cable

headband

on/off

rewind button

play button

fast-forward button

auto reverse

headphone jack

volume control

tuning switch

headphones

cassette

cassette player

AM-FM tuner

earpiece

FM AM
108 160
104 120
100 90
96 70
92 60
88 53
MHZ KHZ

radio/cassette player

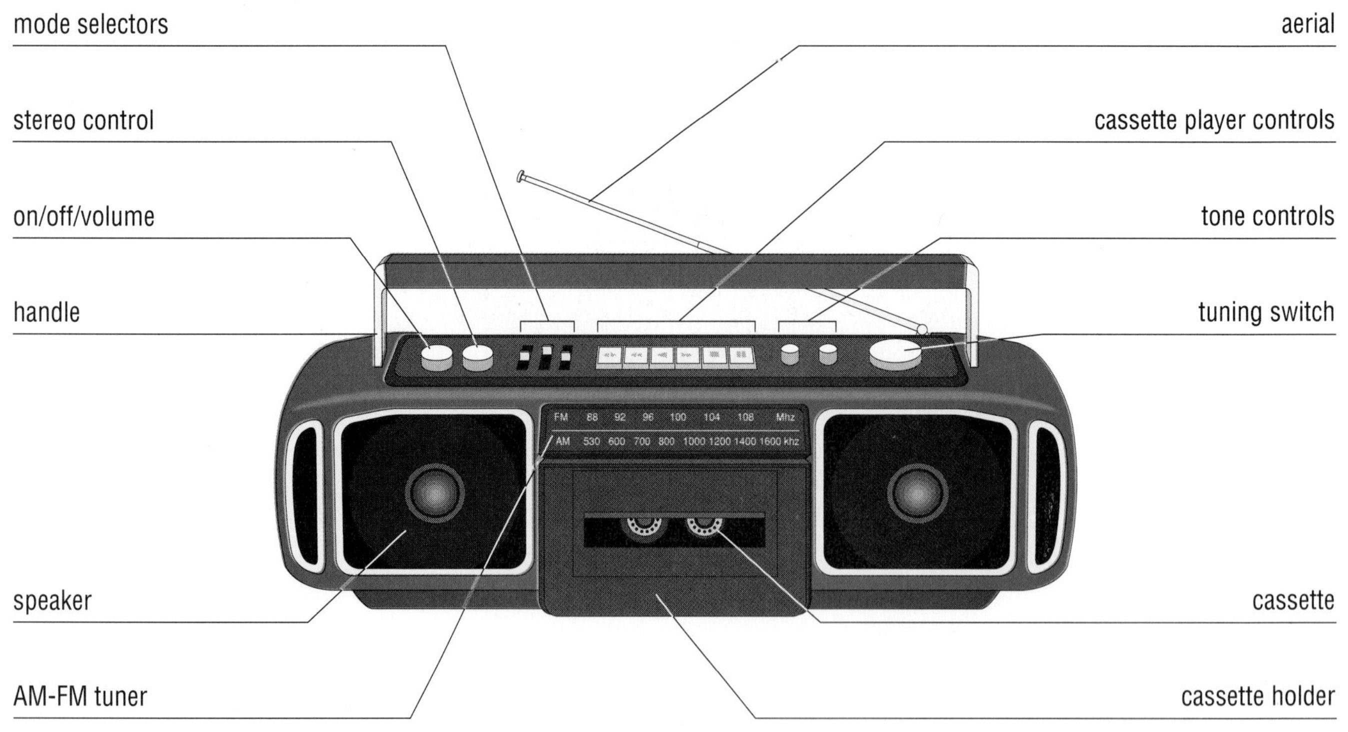

mode selectors

stereo control

on/off/volume

handle

speaker

AM-FM tuner

aerial

cassette player controls

tone controls

tuning switch

cassette

cassette holder

FM 88 92 96 100 104 108 Mhz
AM 530 600 700 800 1000 1200 1400 1600 khz

camera

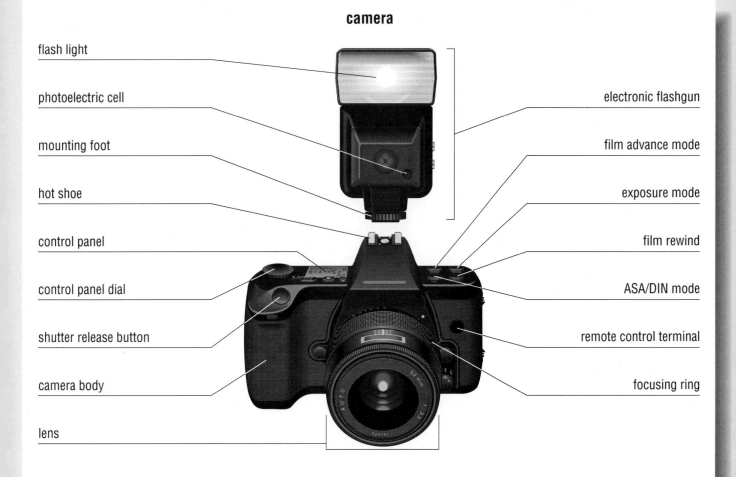

flash light

photoelectric cell

mounting foot

hot shoe

control panel

control panel dial

shutter release button

camera body

lens

electronic flashgun

film advance mode

exposure mode

film rewind

ASA/DIN mode

remote control terminal

focusing ring

slide projector

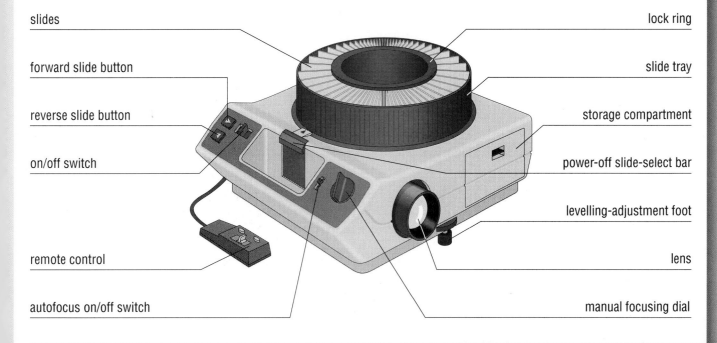

slides

forward slide button

reverse slide button

on/off switch

remote control

autofocus on/off switch

lock ring

slide tray

storage compartment

power-off slide-select bar

levelling-adjustment foot

lens

manual focusing dial

television

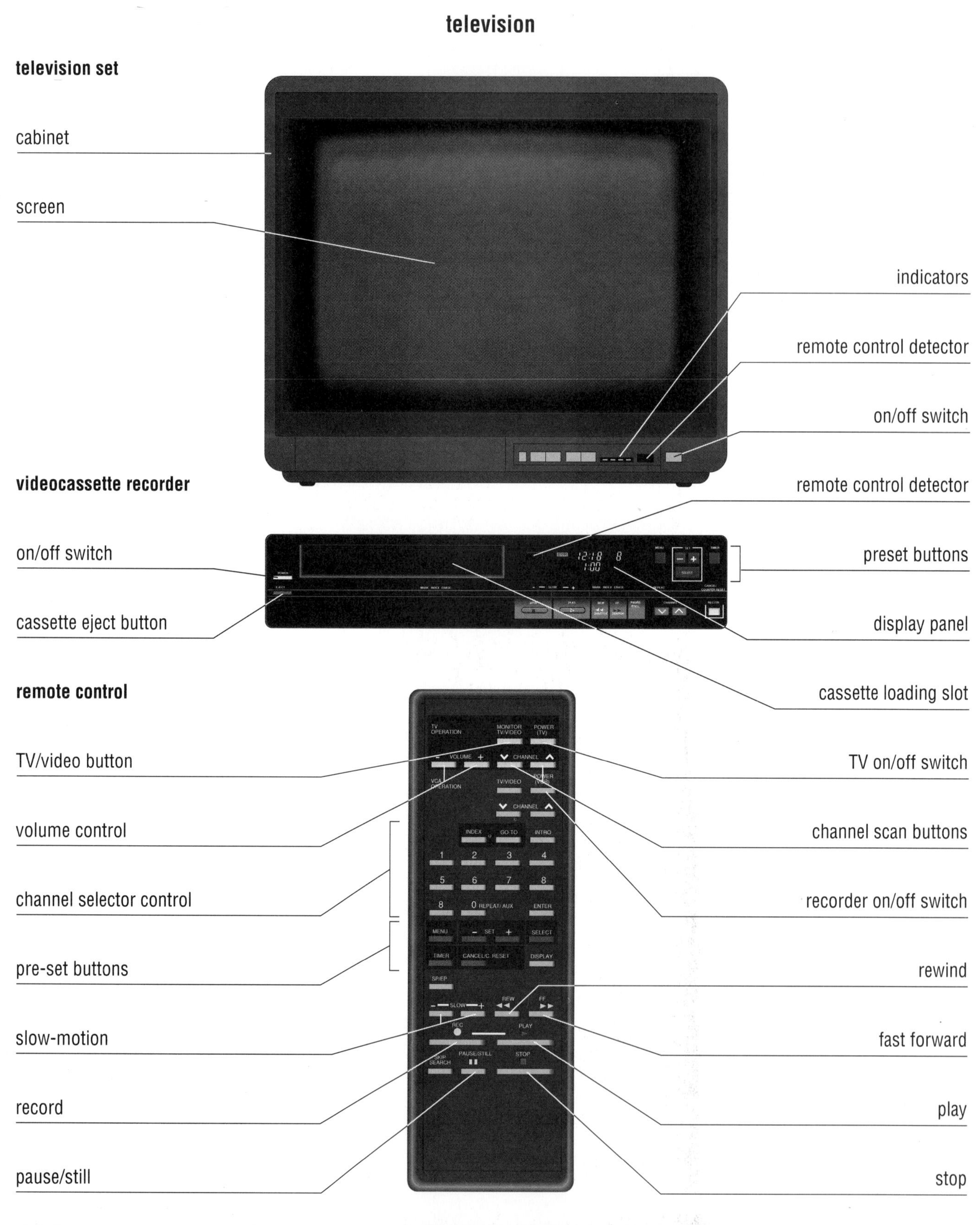

television set

cabinet

screen

indicators

remote control detector

on/off switch

videocassette recorder

remote control detector

on/off switch

preset buttons

cassette eject button

display panel

remote control

cassette loading slot

TV/video button

TV on/off switch

volume control

channel scan buttons

channel selector control

recorder on/off switch

pre-set buttons

rewind

slow-motion

fast forward

record

play

pause/still

stop

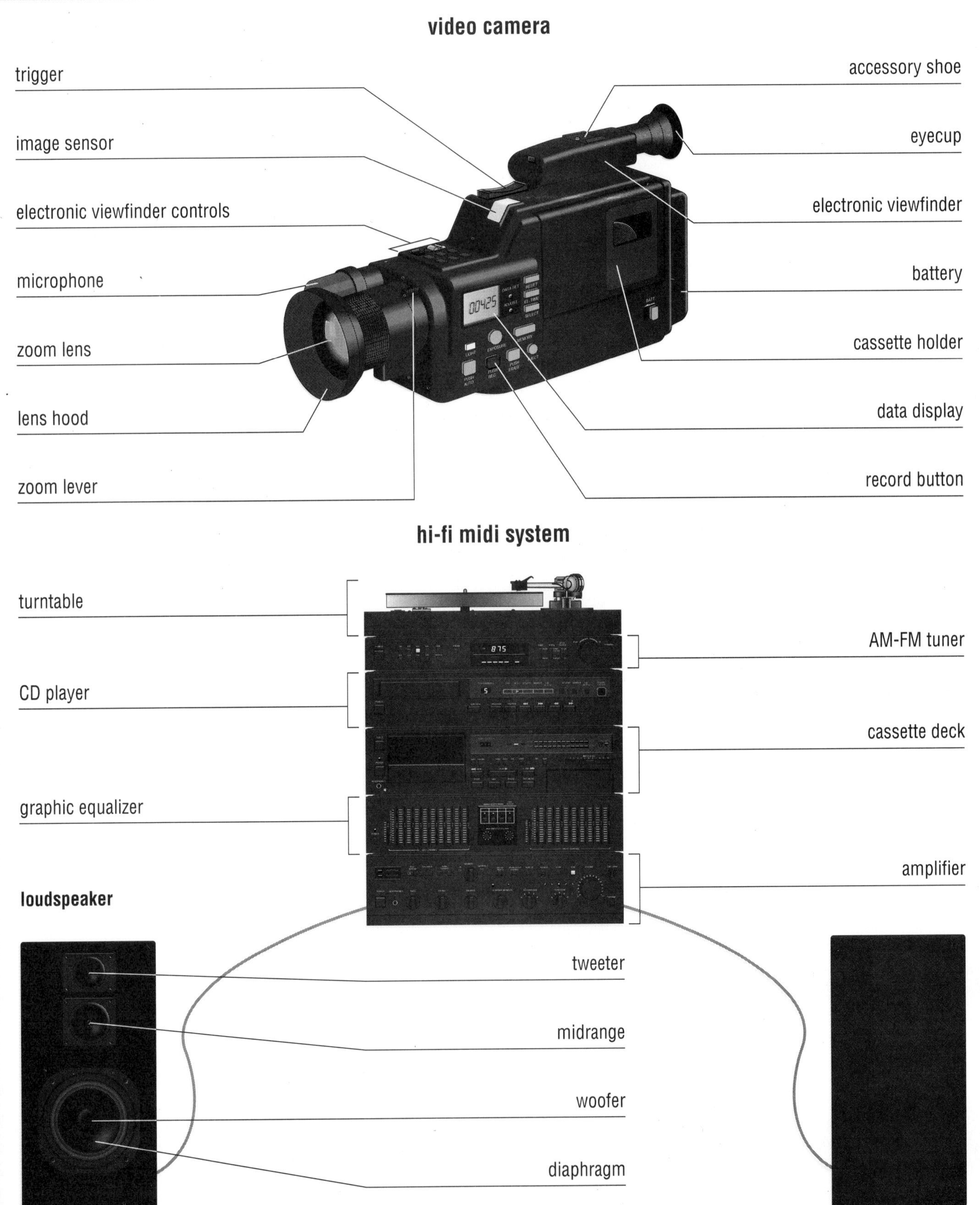

video camera

trigger

image sensor

electronic viewfinder controls

microphone

zoom lens

lens hood

zoom lever

accessory shoe

eyecup

electronic viewfinder

battery

cassette holder

data display

record button

hi-fi midi system

turntable

CD player

graphic equalizer

loudspeaker

AM-FM tuner

cassette deck

amplifier

tweeter

midrange

woofer

diaphragm

car

body

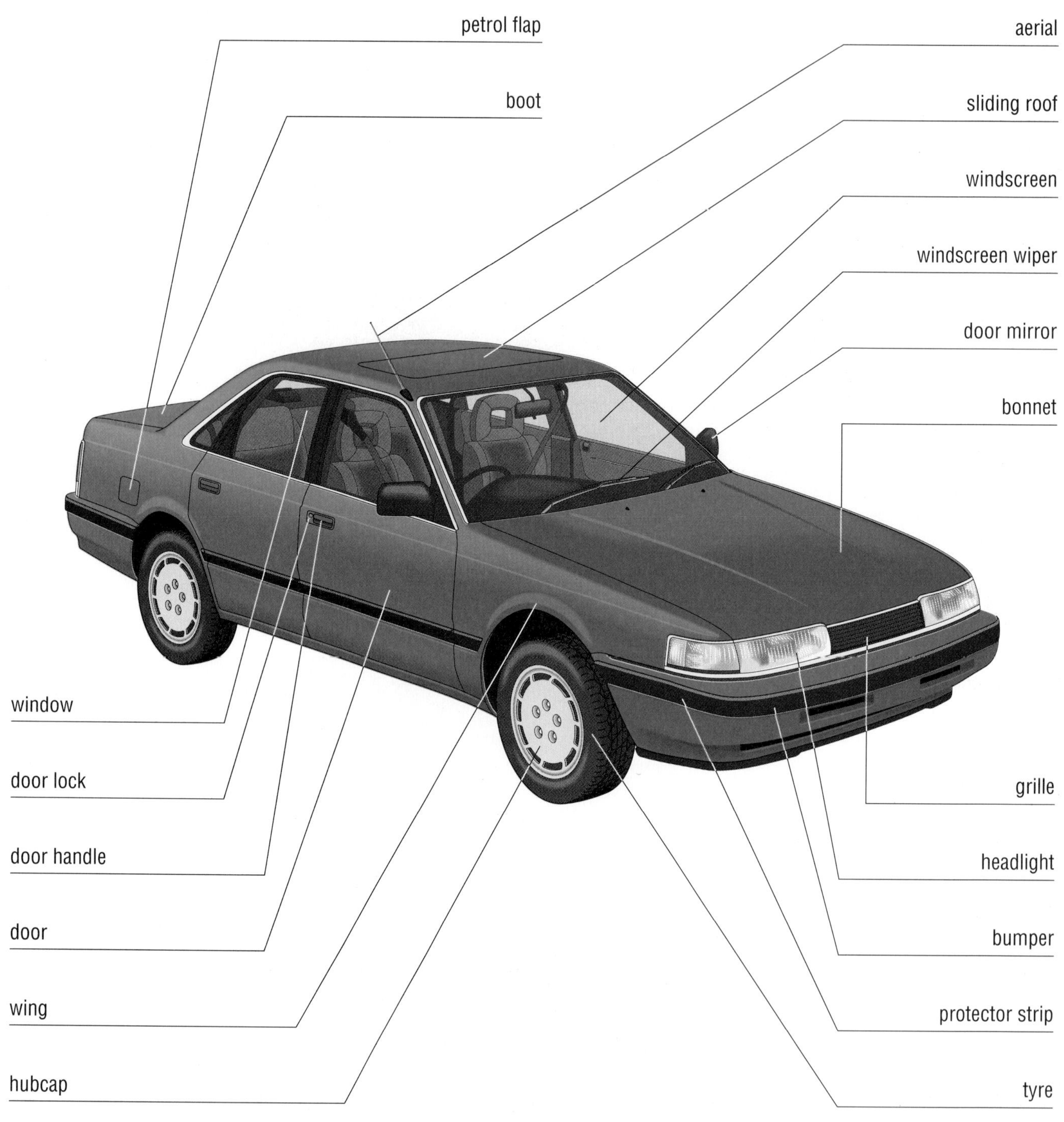

petrol flap

boot

aerial

sliding roof

windscreen

windscreen wiper

door mirror

bonnet

window

door lock

door handle

door

wing

hubcap

grille

headlight

bumper

protector strip

tyre

car

dashboard

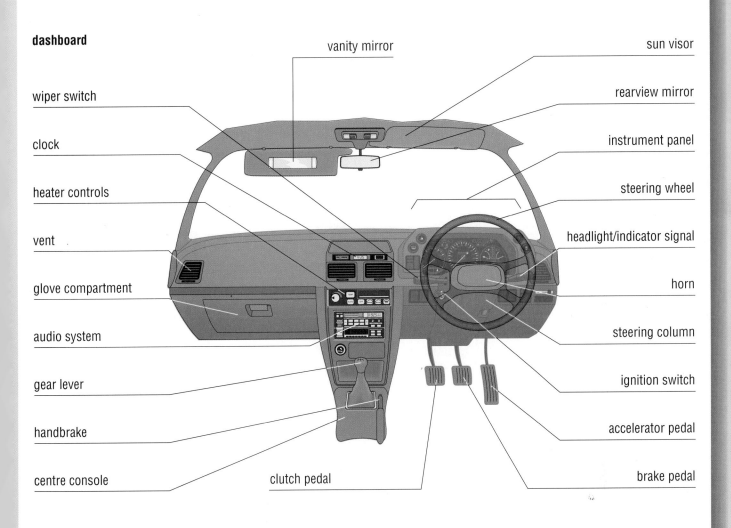

vanity mirror

sun visor

wiper switch

rearview mirror

clock

instrument panel

heater controls

steering wheel

vent

headlight/indicator signal

glove compartment

horn

audio system

steering column

gear lever

ignition switch

handbrake

accelerator pedal

centre console

clutch pedal

brake pedal

instrument panel

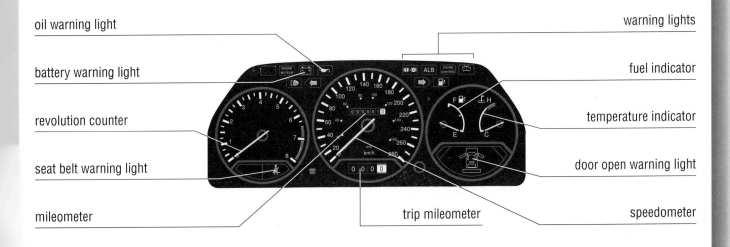

oil warning light

warning lights

battery warning light

fuel indicator

revolution counter

temperature indicator

seat belt warning light

door open warning light

mileometer

trip mileometer

speedometer

ROAD TRANSPORT

car lights

front lights

rear lights

main beam

dipped

indicator

side light

fog lamp

brake light

reversing light

number plate light

indicator

side light

rear light

brake light

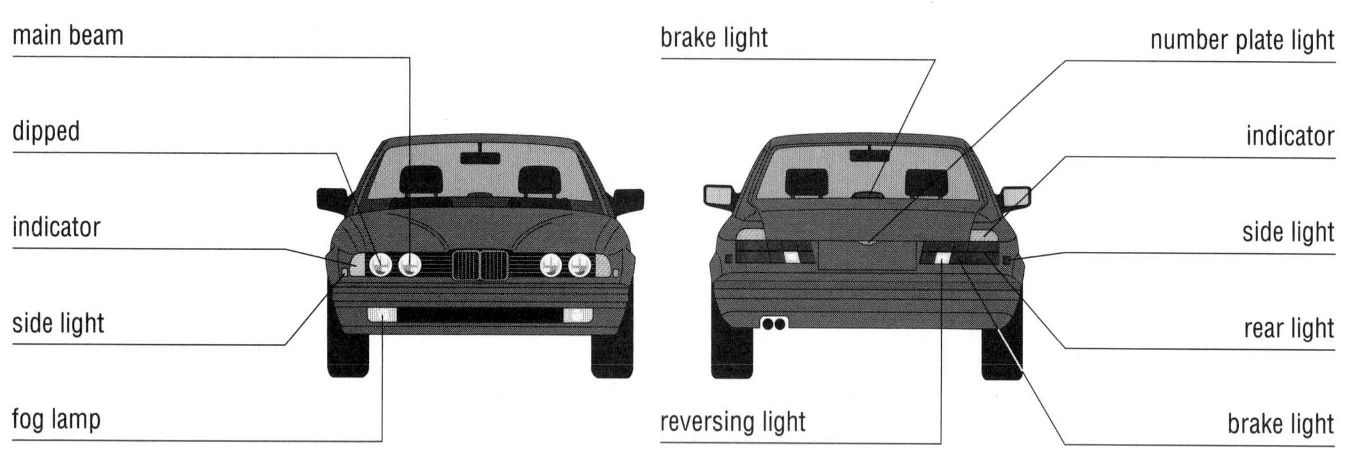

types of bodies

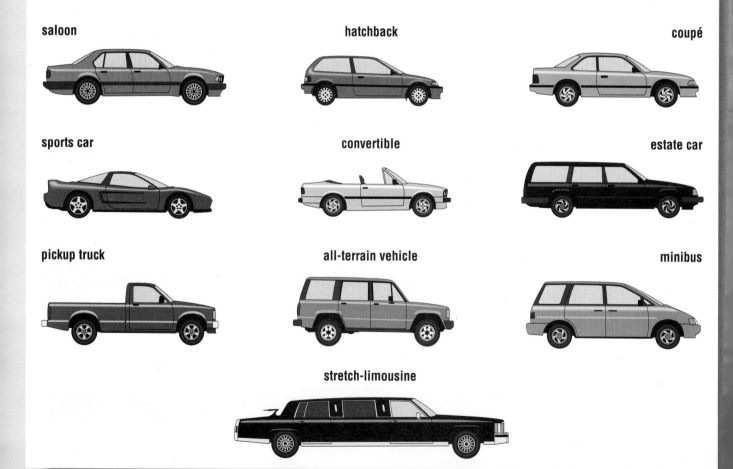

saloon

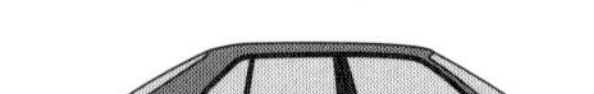

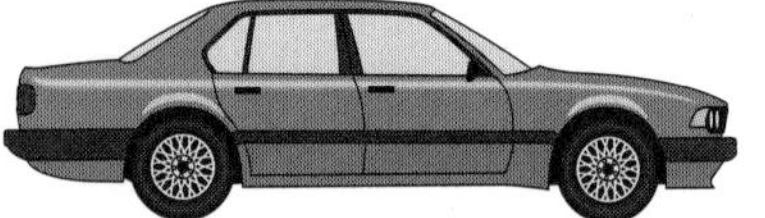

hatchback

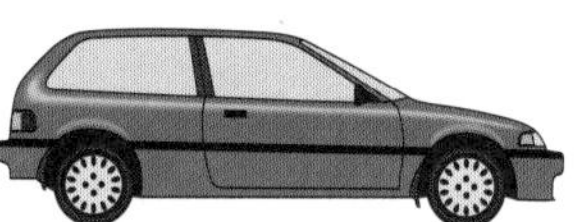

coupé

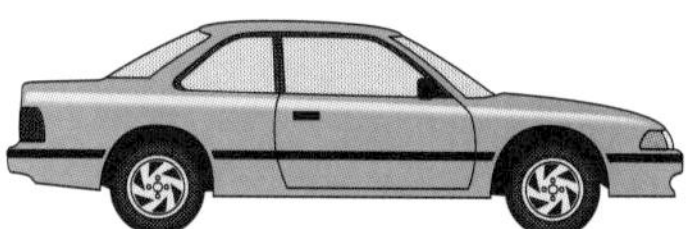

sports car

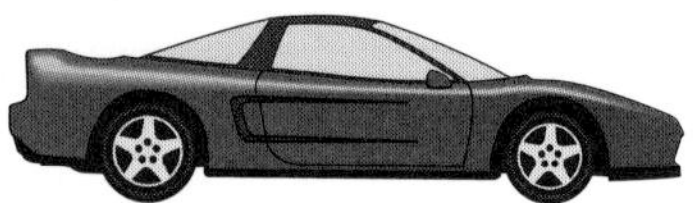

convertible

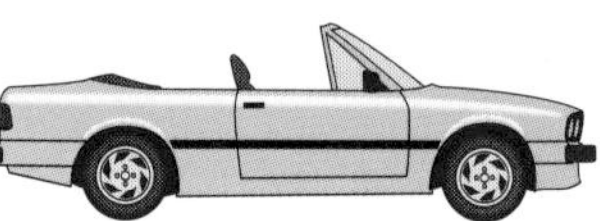

estate car

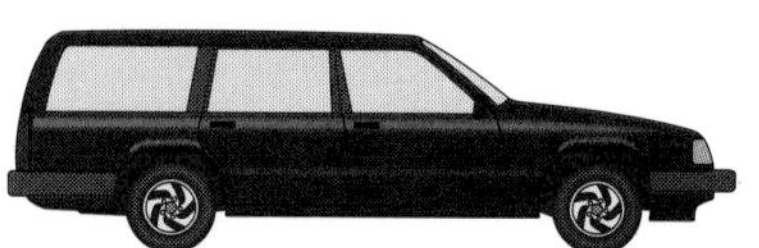

pickup truck

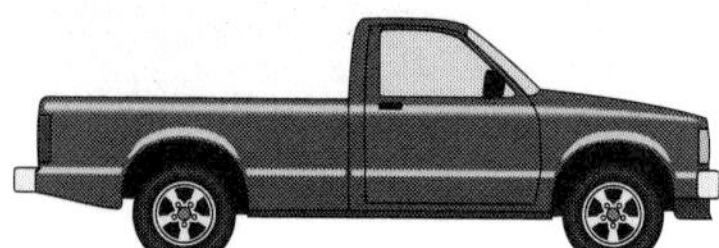

all-terrain vehicle

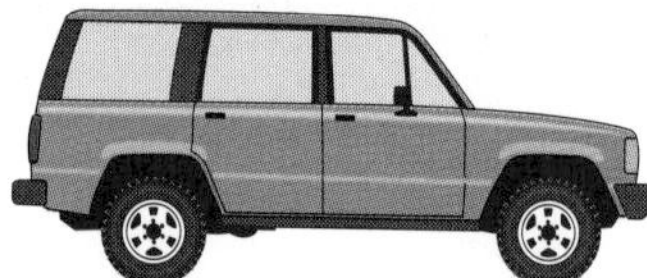

minibus

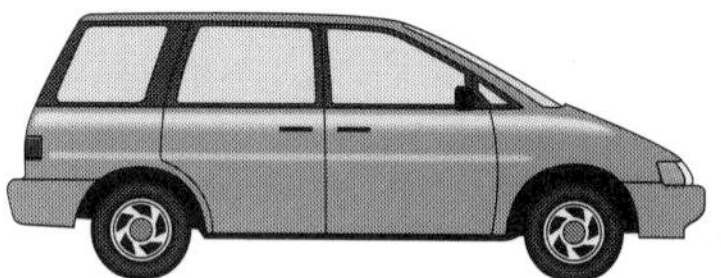

stretch-limousine

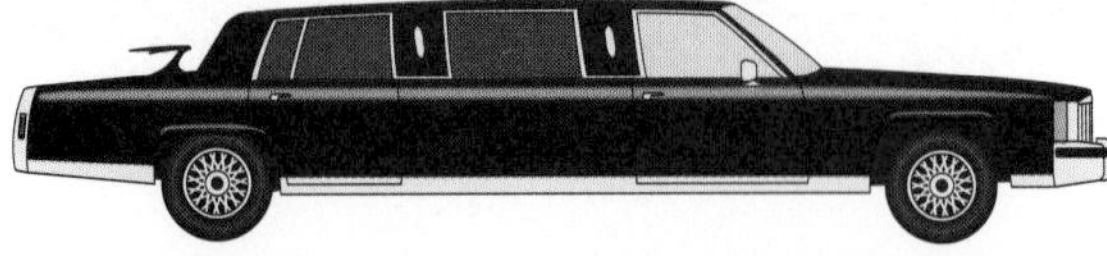

caravan

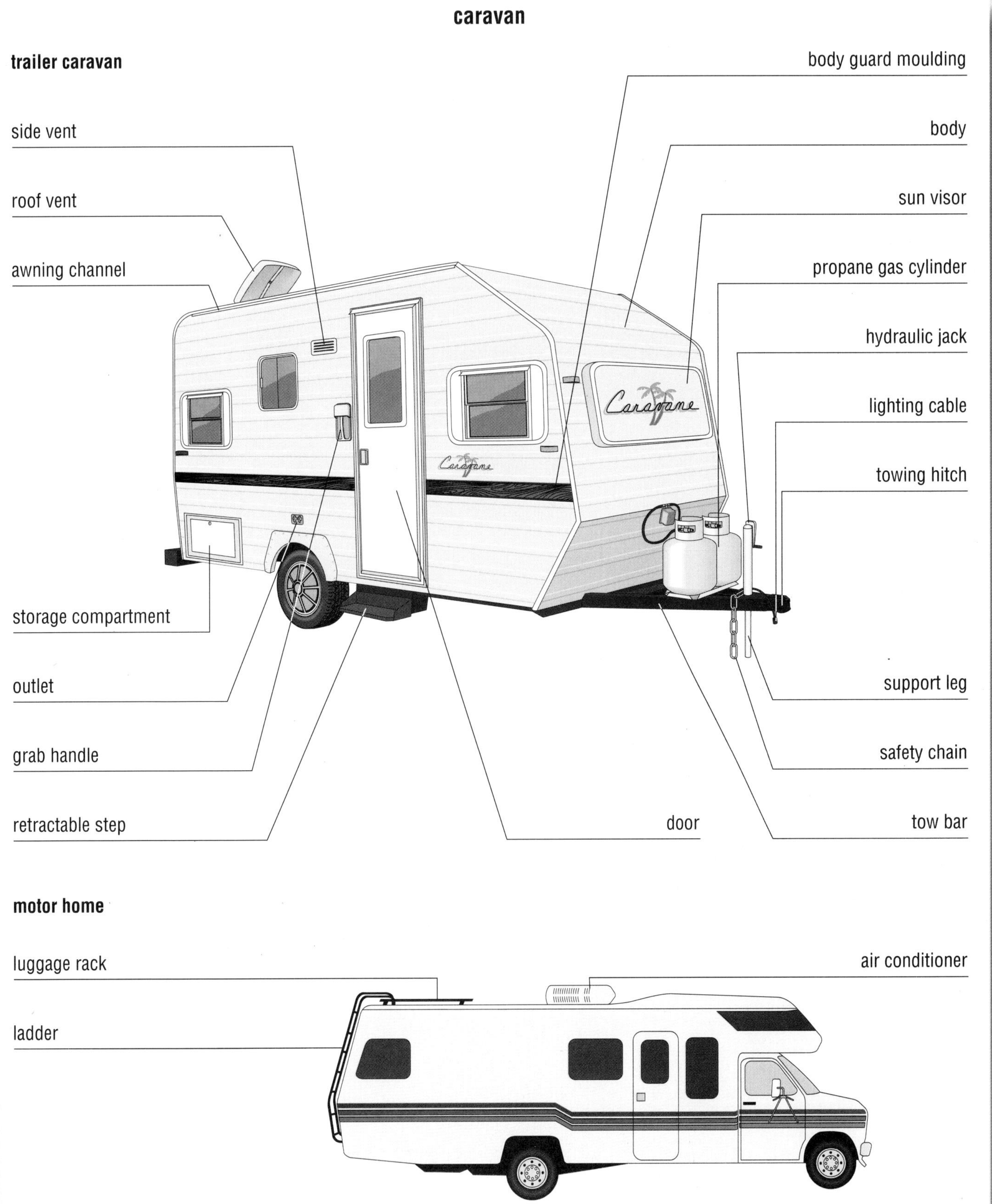

trailer caravan

side vent

roof vent

awning channel

storage compartment

outlet

grab handle

retractable step

body guard moulding

body

sun visor

propane gas cylinder

hydraulic jack

lighting cable

towing hitch

support leg

safety chain

tow bar

door

motor home

luggage rack

ladder

air conditioner

ROAD TRANSPORT

tractor unit

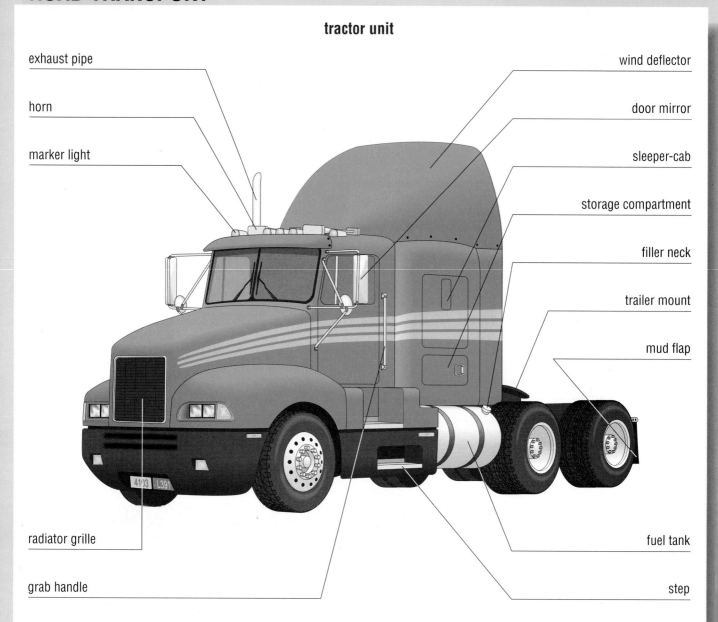

exhaust pipe

horn

marker light

wind deflector

door mirror

sleeper-cab

storage compartment

filler neck

trailer mount

mud flap

radiator grille

grab handle

fuel tank

step

articulated vehicle

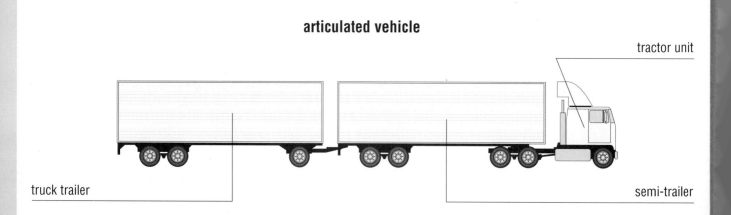

tractor unit

truck trailer

semi-trailer

motorcycle

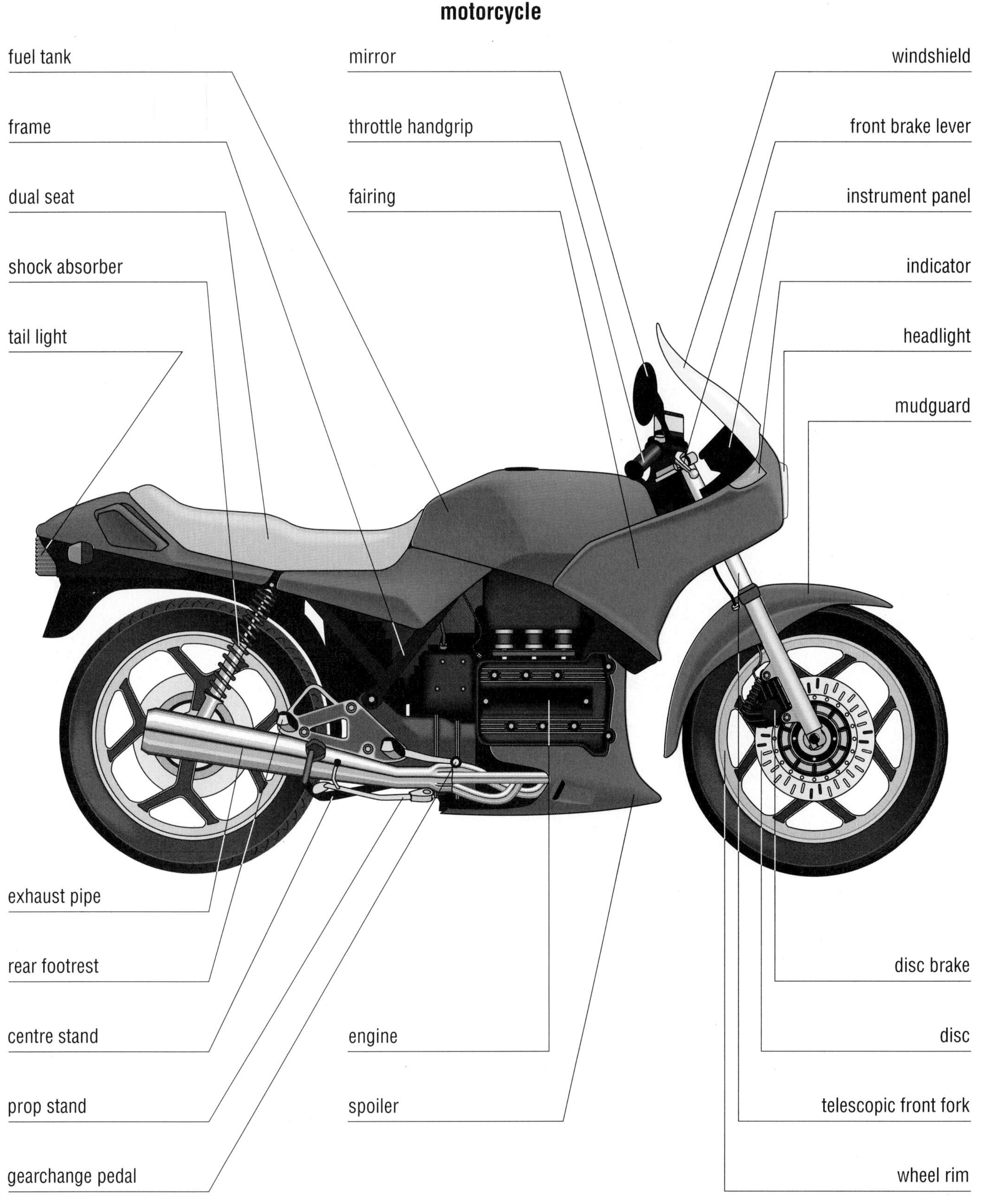

fuel tank

frame

dual seat

shock absorber

tail light

mirror

throttle handgrip

fairing

windshield

front brake lever

instrument panel

indicator

headlight

mudguard

exhaust pipe

rear footrest

centre stand

prop stand

gearchange pedal

engine

spoiler

disc brake

disc

telescopic front fork

wheel rim

petrol station

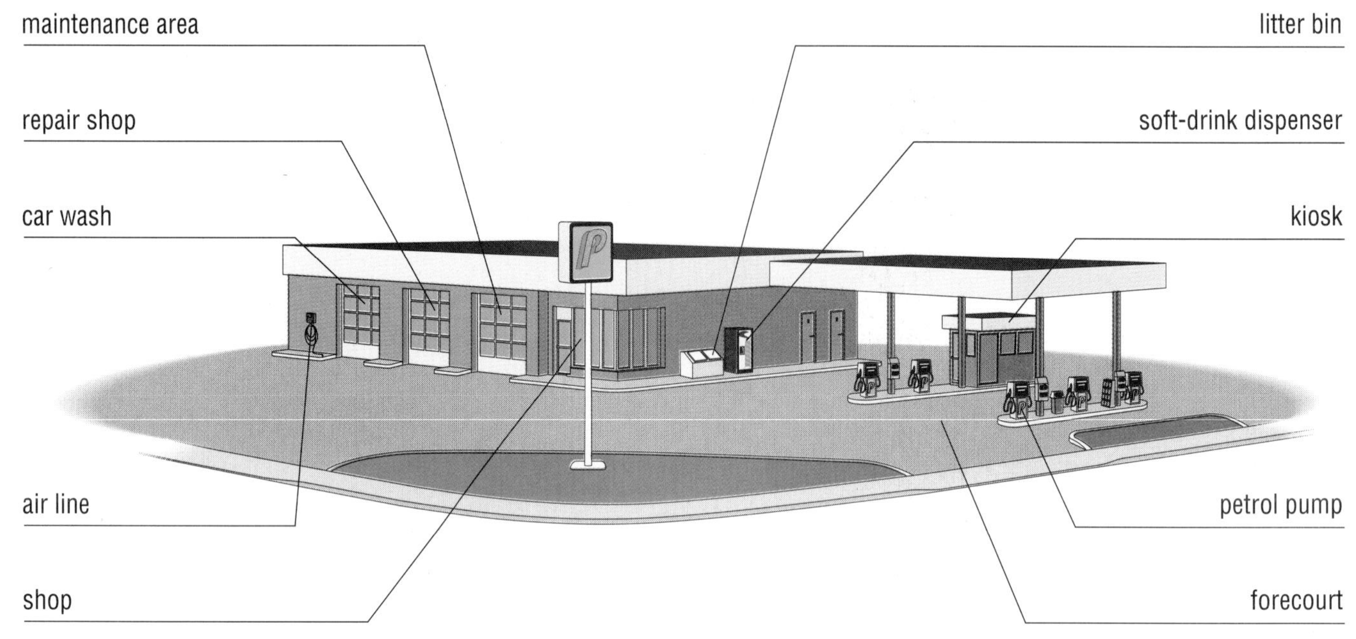

maintenance area

repair shop

car wash

air line

shop

litter bin

soft-drink dispenser

kiosk

petrol pump

forecourt

petrol pump

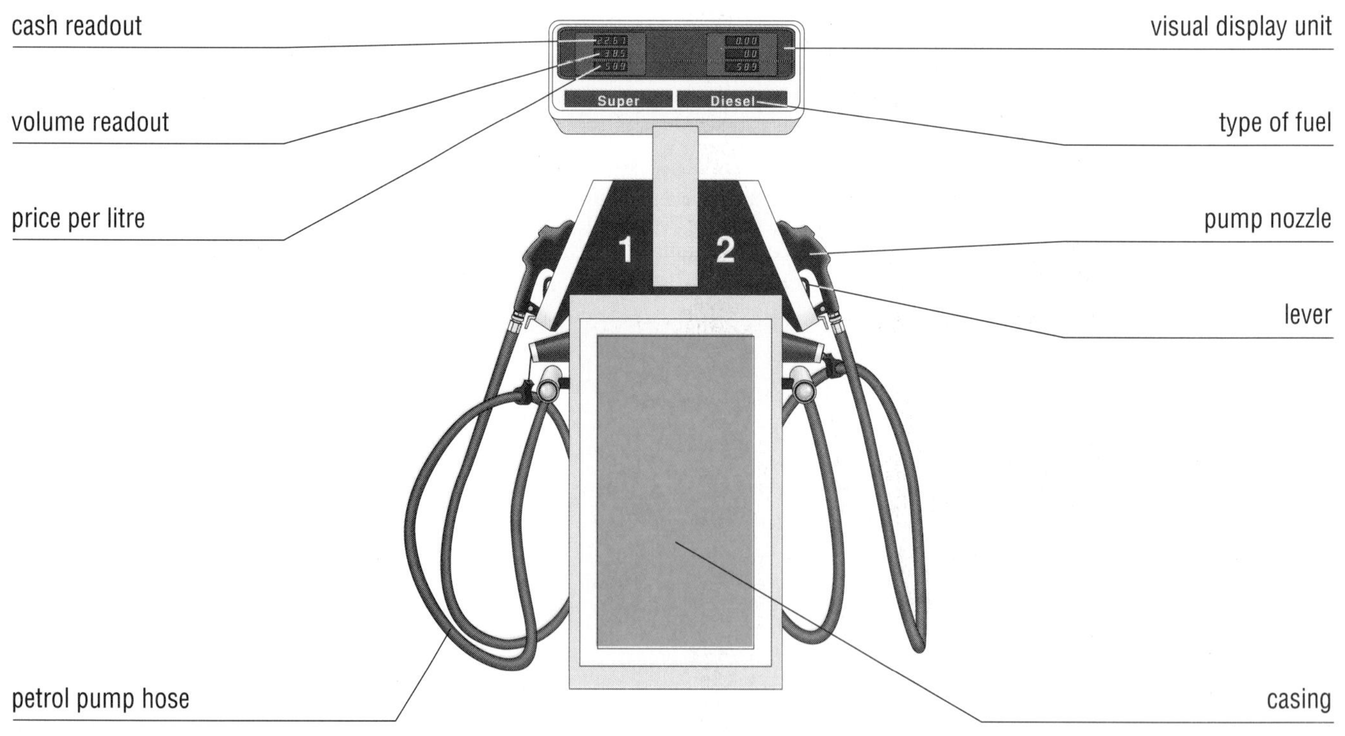

cash readout

volume readout

price per litre

petrol pump hose

visual display unit

type of fuel

pump nozzle

lever

casing

Super   Diesel

1   2

bridges

simple-span beam

deck

parapet

underpass

arch

arch

pier

upper chord

bearing

lower chord

abutment

deck

cantilever

cantilever span

suspended span

suspension

suspension cable

deck

suspender

stiffening girder

abutment

side span

tower

centre span

bicycle

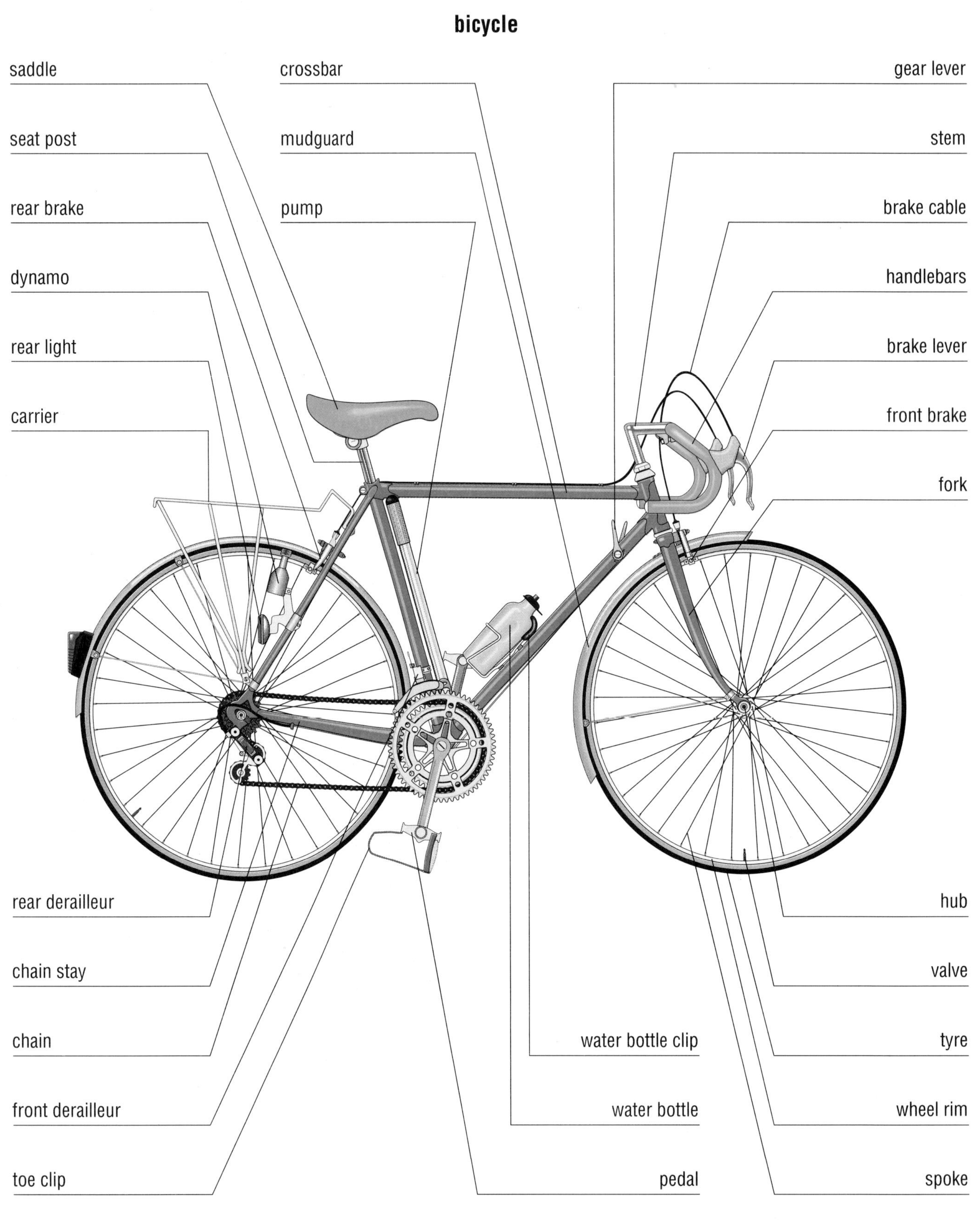

saddle

seat post

rear brake

dynamo

rear light

carrier

crossbar

mudguard

pump

gear lever

stem

brake cable

handlebars

brake lever

front brake

fork

rear derailleur

chain stay

chain

front derailleur

toe clip

water bottle clip

water bottle

pedal

hub

valve

tyre

wheel rim

spoke

bicycle

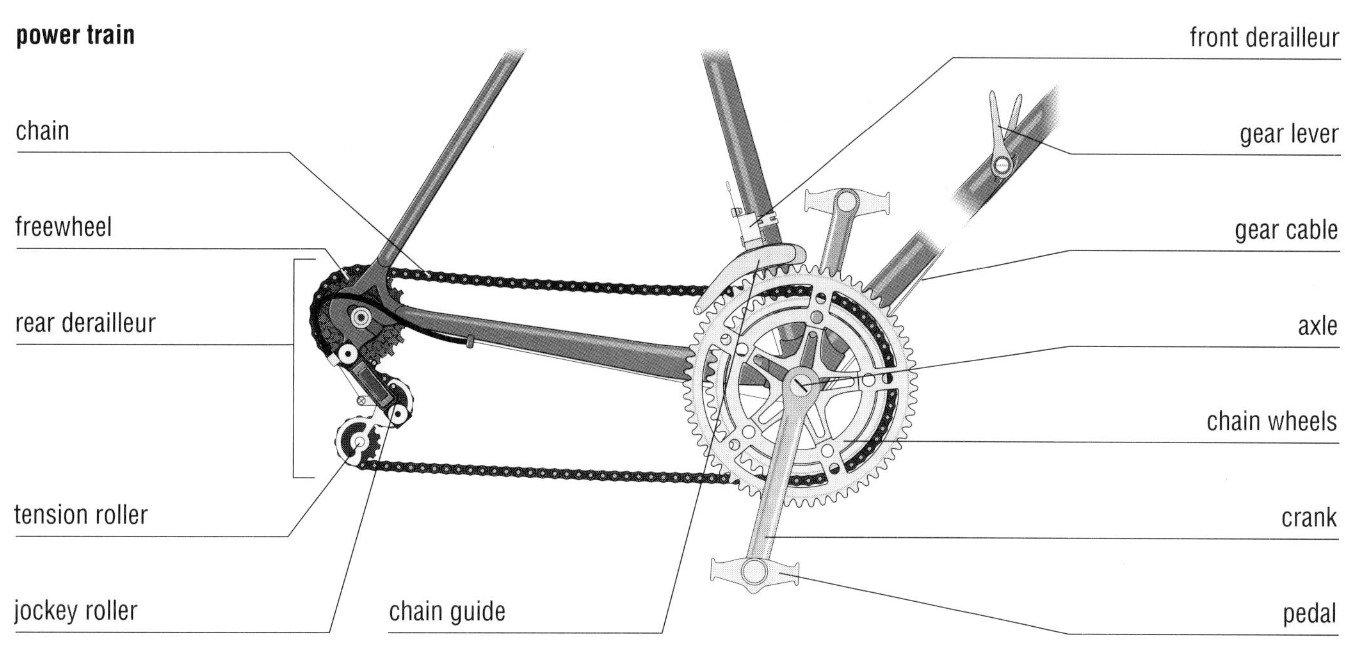

power train

chain

freewheel

rear derailleur

tension roller

jockey roller

chain guide

front derailleur

gear lever

gear cable

axle

chain wheels

crank

pedal

protective helmet

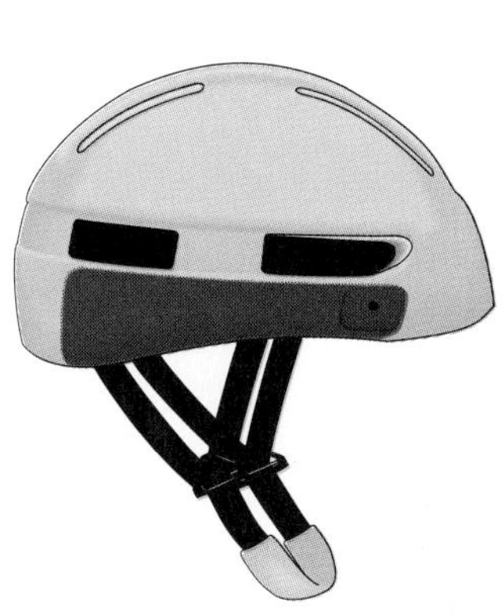

pannier bag

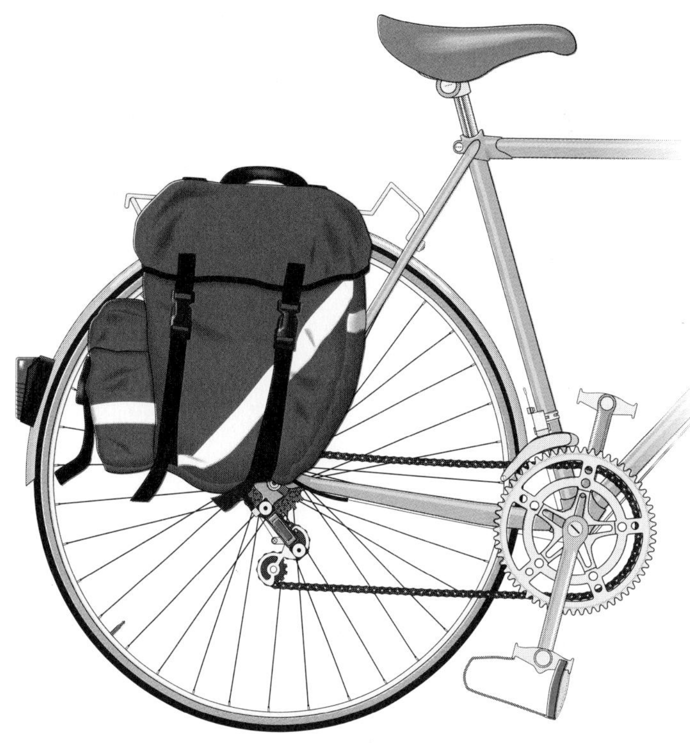

'U' lock

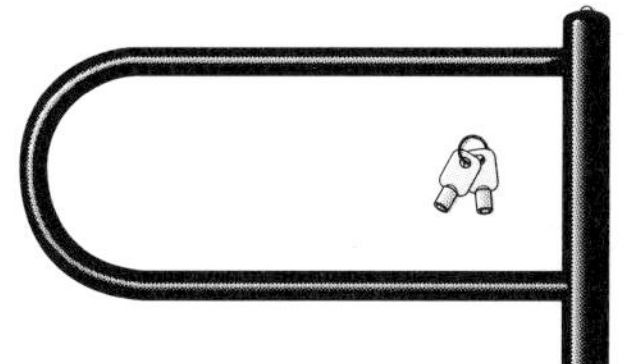

RAIL TRANSPORT

high-speed train

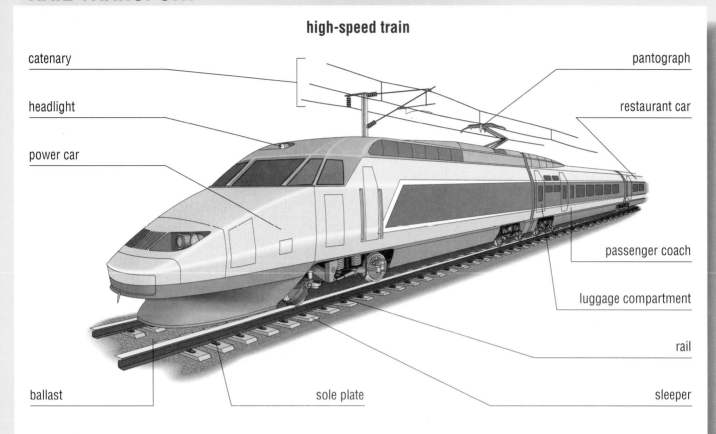

catenary

headlight

power car

pantograph

restaurant car

passenger coach

luggage compartment

rail

ballast

sole plate

sleeper

diesel-electric locomotive

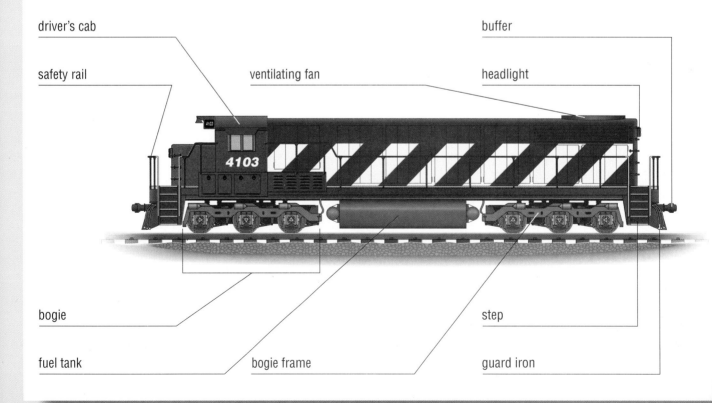

driver's cab

safety rail

ventilating fan

buffer

headlight

4103

bogie

step

fuel tank

bogie frame

guard iron

types of freight wagons

hopper wagon

bulkhead flat wagon

bogie well wagon

bogie flat wagon

piggyback flat wagon

refrigerator van

bogie tank wagon

bogie car-carrying wagon

container flat wagon

livestock van

bogie wagon

gondola open wagon

brake van

passenger liner

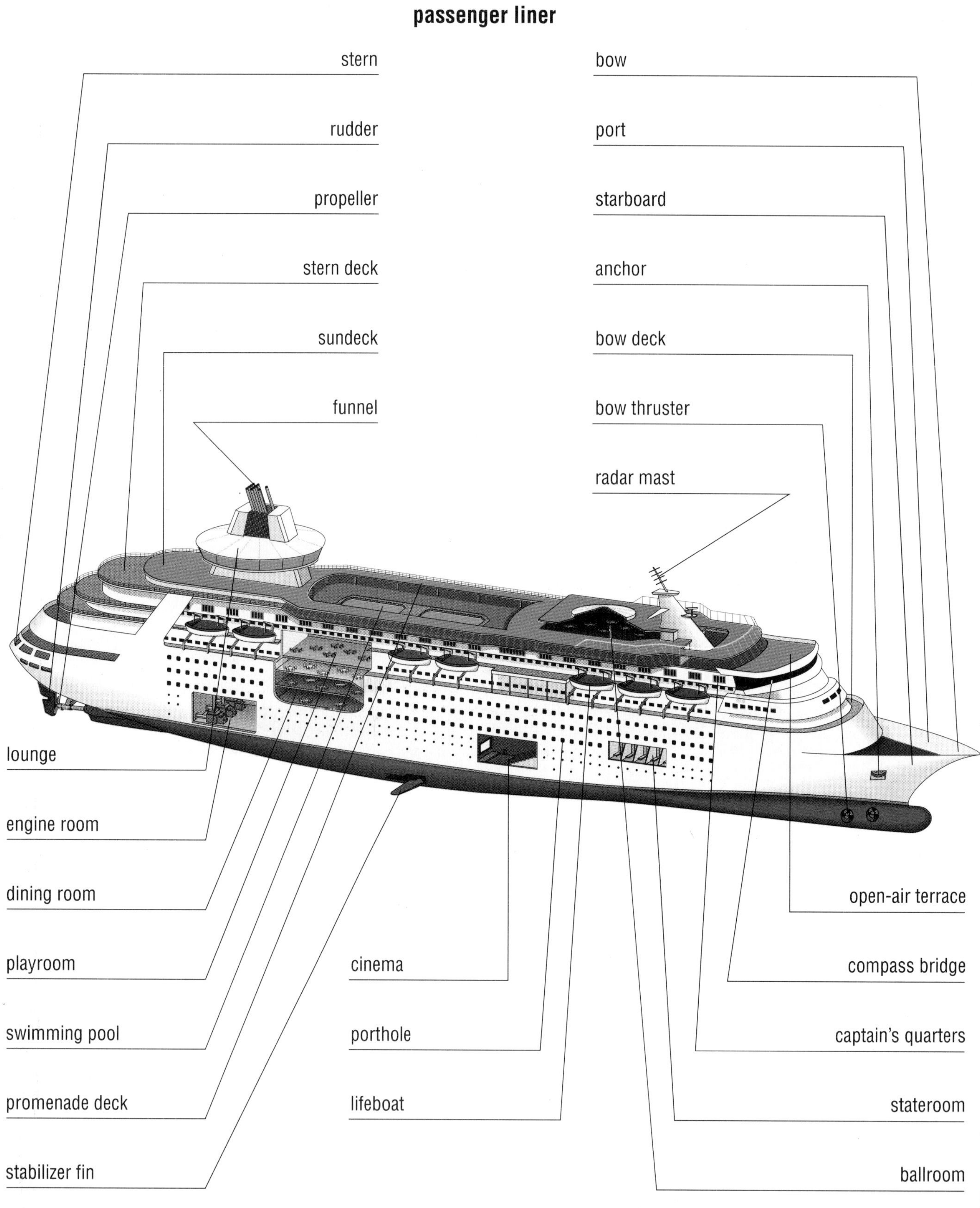

stern

rudder

propeller

stern deck

sundeck

funnel

bow

port

starboard

anchor

bow deck

bow thruster

radar mast

lounge

engine room

dining room

playroom

swimming pool

promenade deck

stabilizer fin

cinema

porthole

lifeboat

open-air terrace

compass bridge

captain's quarters

stateroom

ballroom

submarine

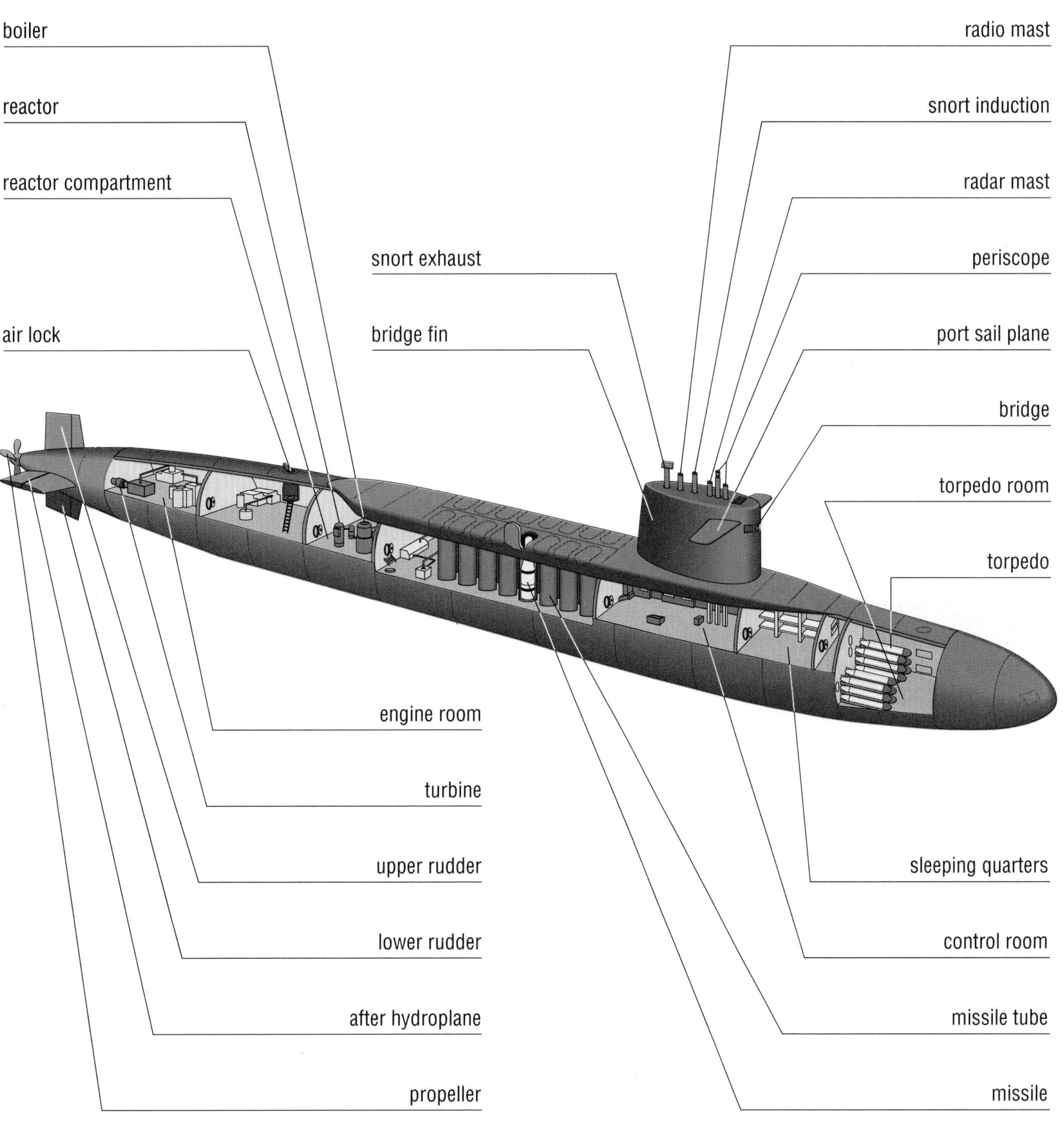

boiler

reactor

reactor compartment

air lock

snort exhaust

bridge fin

radio mast

snort induction

radar mast

periscope

port sail plane

bridge

torpedo room

torpedo

engine room

turbine

upper rudder

lower rudder

after hydroplane

propeller

sleeping quarters

control room

missile tube

missile

long-range aircraft

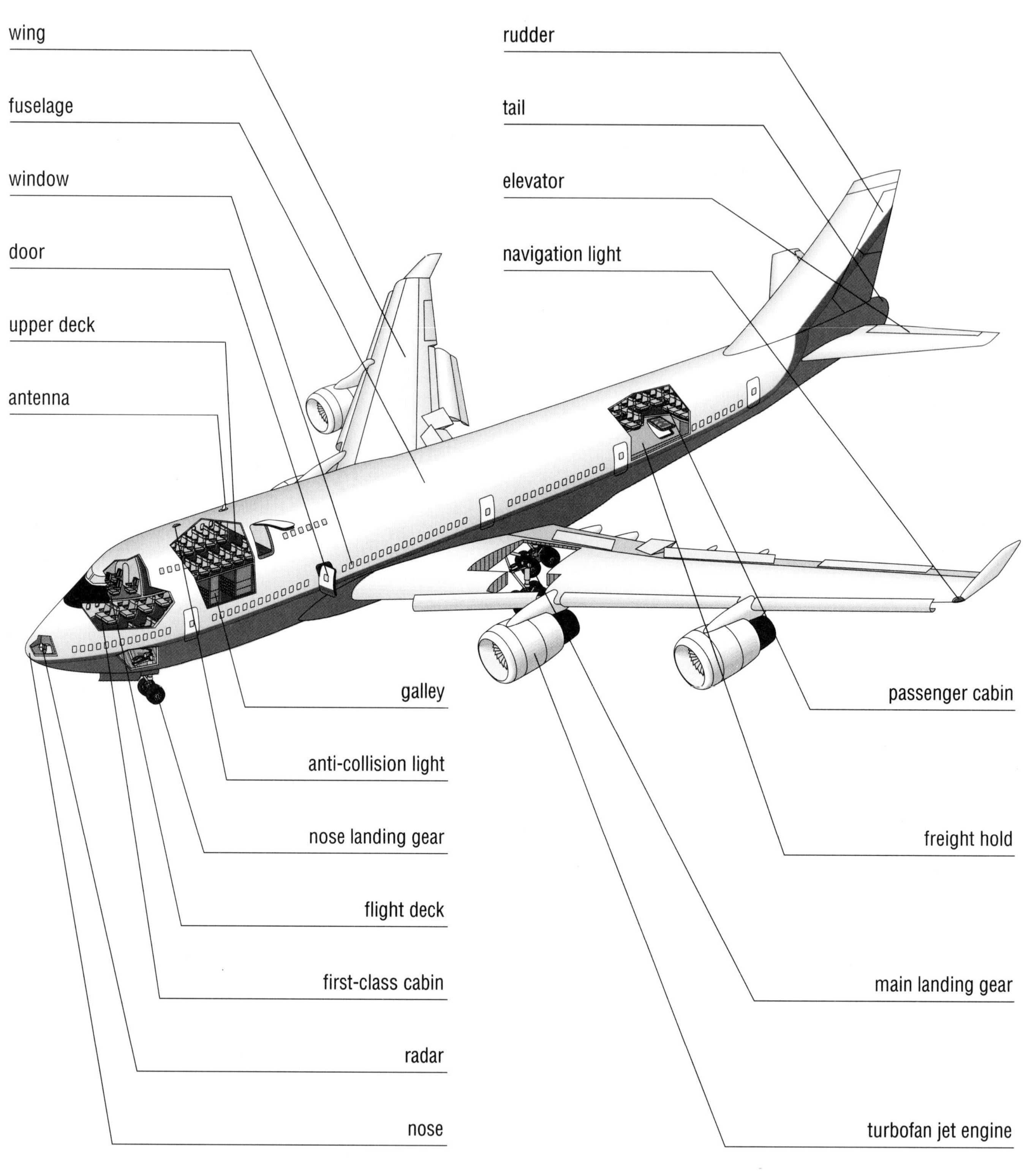

wing

fuselage

window

door

upper deck

antenna

rudder

tail

elevator

navigation light

galley

anti-collision light

nose landing gear

flight deck

first-class cabin

radar

nose

passenger cabin

freight hold

main landing gear

turbofan jet engine

helicopter

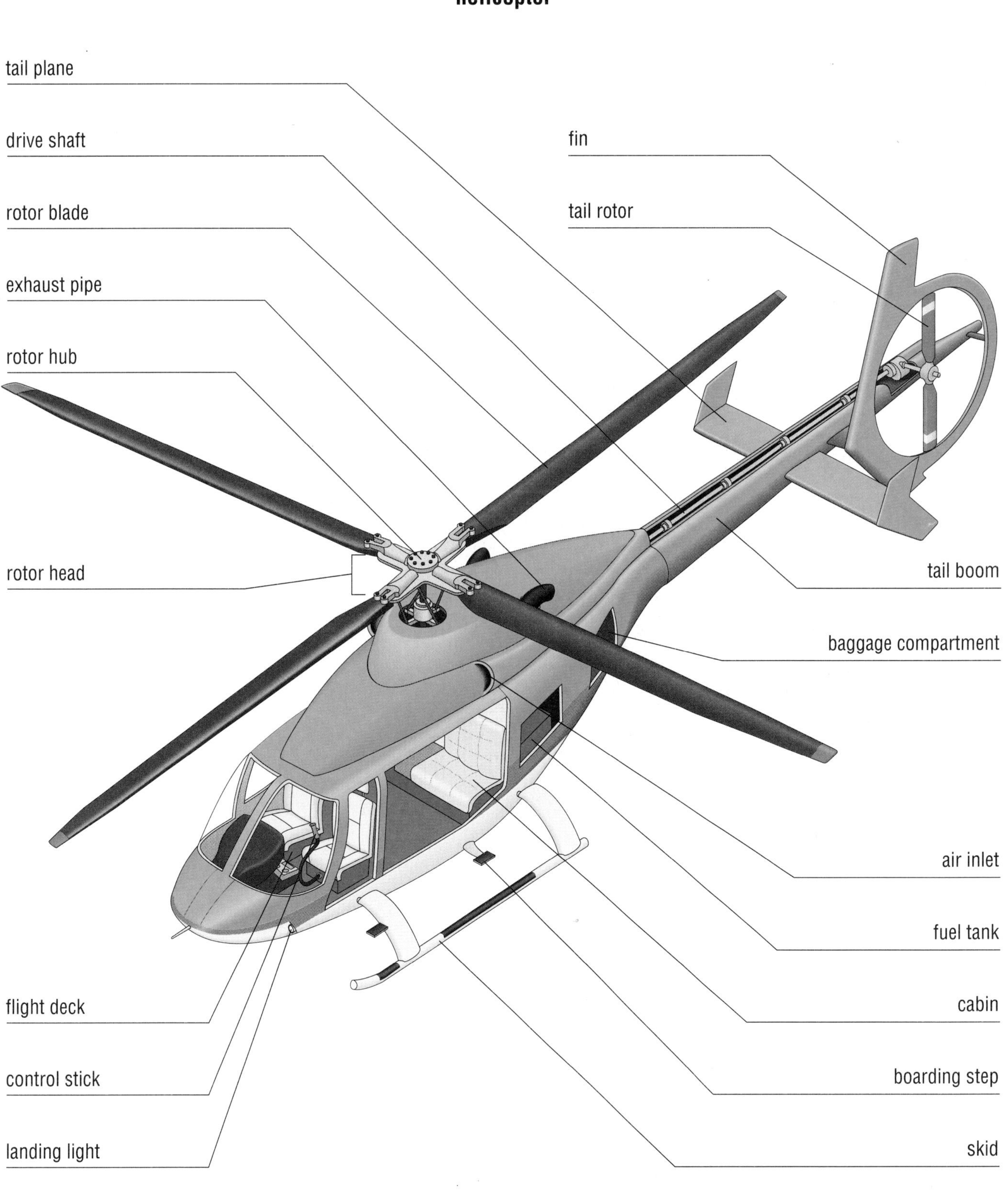

tail plane

drive shaft

rotor blade

exhaust pipe

rotor hub

rotor head

flight deck

control stick

landing light

fin

tail rotor

tail boom

baggage compartment

air inlet

fuel tank

cabin

boarding step

skid

SPACE TRANSPORT

rocket

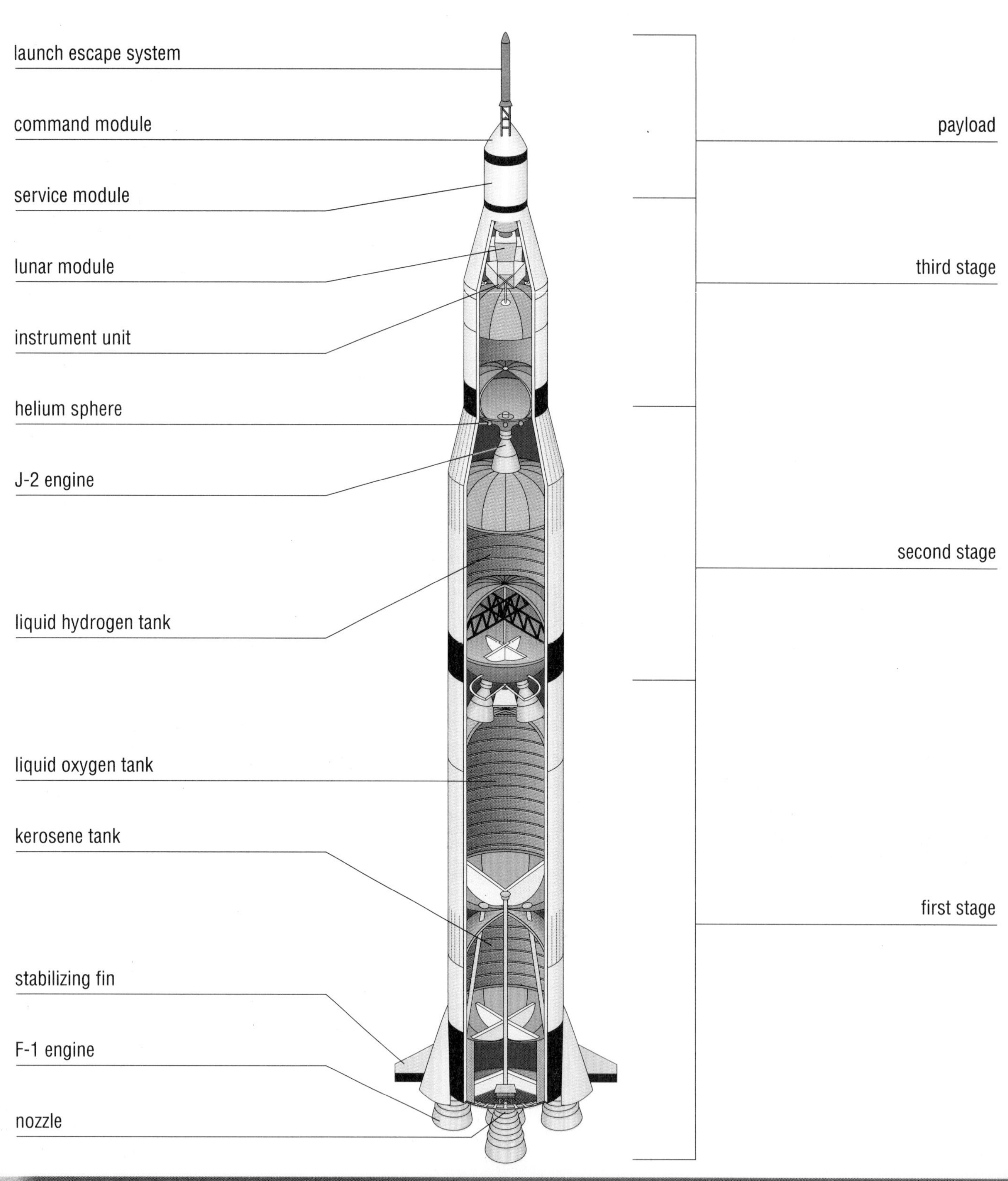

launch escape system

command module

service module

lunar module

instrument unit

helium sphere

J-2 engine

liquid hydrogen tank

liquid oxygen tank

kerosene tank

stabilizing fin

F-1 engine

nozzle

payload

third stage

second stage

first stage

space shuttle

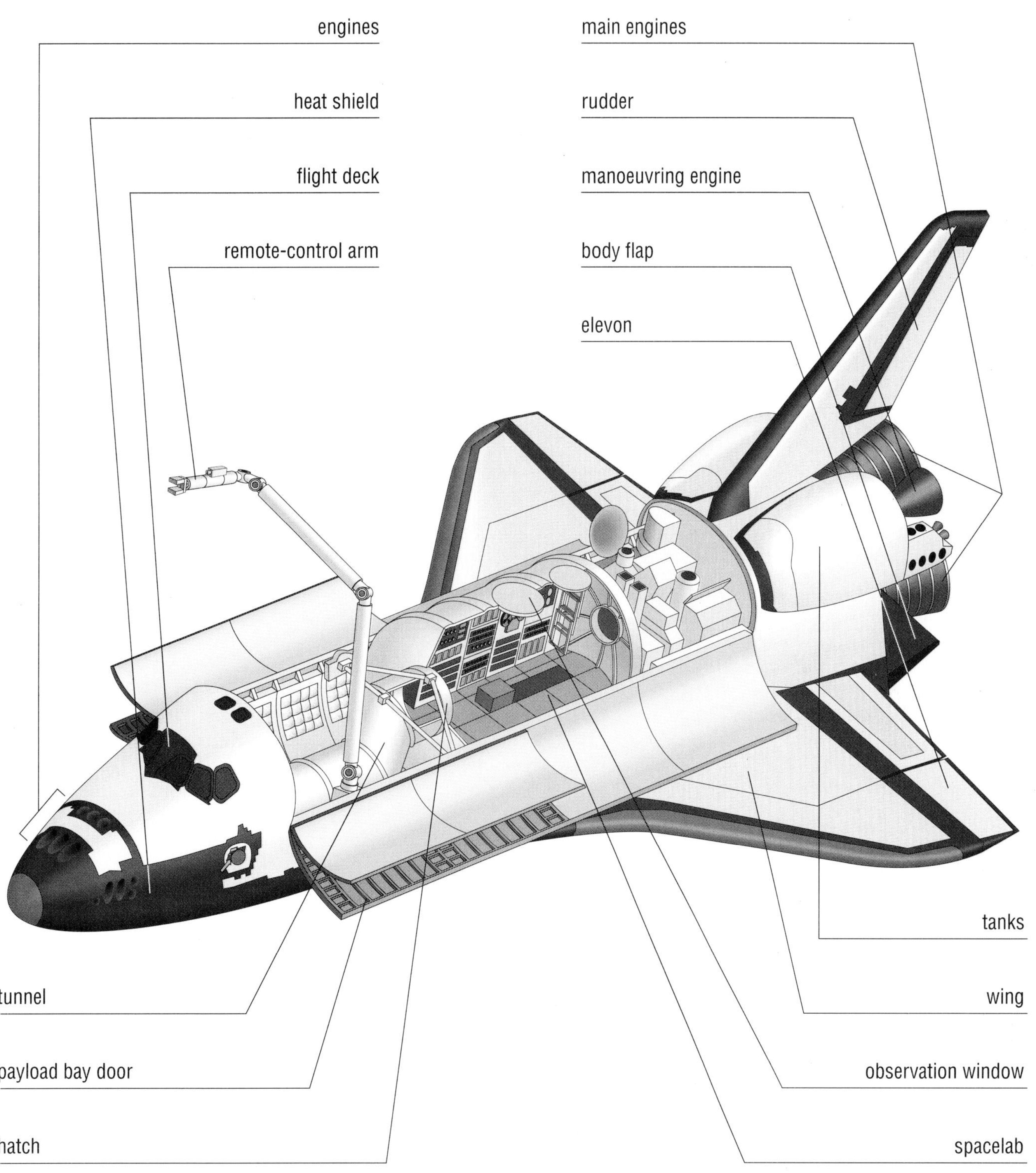

engines

heat shield

flight deck

remote-control arm

main engines

rudder

manoeuvring engine

body flap

elevon

tunnel

payload bay door

hatch

tanks

wing

observation window

spacelab

WEPONS

armour

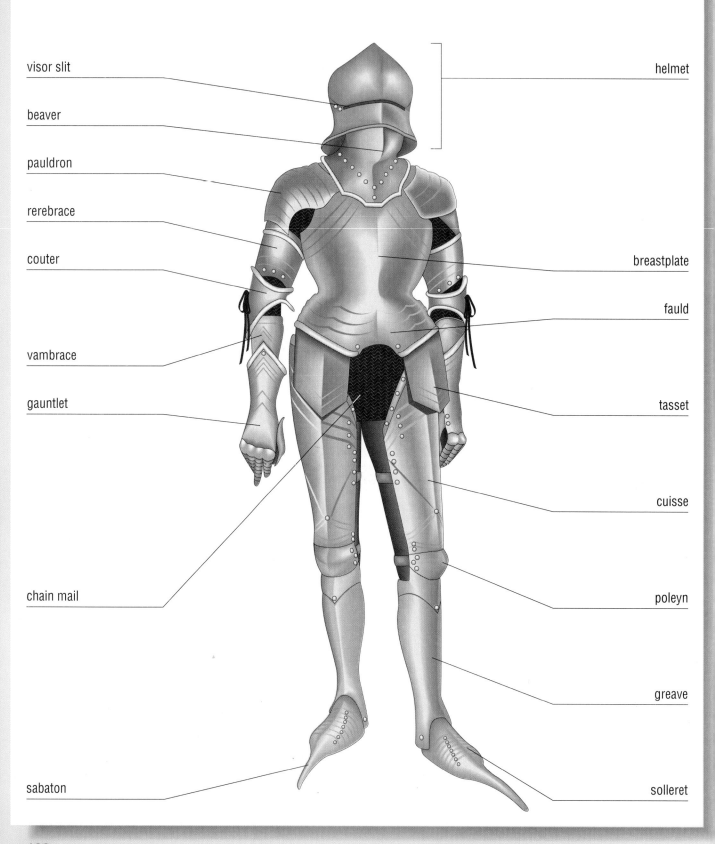

visor slit

beaver

pauldron

rerebrace

couter

vambrace

gauntlet

chain mail

sabaton

helmet

breastplate

fauld

tasset

cuisse

poleyn

greave

solleret

thrusting weapons

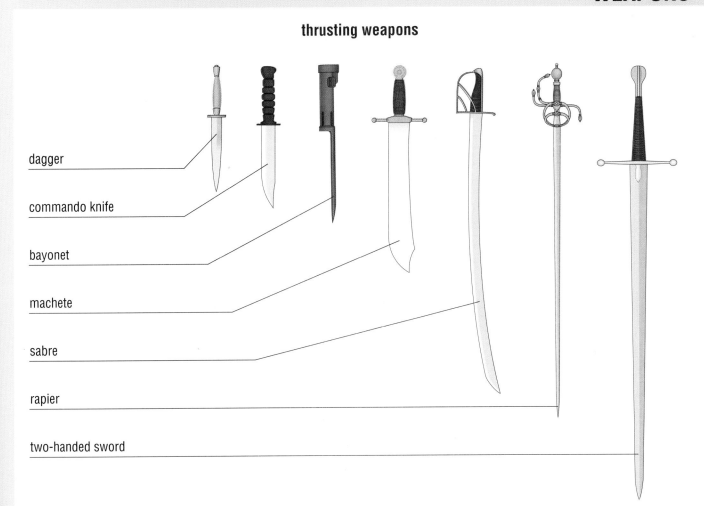

dagger

commando knife

bayonet

machete

sabre

rapier

two-handed sword

crossbow

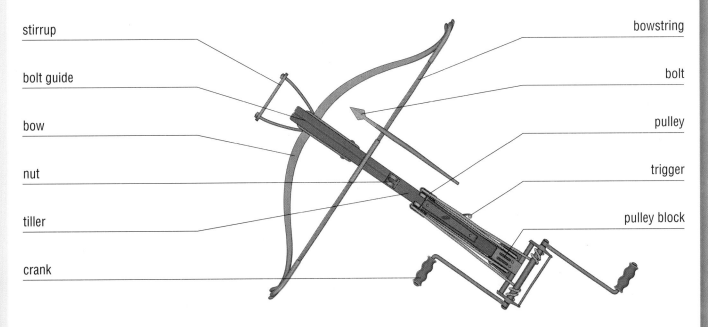

stirrup

bolt guide

bow

nut

tiller

crank

bowstring

bolt

pulley

trigger

pulley block

WEAPONS

revolver

hammer

front sight

butt

muzzle

barrel

cylinder

loading gate

trigger guard

trigger

pistol

rear sight

barrel

hammer

front sight

magazine

slide

trigger guard

trigger

magazine base

bullet

butt

magazine catch

tank

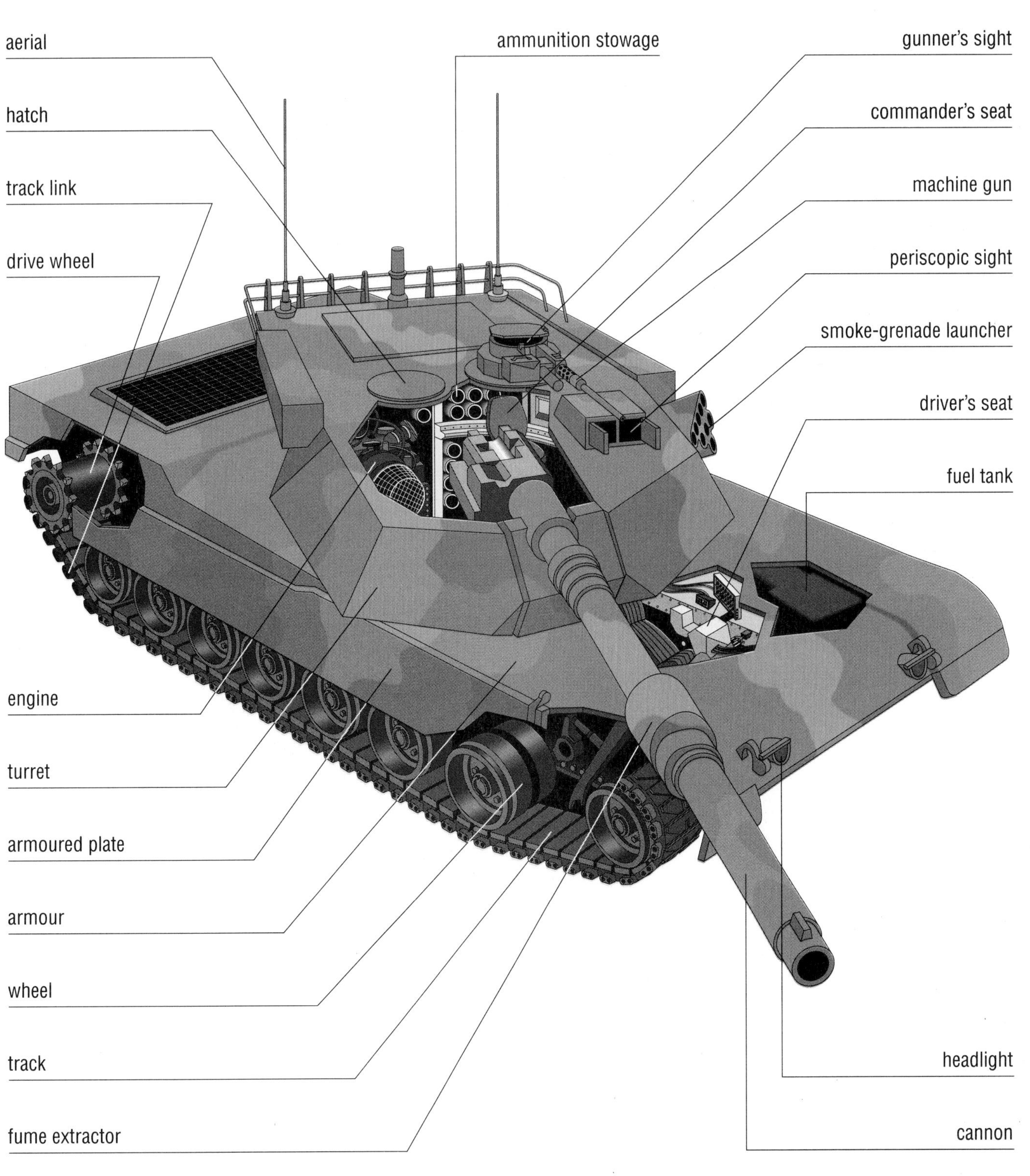

aerial

hatch

track link

drive wheel

ammunition stowage

gunner's sight

commander's seat

machine gun

periscopic sight

smoke-grenade launcher

driver's seat

fuel tank

engine

turret

armoured plate

armour

wheel

track

headlight

fume extractor

cannon

MUSIC

musical notation

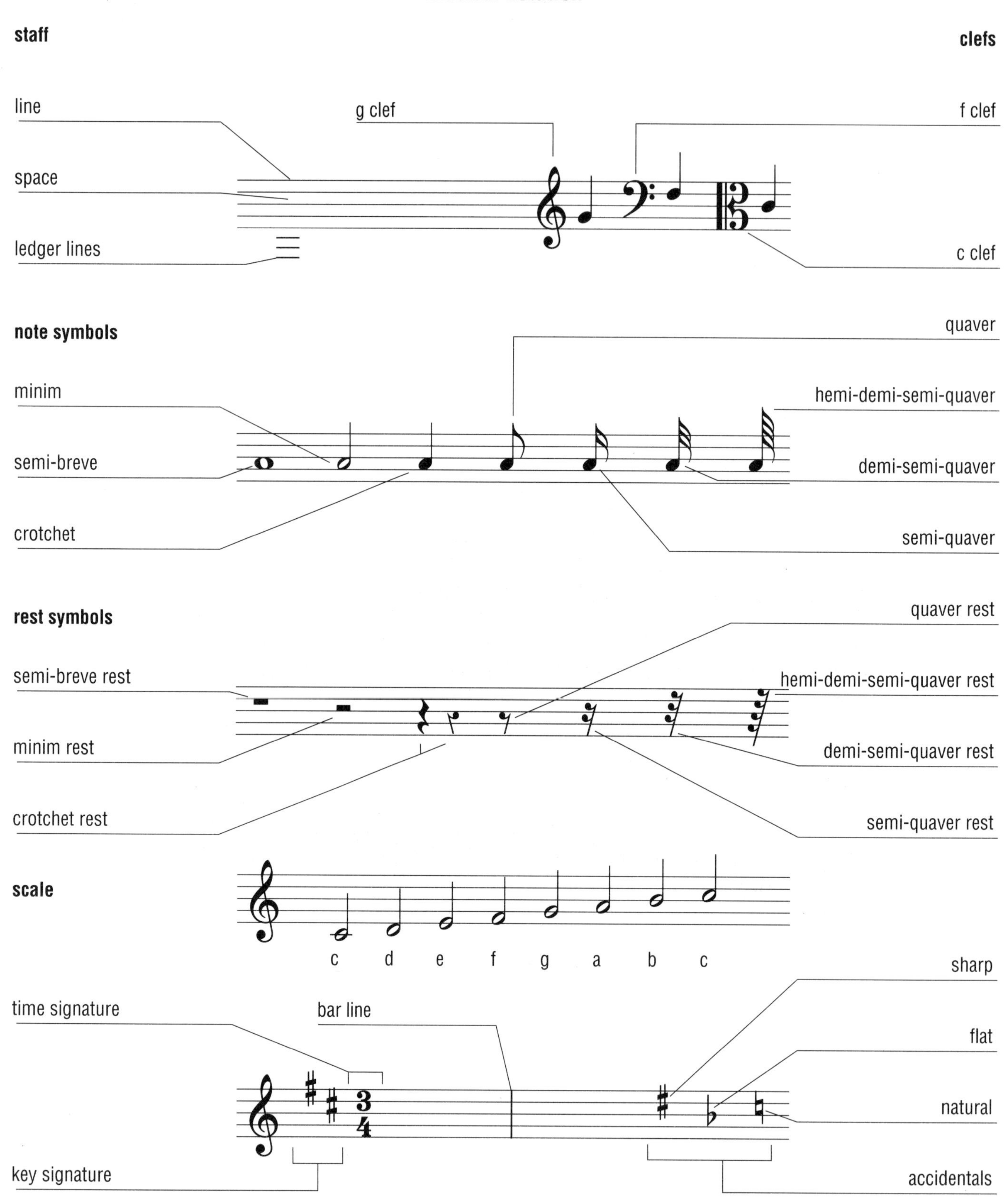

staff

line

space

ledger lines

g clef

clefs

f clef

c clef

note symbols

minim

semi-breve

crotchet

quaver

hemi-demi-semi-quaver

demi-semi-quaver

semi-quaver

rest symbols

semi-breve rest

minim rest

crotchet rest

quaver rest

hemi-demi-semi-quaver rest

demi-semi-quaver rest

semi-quaver rest

scale

c d e f g a b c

time signature

bar line

key signature

sharp

flat

natural

accidentals

upright piano

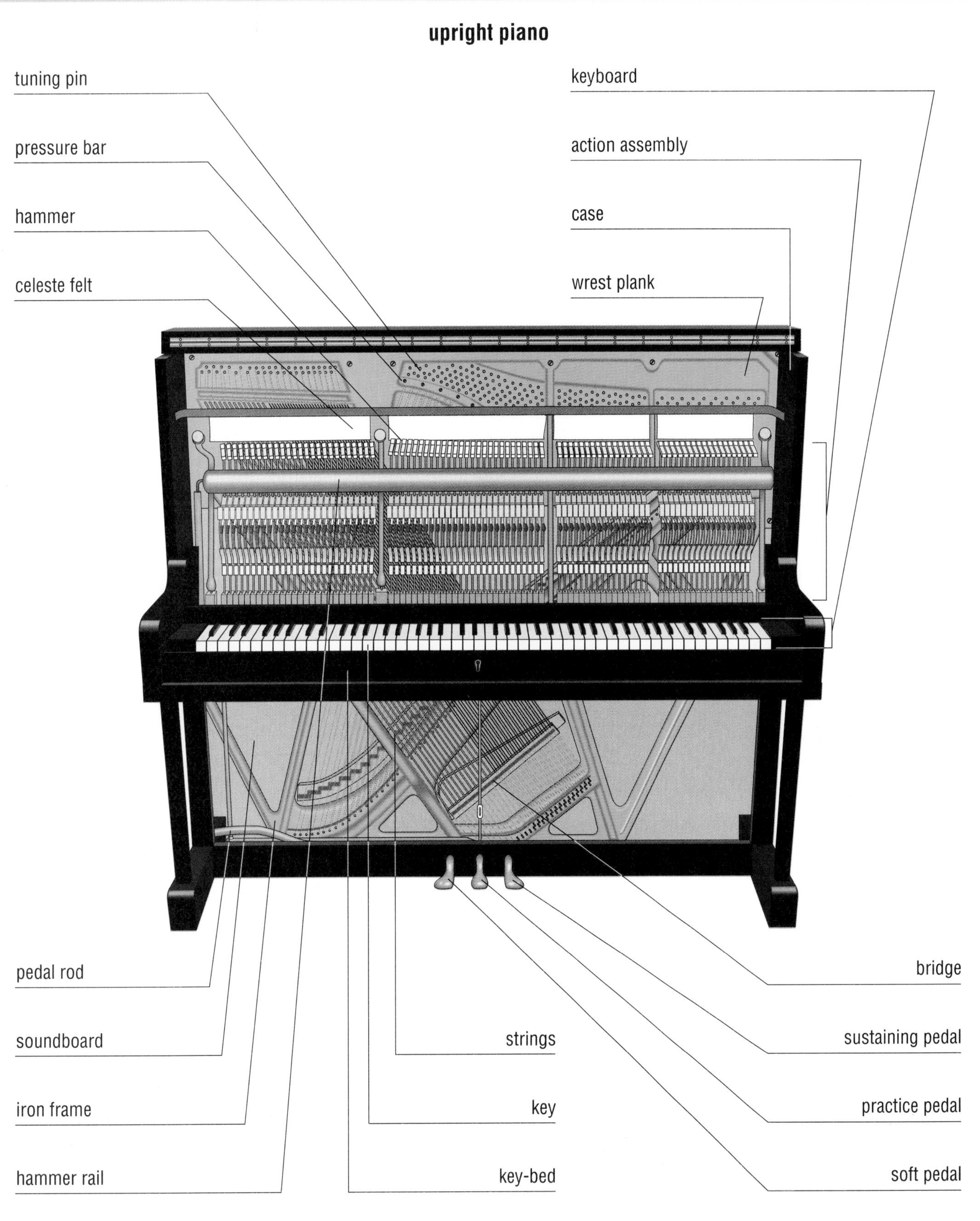

tuning pin

pressure bar

hammer

celeste felt

keyboard

action assembly

case

wrest plank

pedal rod

soundboard

iron frame

hammer rail

strings

key

key-bed

bridge

sustaining pedal

practice pedal

soft pedal

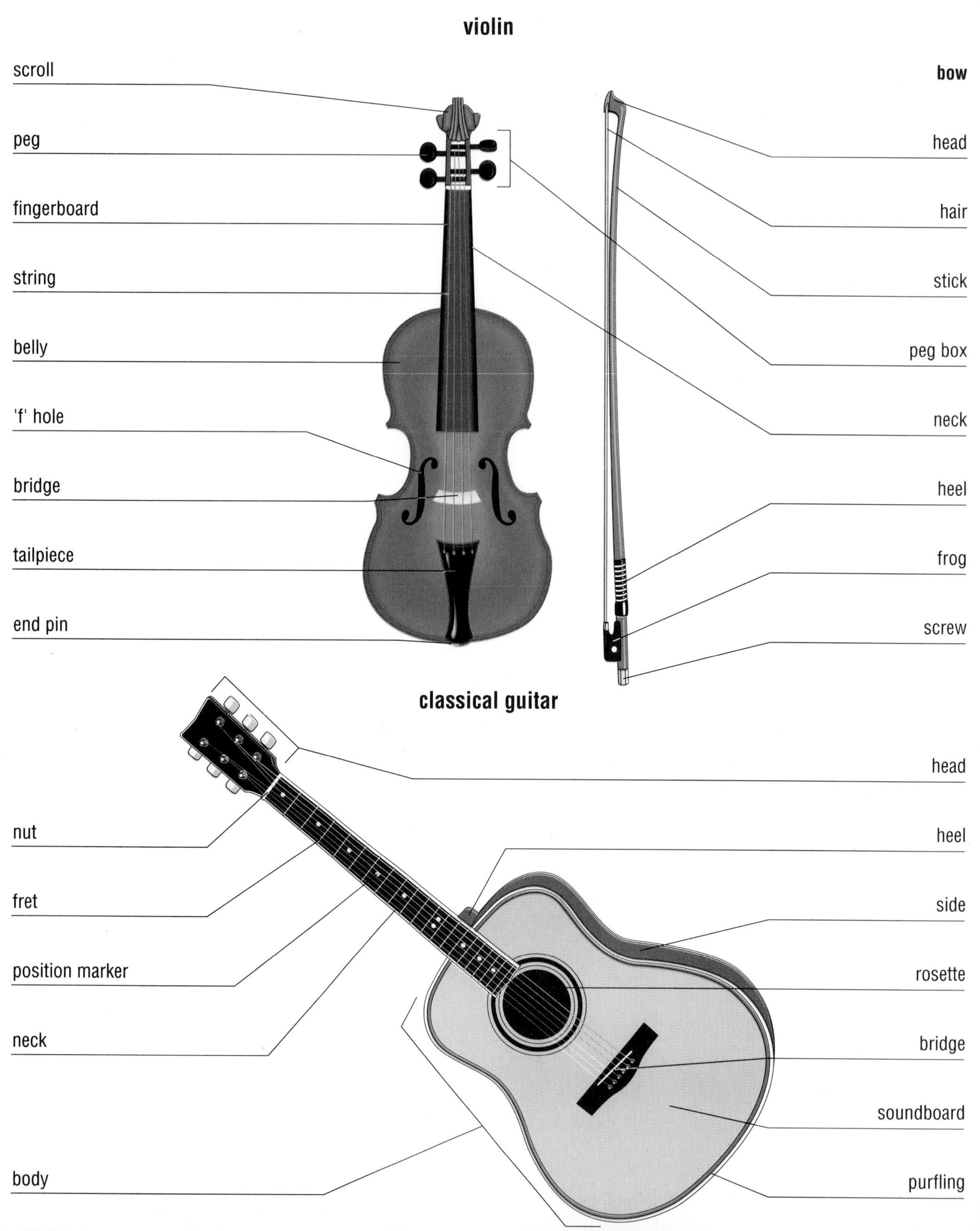

violin

scroll

peg

fingerboard

string

belly

'f' hole

bridge

tailpiece

end pin

bow

head

hair

stick

peg box

neck

heel

frog

screw

classical guitar

head

heel

side

rosette

bridge

soundboard

purfling

nut

fret

position marker

neck

body

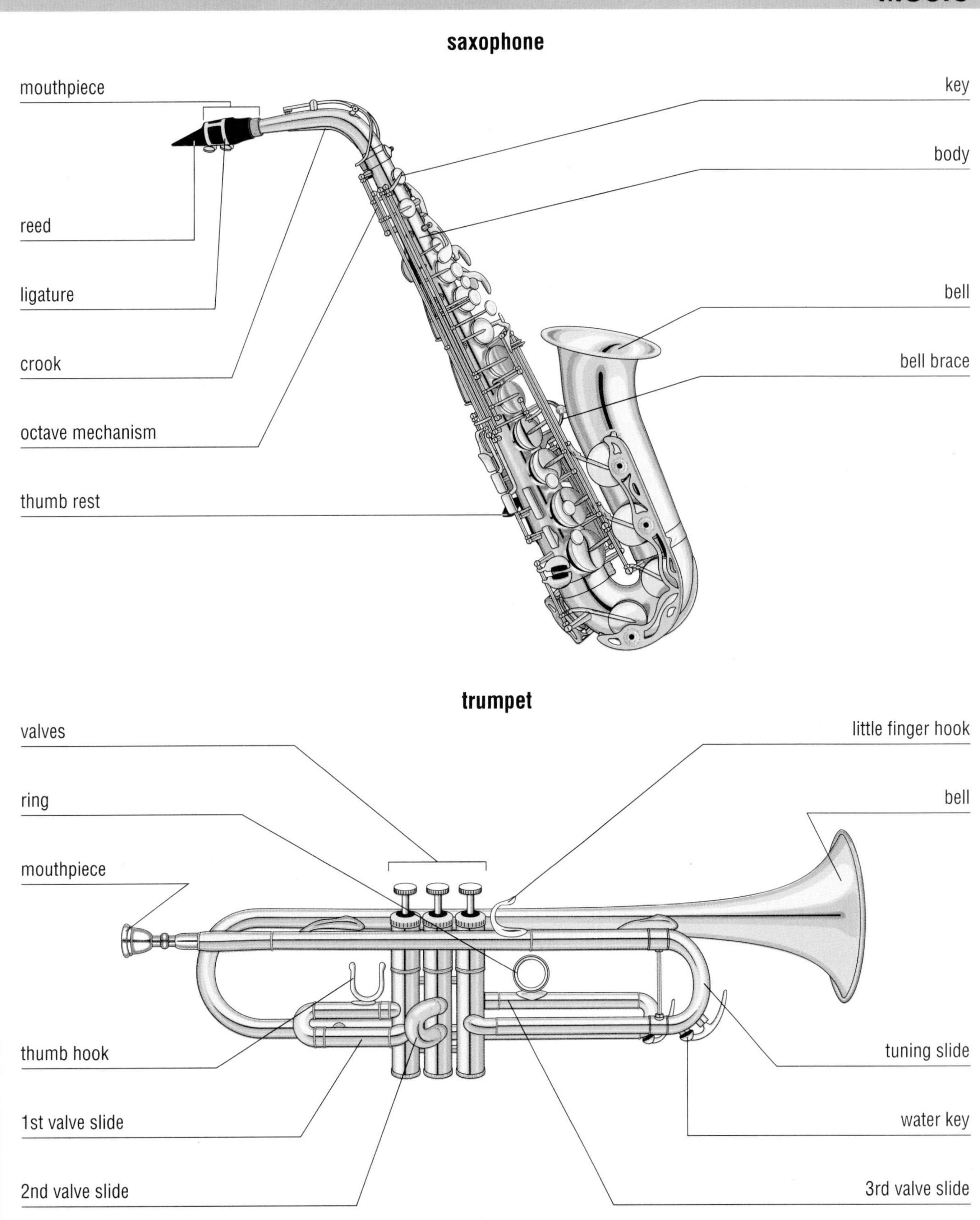

saxophone

mouthpiece

key

body

reed

ligature

bell

crook

bell brace

octave mechanism

thumb rest

trumpet

valves

little finger hook

ring

bell

mouthpiece

thumb hook

tuning slide

1st valve slide

water key

2nd valve slide

3rd valve slide

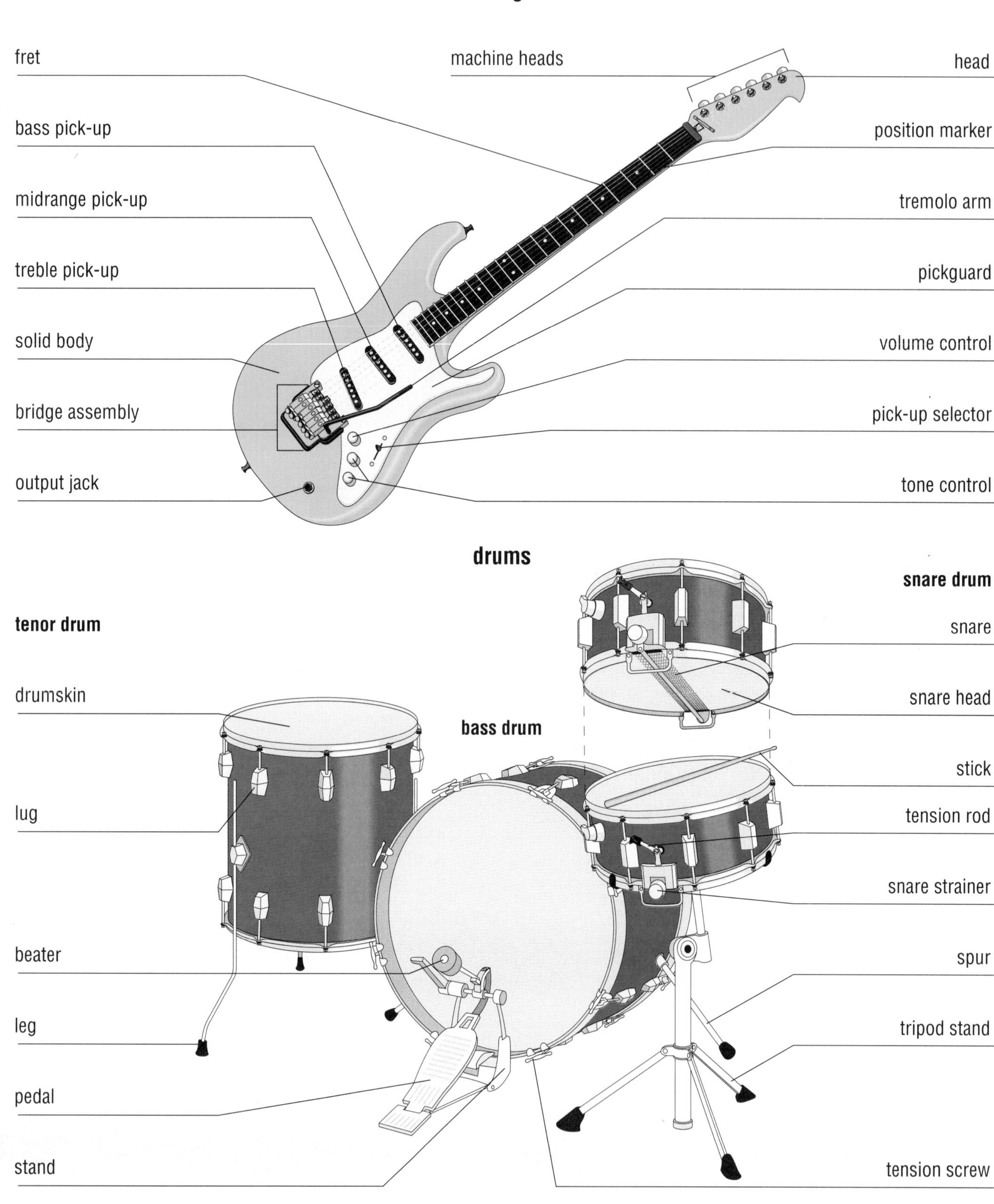

electric guitar

fret

bass pick-up

midrange pick-up

treble pick-up

solid body

bridge assembly

output jack

machine heads

head

position marker

tremolo arm

pickguard

volume control

pick-up selector

tone control

drums

tenor drum

drumskin

lug

beater

leg

pedal

stand

snare drum

snare

snare head

bass drum

stick

tension rod

snare strainer

spur

tripod stand

tension screw

orchestra

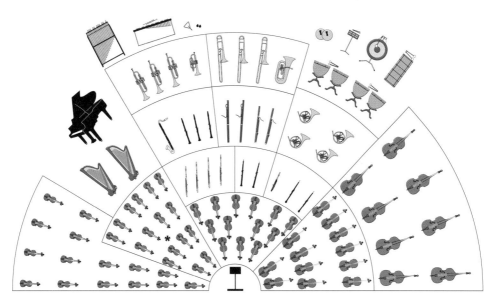

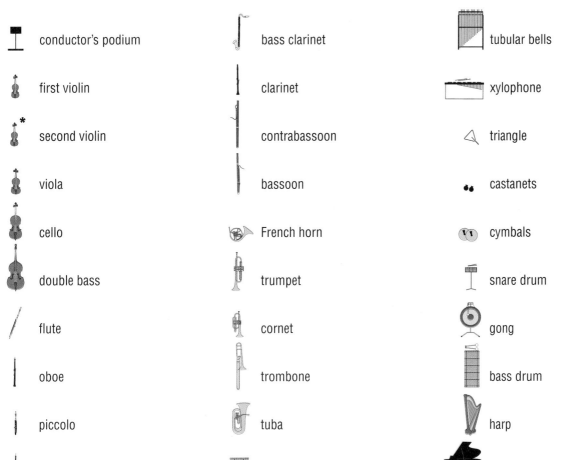

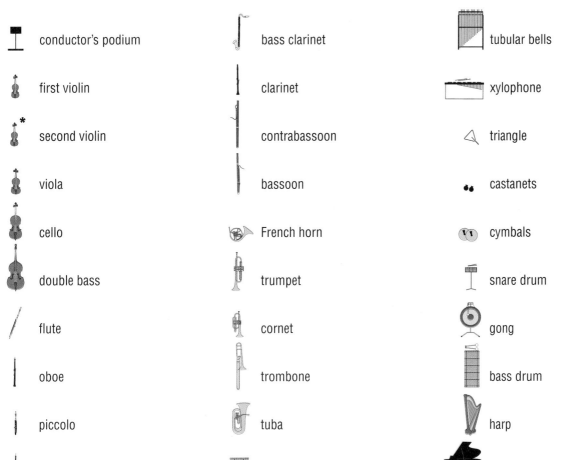 conductor's podium

first violin

second violin *

viola

cello

double bass

flute

oboe

piccolo

cor anglais

bass clarinet

clarinet

contrabassoon

bassoon

French horn

trumpet

cornet

trombone

tuba

timpani

tubular bells

xylophone

triangle

castanets

cymbals

snare drum

gong

bass drum

harp

piano

SPORTS

soccer

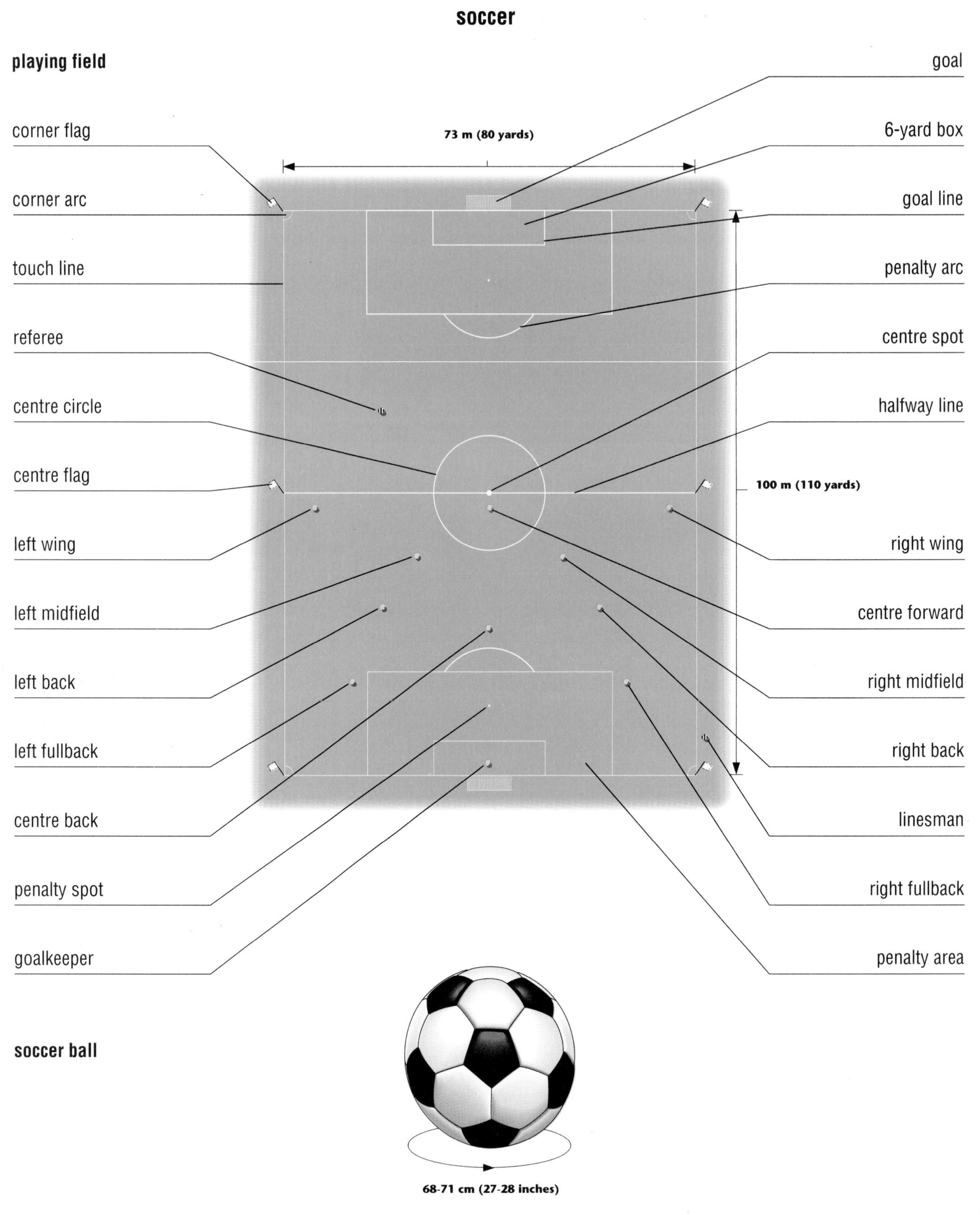

playing field

goal

corner flag

6-yard box

73 m (80 yards)

corner arc

goal line

touch line

penalty arc

referee

centre spot

centre circle

halfway line

centre flag

100 m (110 yards)

left wing

right wing

left midfield

centre forward

left back

right midfield

left fullback

right back

centre back

linesman

penalty spot

right fullback

goalkeeper

penalty area

soccer ball

68-71 cm (27-28 inches)

rugby union

playing field

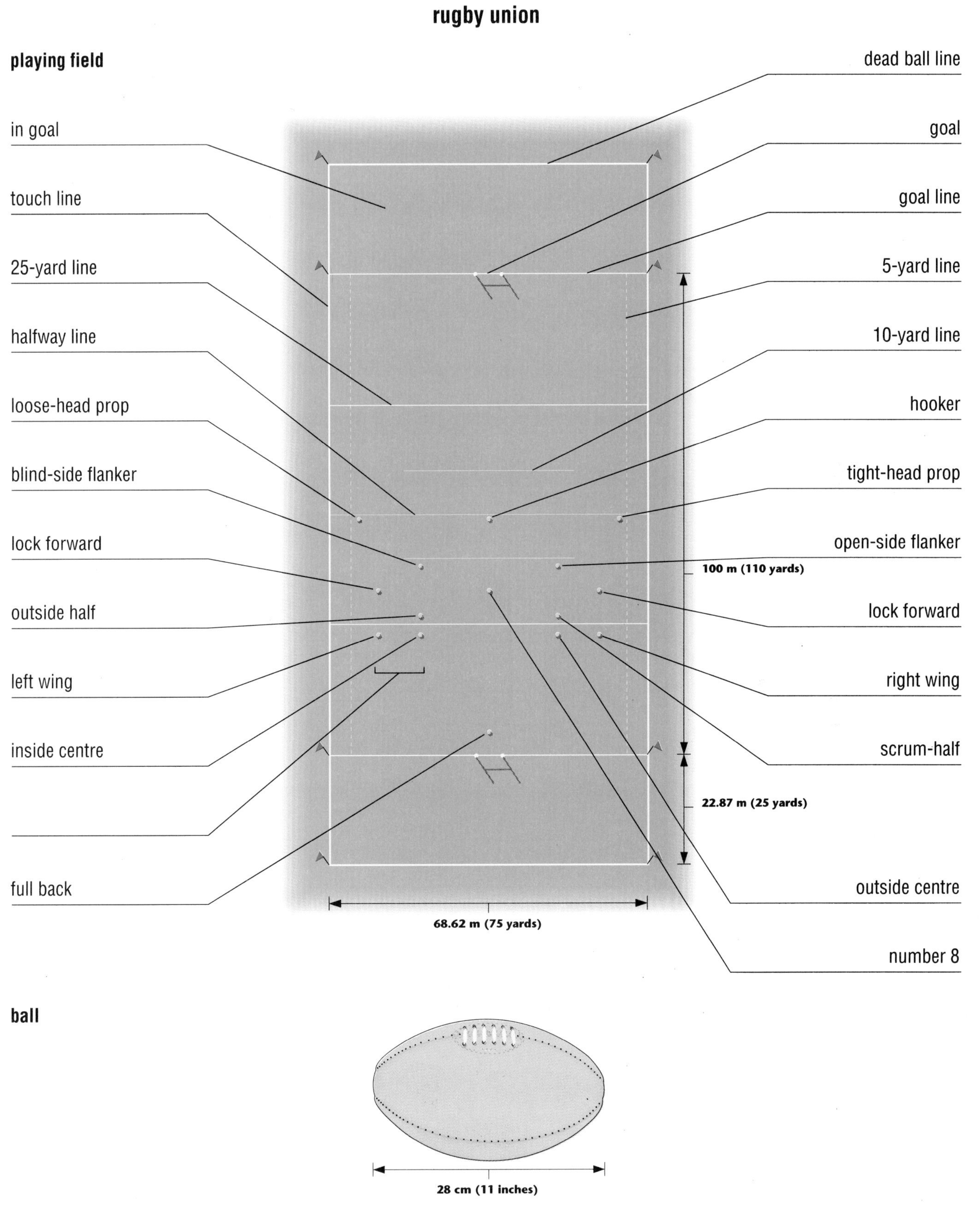

in goal

touch line

25-yard line

halfway line

loose-head prop

blind-side flanker

lock forward

outside half

left wing

inside centre

full back

dead ball line

goal

goal line

5-yard line

10-yard line

hooker

tight-head prop

open-side flanker

100 m (110 yards)

lock forward

right wing

scrum-half

22.87 m (25 yards)

outside centre

68.62 m (75 yards)

number 8

ball

28 cm (11 inches)

American football

offensive

defensive

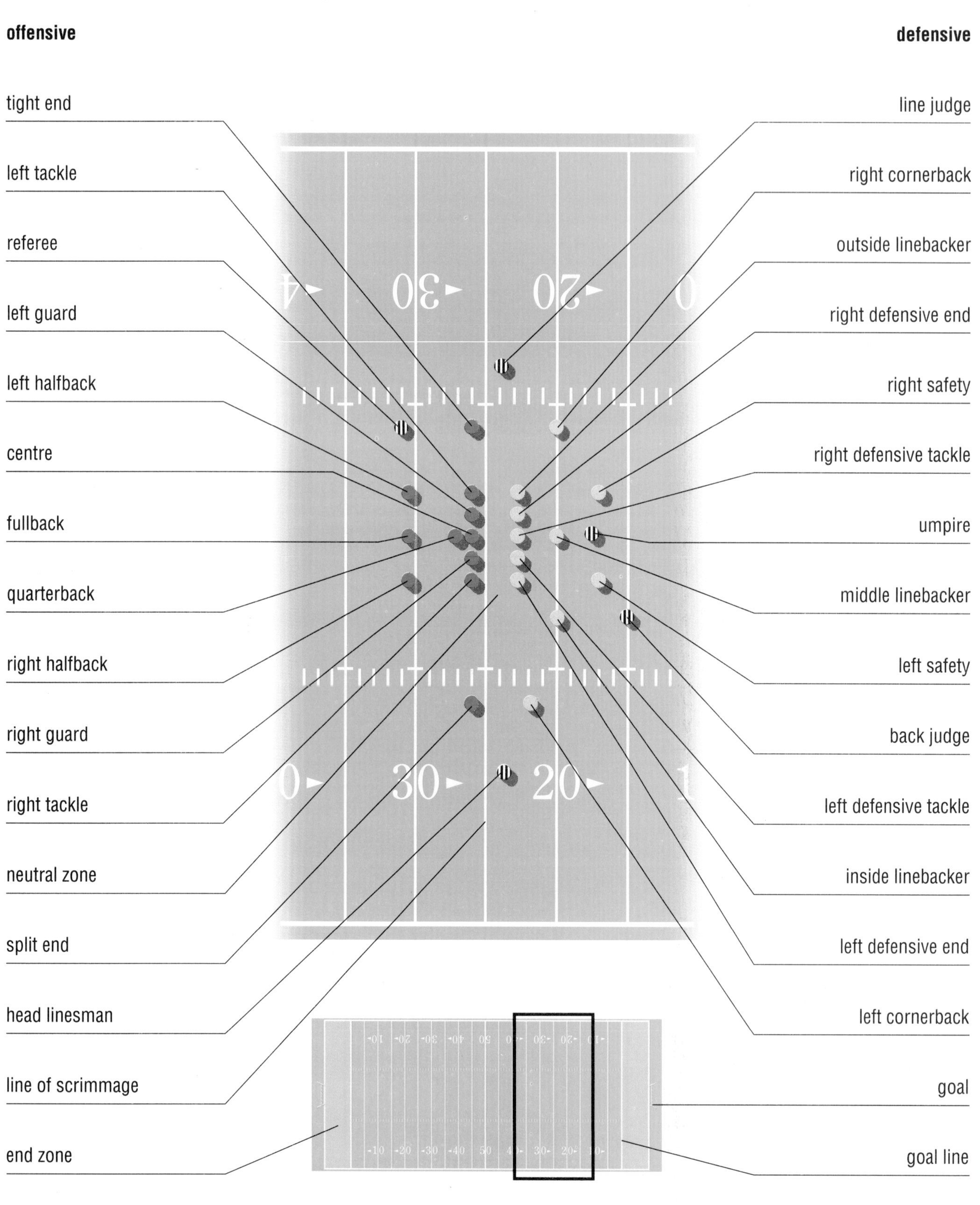

tight end

left tackle

referee

left guard

left halfback

centre

fullback

quarterback

right halfback

right guard

right tackle

neutral zone

split end

head linesman

line of scrimmage

end zone

line judge

right cornerback

outside linebacker

right defensive end

right safety

right defensive tackle

umpire

middle linebacker

left safety

back judge

left defensive tackle

inside linebacker

left defensive end

left cornerback

goal

goal line

American football

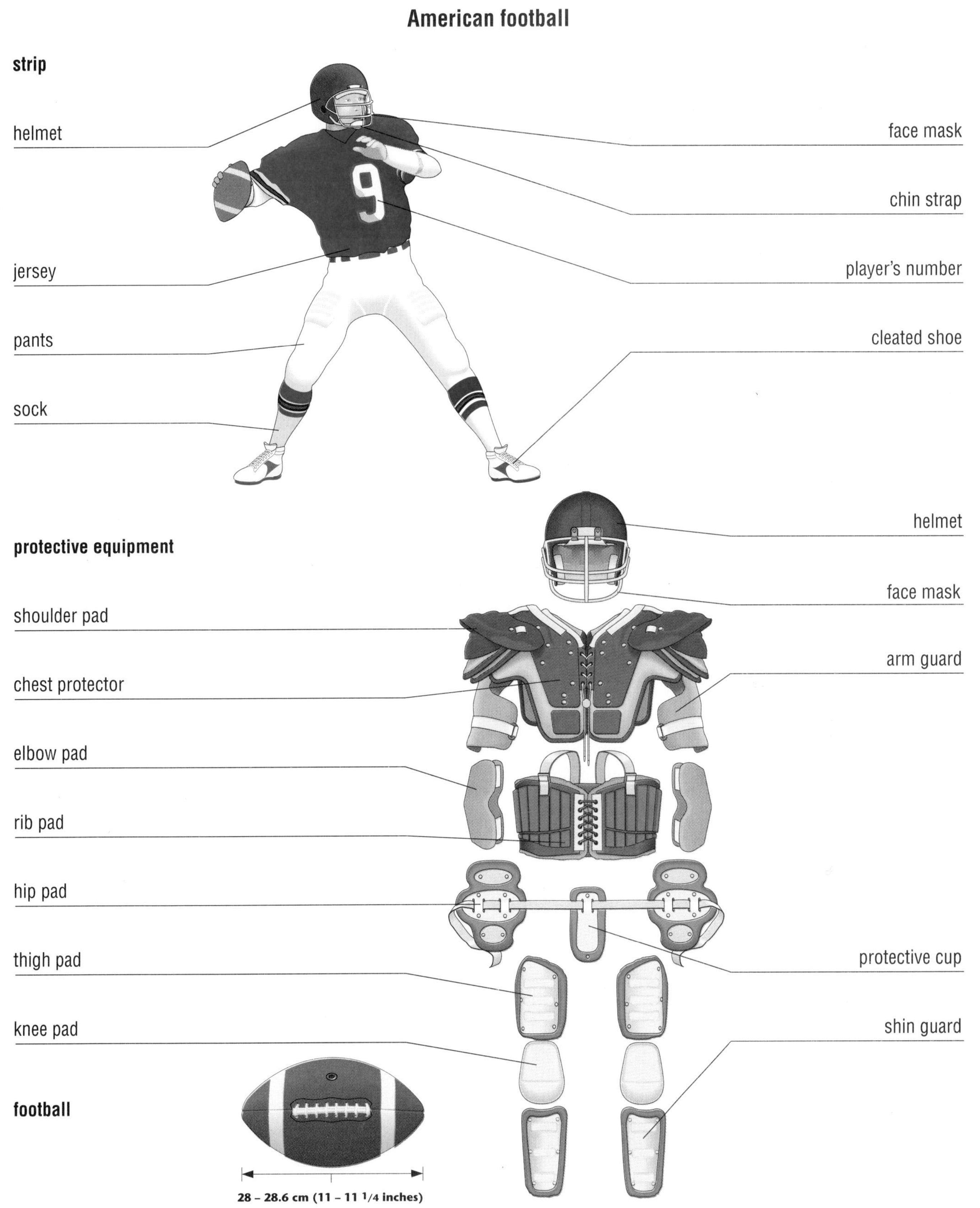

strip

helmet

jersey

pants

sock

face mask

chin strap

player's number

cleated shoe

protective equipment

shoulder pad

chest protector

elbow pad

rib pad

hip pad

thigh pad

knee pad

helmet

face mask

arm guard

protective cup

shin guard

football

28 – 28.6 cm (11 – 11 ¹/4 inches)

baseball

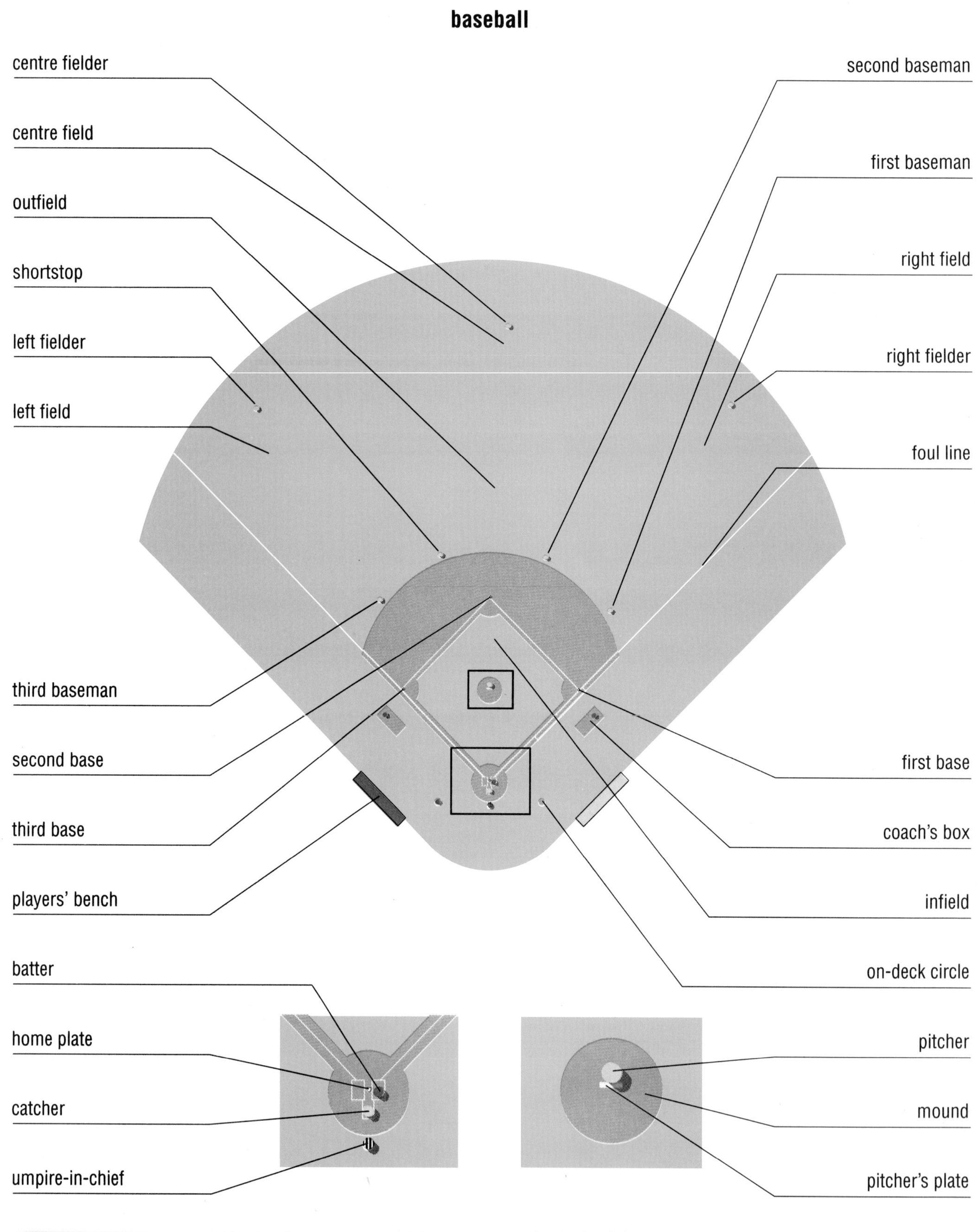

centre fielder

centre field

outfield

shortstop

left fielder

left field

third baseman

second base

third base

players' bench

batter

home plate

catcher

umpire-in-chief

second baseman

first baseman

right field

right fielder

foul line

first base

coach's box

infield

on-deck circle

pitcher

mound

pitcher's plate

baseball

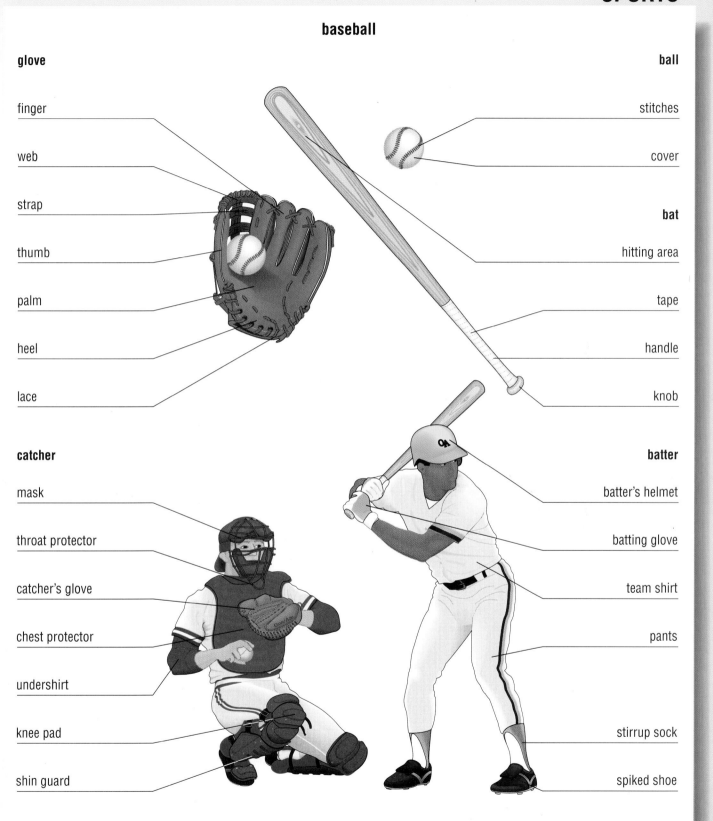

glove

finger

web

strap

thumb

palm

heel

lace

ball

stitches

cover

bat

hitting area

tape

handle

knob

catcher

mask

throat protector

catcher's glove

chest protector

undershirt

knee pad

shin guard

batter

batter's helmet

batting glove

team shirt

pants

stirrup sock

spiked shoe

cricket

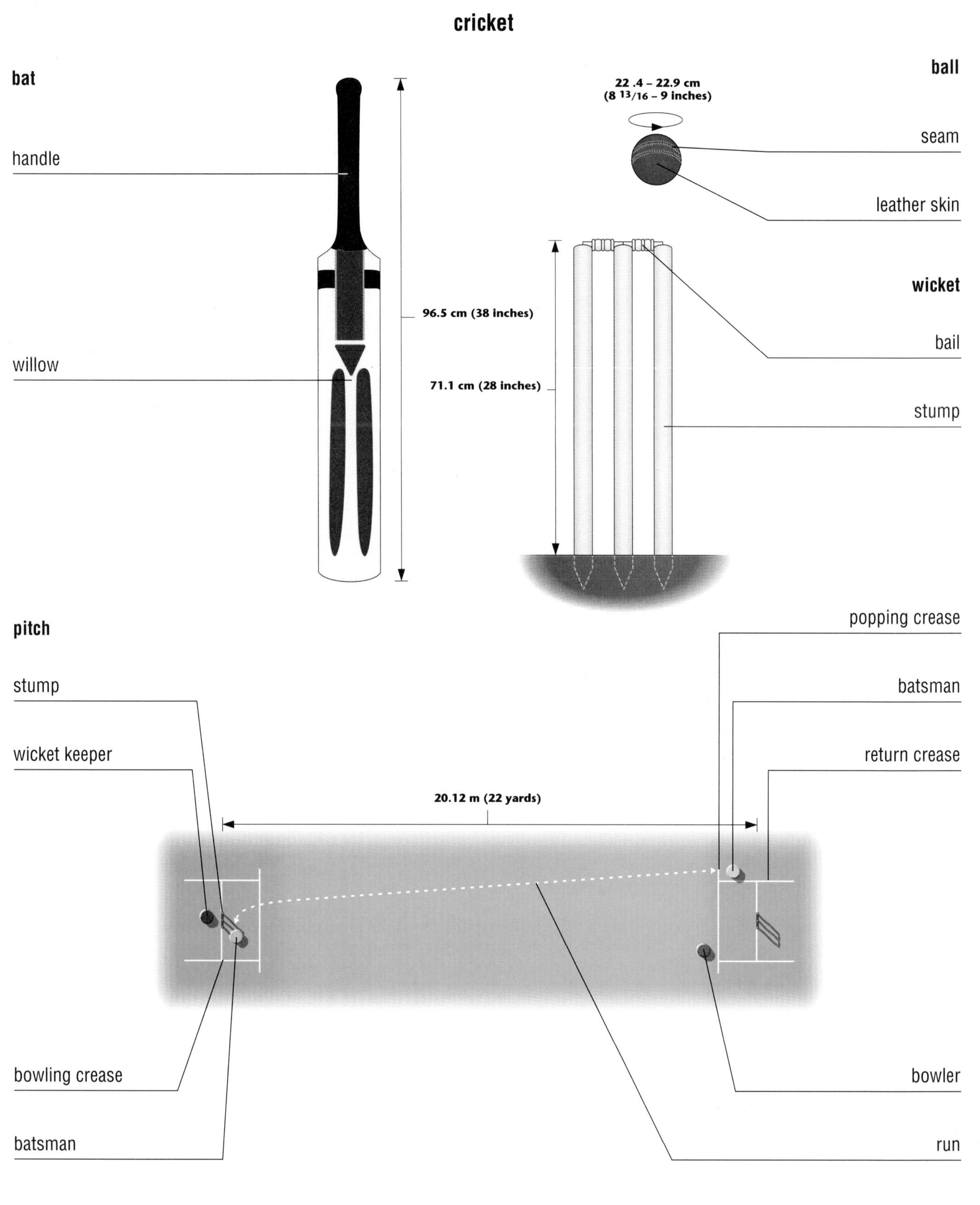

bat

handle

willow

96.5 cm (38 inches)

71.1 cm (28 inches)

ball

22 .4 – 22.9 cm
(8 13/16 – 9 inches)

seam

leather skin

wicket

bail

stump

pitch

stump

wicket keeper

20.12 m (22 yards)

popping crease

batsman

return crease

bowling crease

batsman

bowler

run

hockey

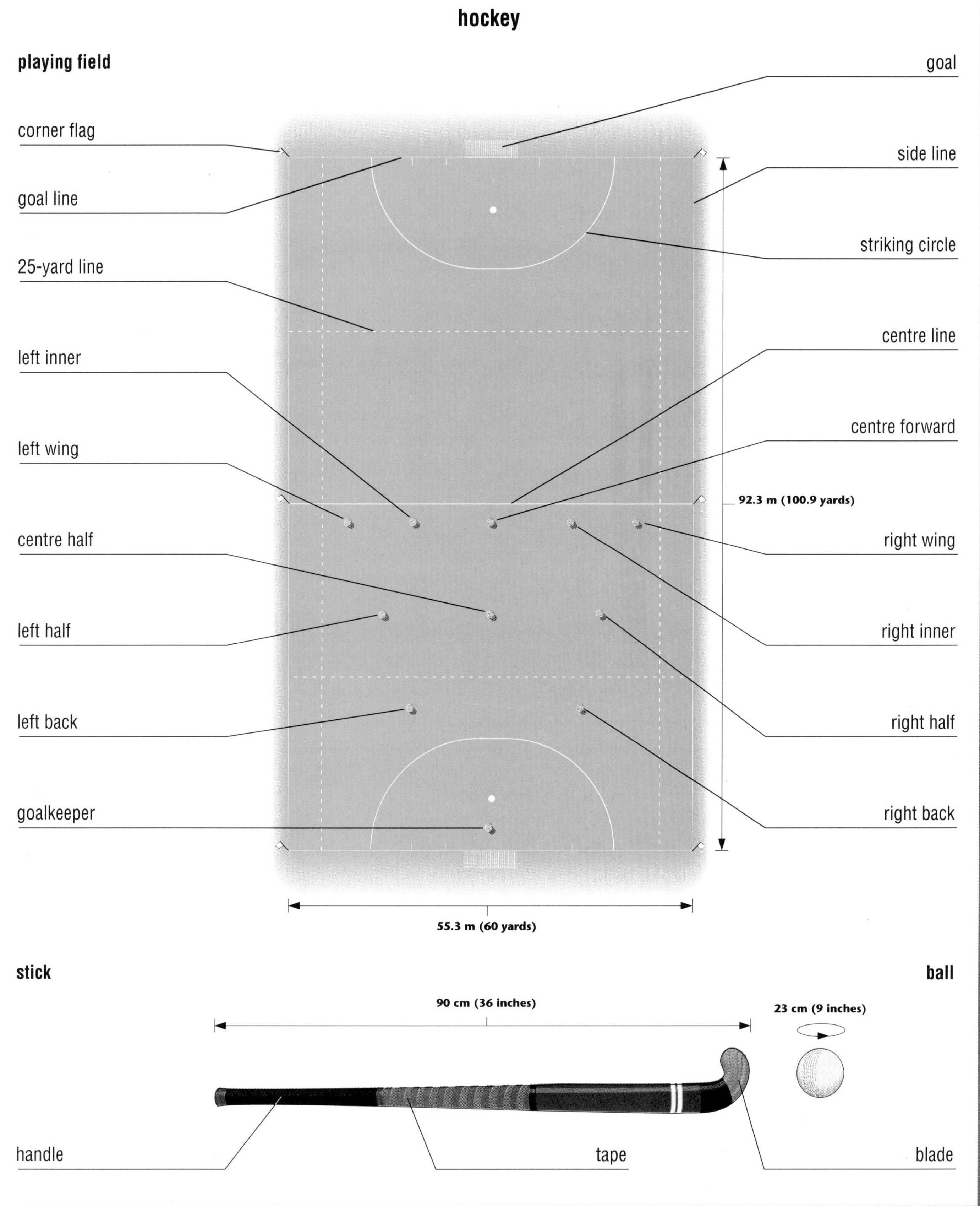

playing field

goal

corner flag

goal line

side line

striking circle

25-yard line

centre line

left inner

centre forward

left wing

92.3 m (100.9 yards)

right wing

centre half

left half

right inner

left back

right half

goalkeeper

right back

55.3 m (60 yards)

stick

ball

90 cm (36 inches)

23 cm (9 inches)

handle

tape

blade

ice hockey

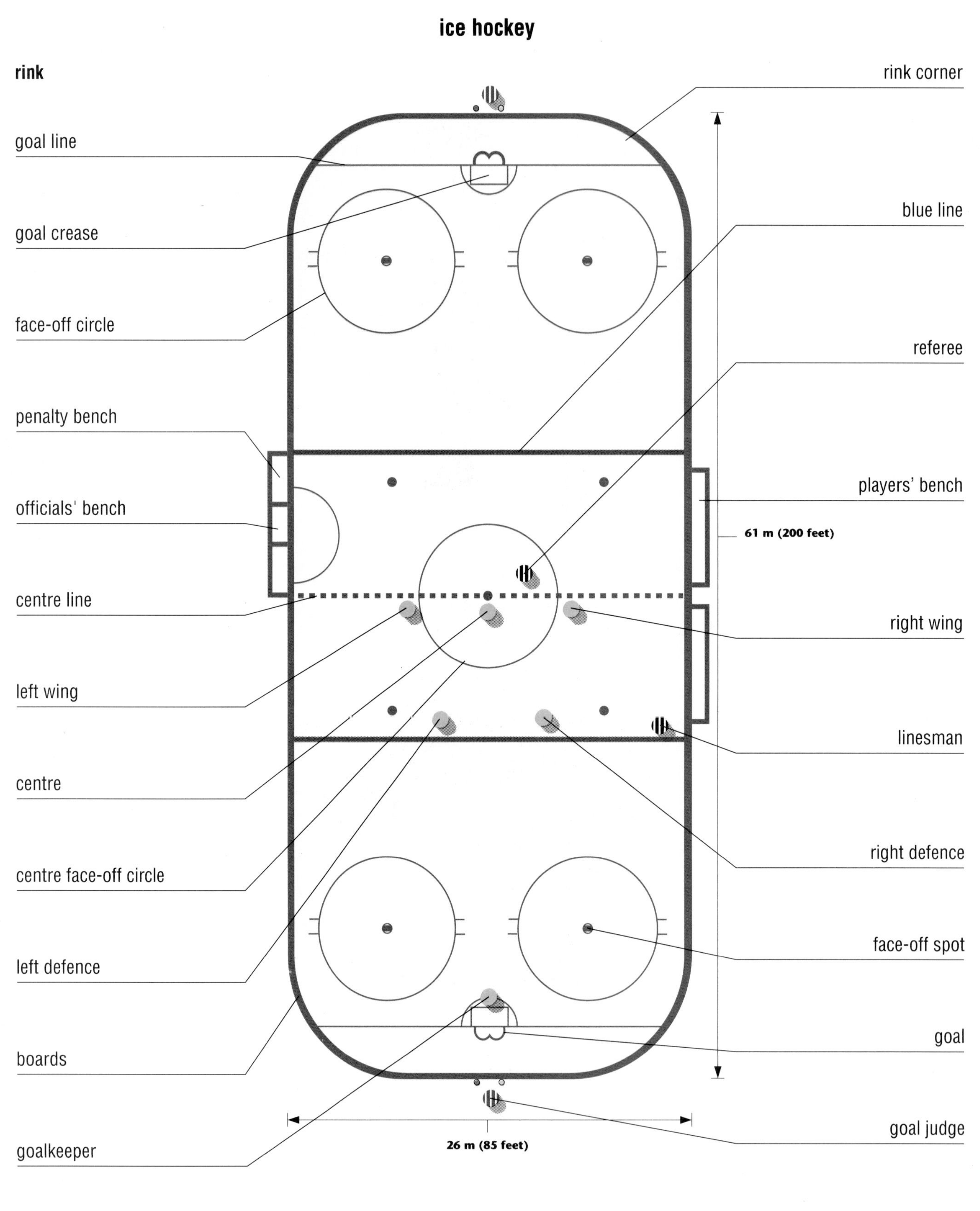

rink

goal line

goal crease

face-off circle

penalty bench

officials' bench

centre line

left wing

centre

centre face-off circle

left defence

boards

goalkeeper

rink corner

blue line

referee

players' bench

61 m (200 feet)

right wing

linesman

right defence

face-off spot

goal

goal judge

26 m (85 feet)

ice hockey

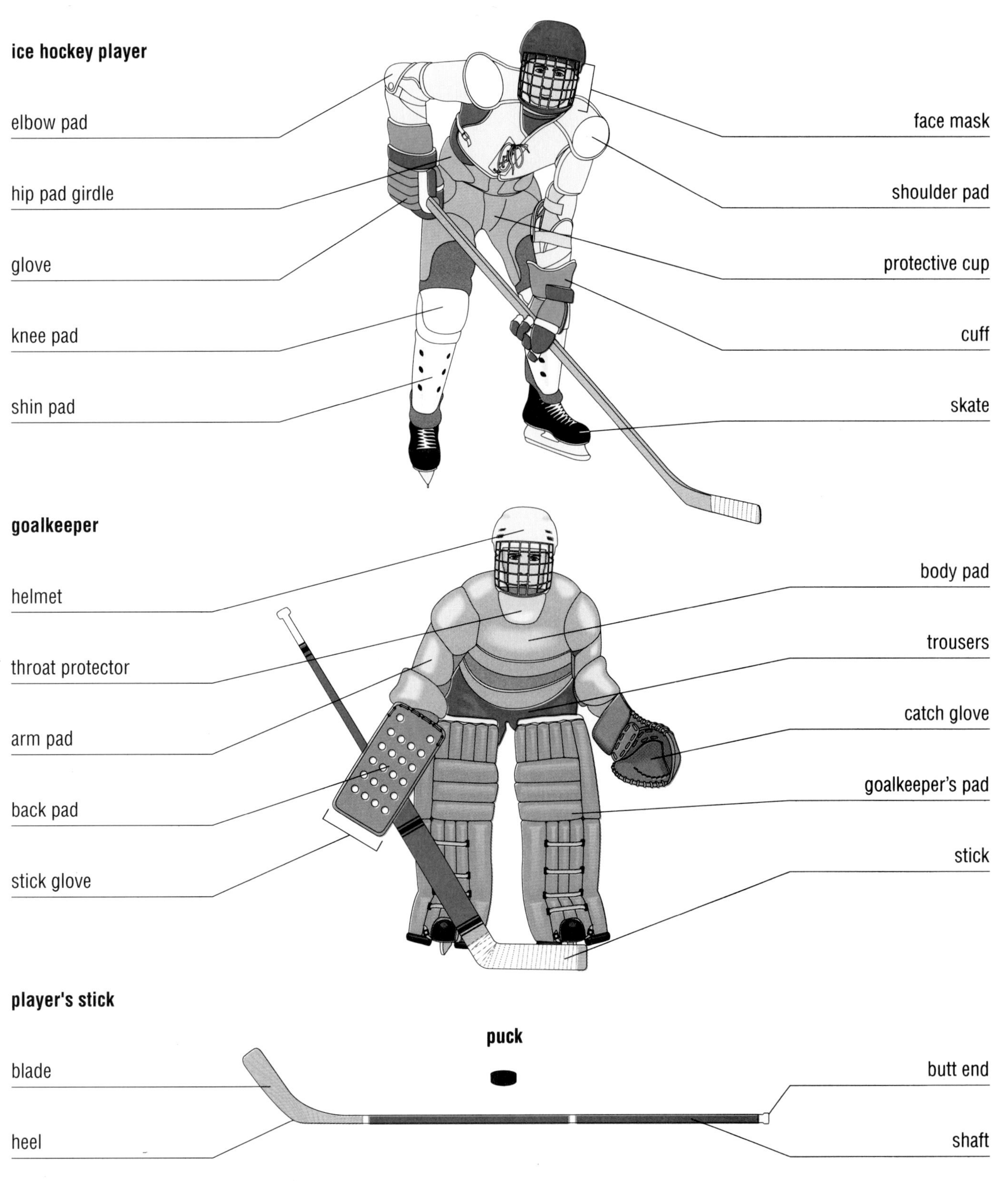

ice hockey player

elbow pad

hip pad girdle

glove

knee pad

shin pad

face mask

shoulder pad

protective cup

cuff

skate

goalkeeper

helmet

throat protector

arm pad

back pad

stick glove

body pad

trousers

catch glove

goalkeeper's pad

stick

player's stick

puck

blade

heel

butt end

shaft

skating

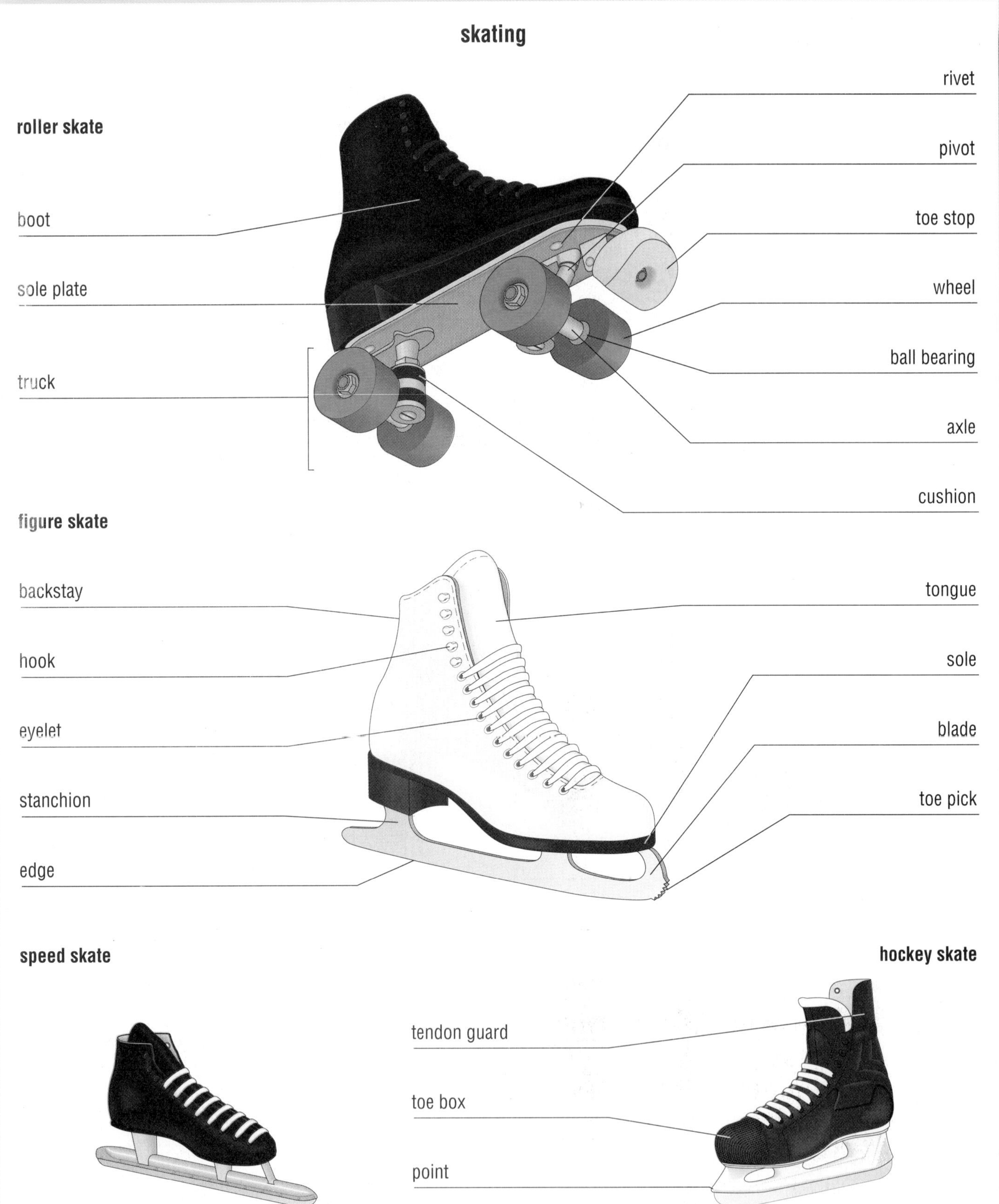

roller skate

rivet

pivot

toe stop

boot

sole plate

wheel

ball bearing

truck

axle

cushion

figure skate

backstay

tongue

hook

sole

eyelet

blade

stanchion

toe pick

edge

speed skate

hockey skate

tendon guard

toe box

point

basketball

court

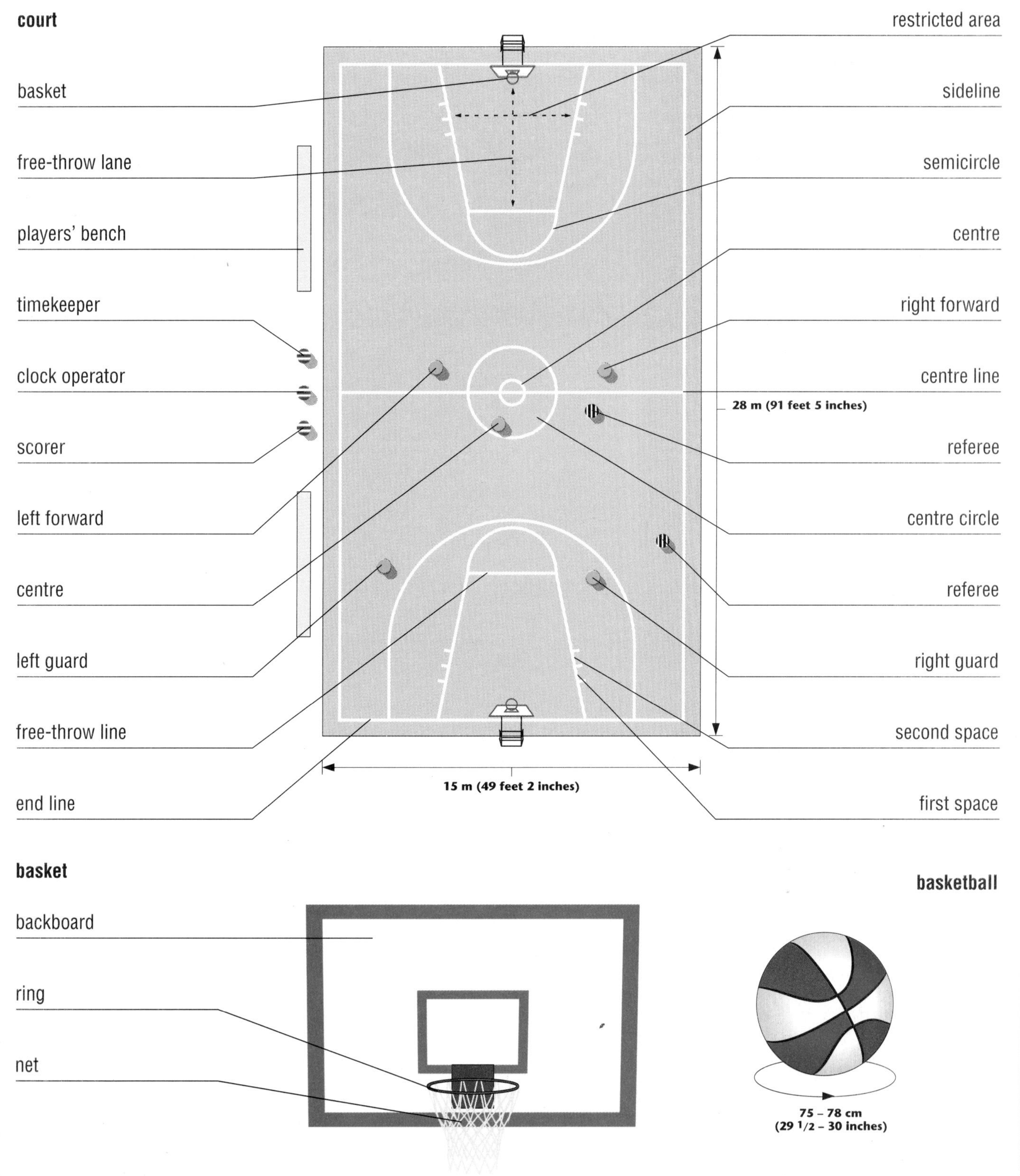

restricted area

basket

sideline

free-throw lane

semicircle

players' bench

centre

timekeeper

right forward

clock operator

centre line

28 m (91 feet 5 inches)

scorer

referee

left forward

centre circle

centre

referee

left guard

right guard

free-throw line

second space

15 m (49 feet 2 inches)

end line

first space

basket

basketball

backboard

ring

net

75 – 78 cm
(29 1/2 – 30 inches)

tennis

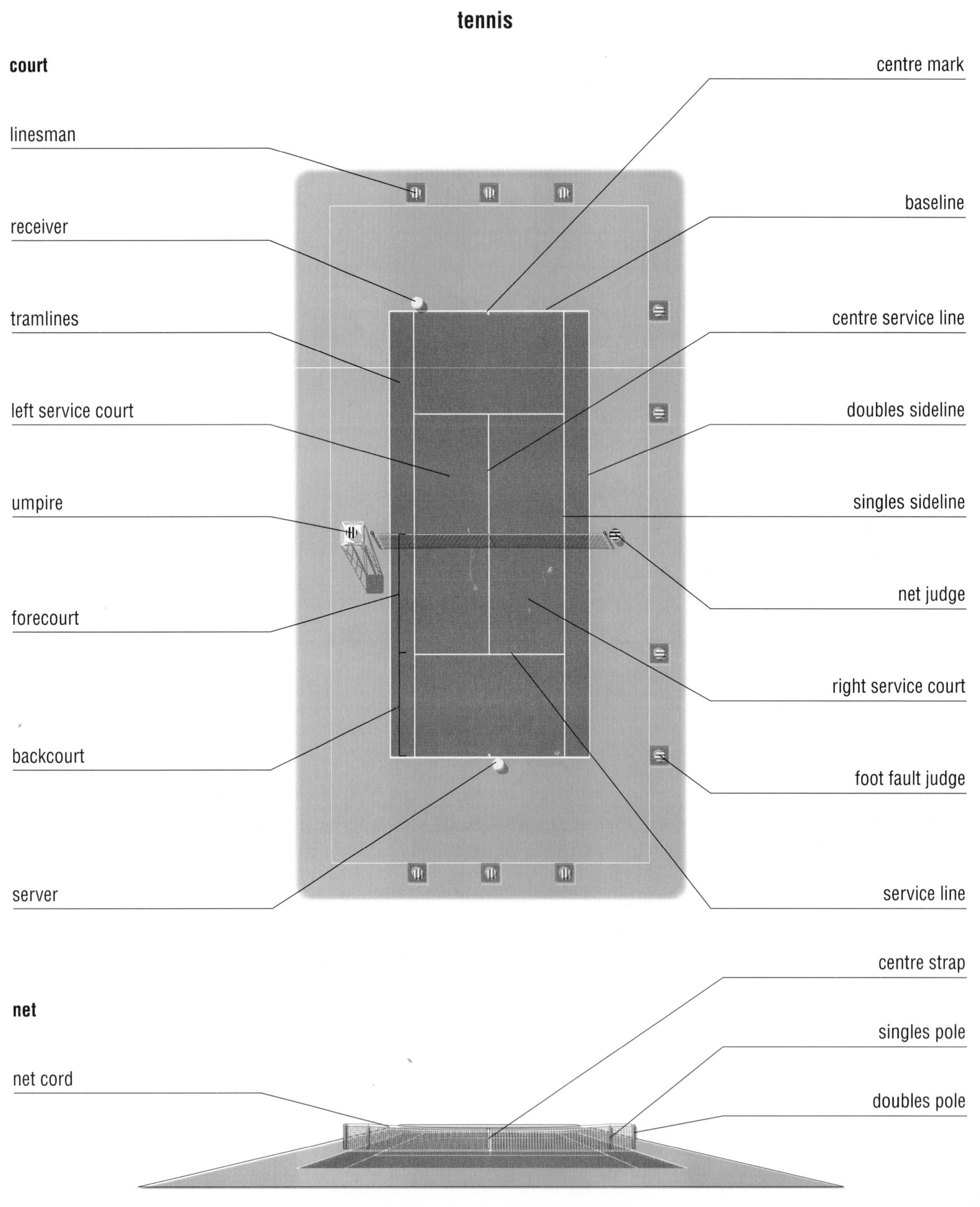

court

linesman

receiver

tramlines

left service court

umpire

forecourt

backcourt

server

centre mark

baseline

centre service line

doubles sideline

singles sideline

net judge

right service court

foot fault judge

service line

centre strap

singles pole

doubles pole

net

net cord

tennis

tennis player

wristband

headband

skirt

shirt

tennis shoe

sock

tennis racquet

throat

shoulder

butt

frame

handle

stringing

shaft

head

tennis ball

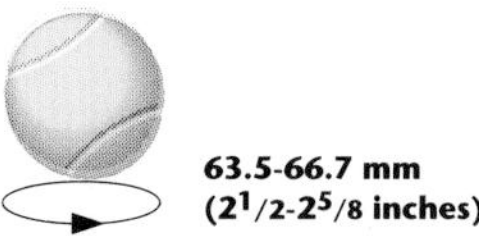

63.5-66.7 mm
($2^1/2$-$2^5/8$ inches)

downhill skiing

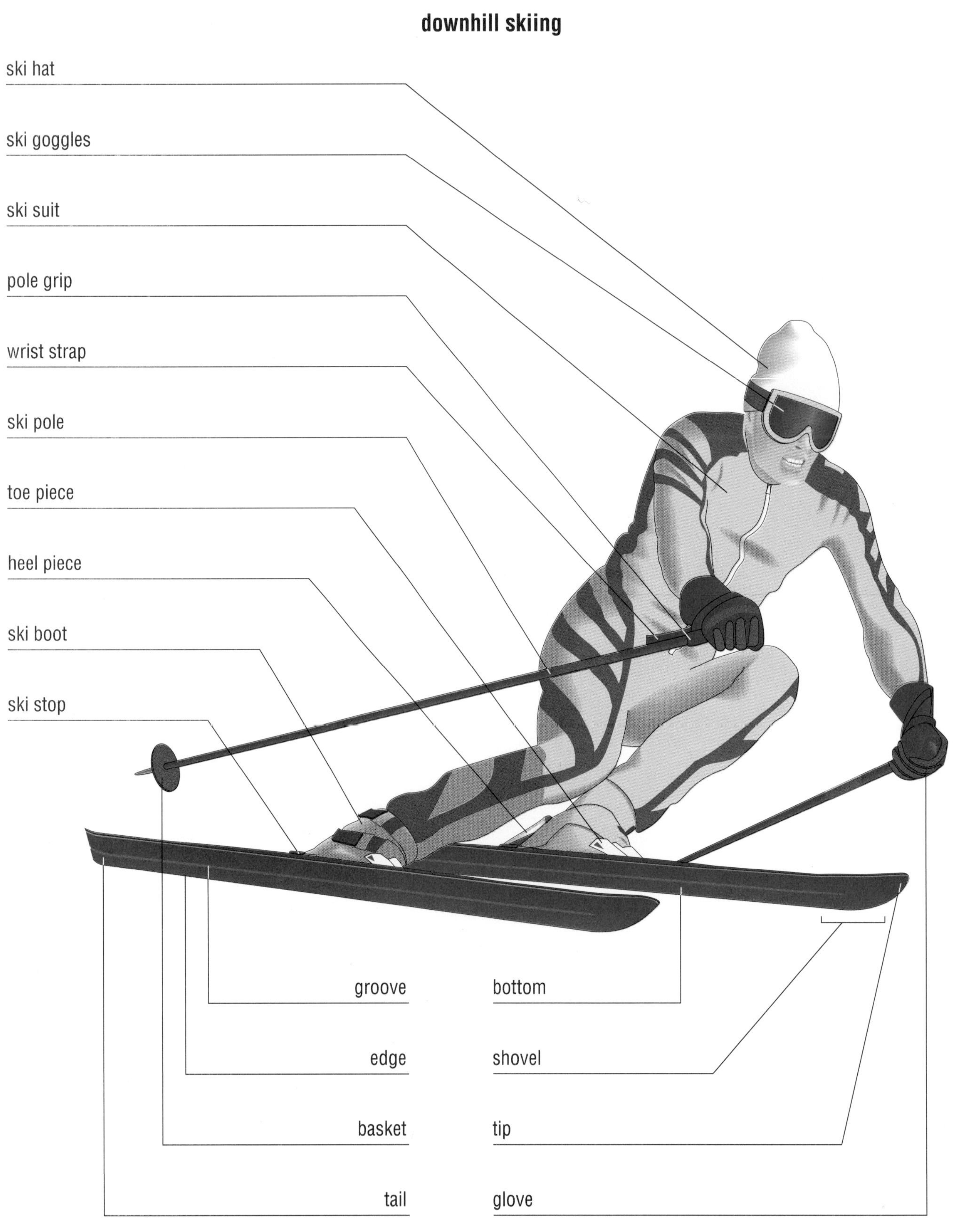

ski hat

ski goggles

ski suit

pole grip

wrist strap

ski pole

toe piece

heel piece

ski boot

ski stop

groove   bottom

edge   shovel

basket   tip

tail   glove

cross-country skiing

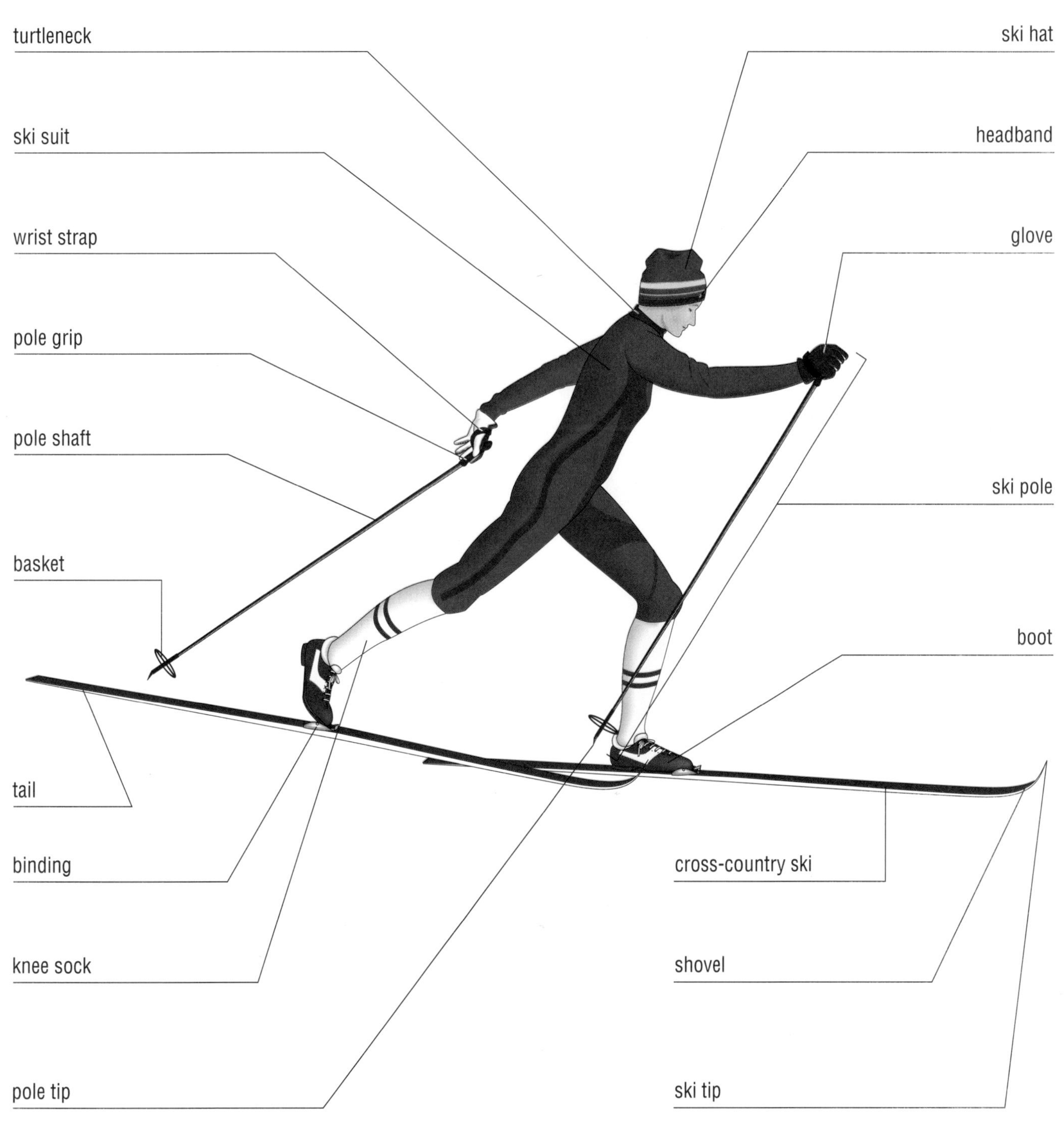

turtleneck

ski hat

ski suit

headband

wrist strap

glove

pole grip

pole shaft

ski pole

basket

boot

tail

binding

cross-country ski

knee sock

shovel

pole tip

ski tip

SPORTS

diving

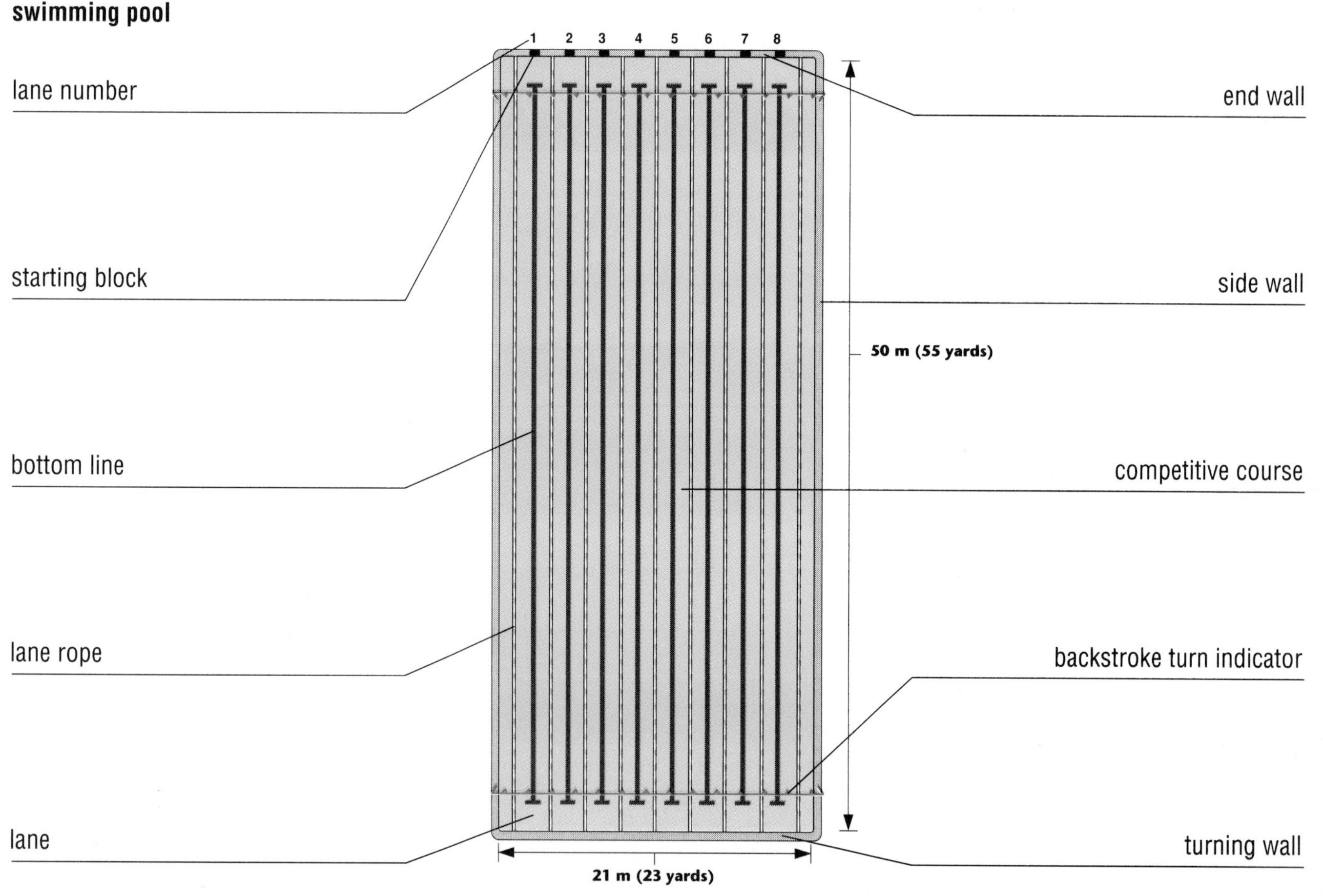

10-metre platform

7.5-metre platform

fulcrum

5-metre platform

3-metre platform

3-metre springboard

surface of the water

1-metre springboard

swimming

swimming pool

lane number

end wall

starting block

side wall

50 m (55 yards)

bottom line

competitive course

lane rope

backstroke turn indicator

lane

turning wall

21 m (23 yards)

skin diving

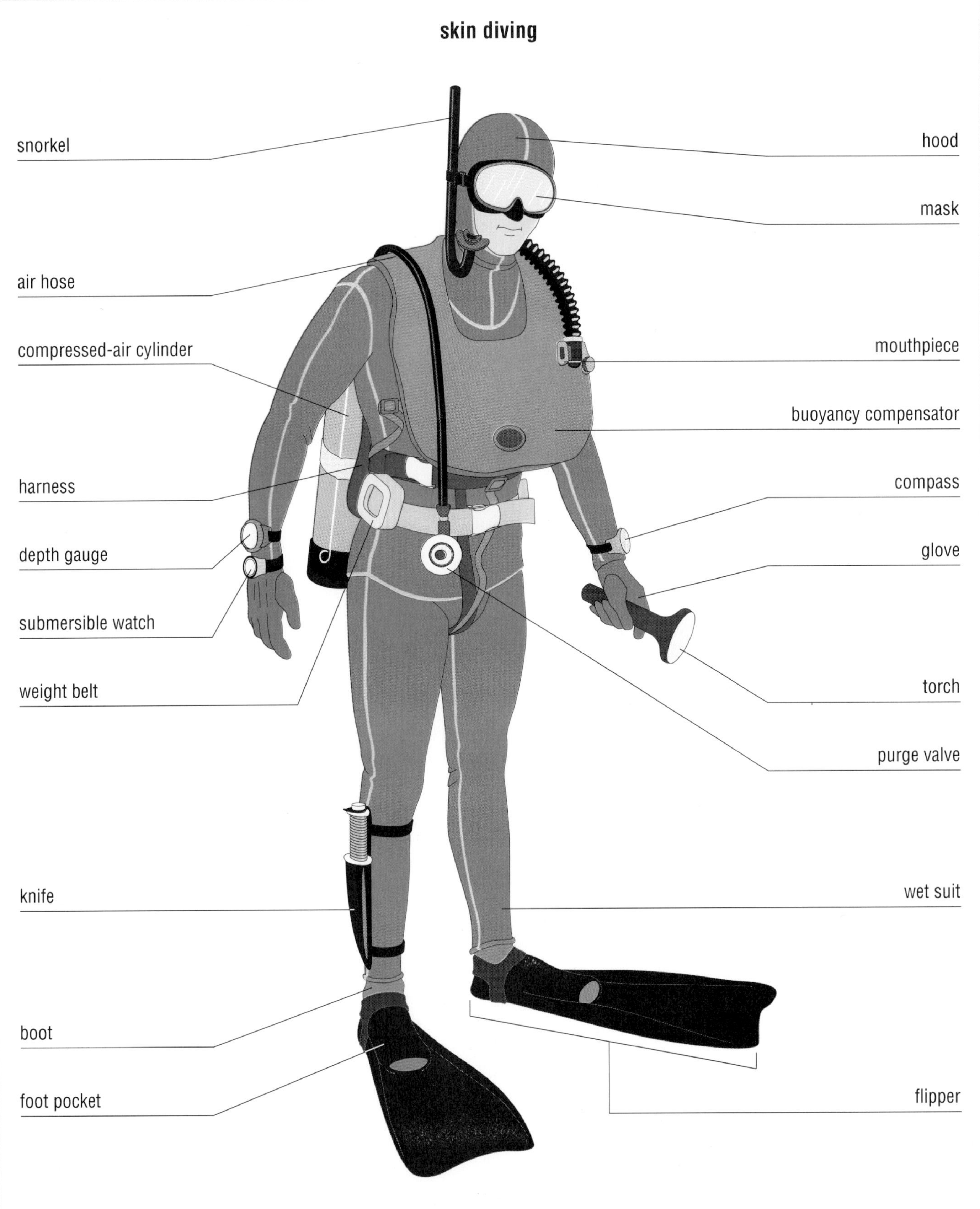

snorkel

hood

mask

air hose

mouthpiece

compressed-air cylinder

buoyancy compensator

harness

compass

depth gauge

glove

submersible watch

weight belt

torch

purge valve

knife

wet suit

boot

foot pocket

flipper

windsurfing

sailboard

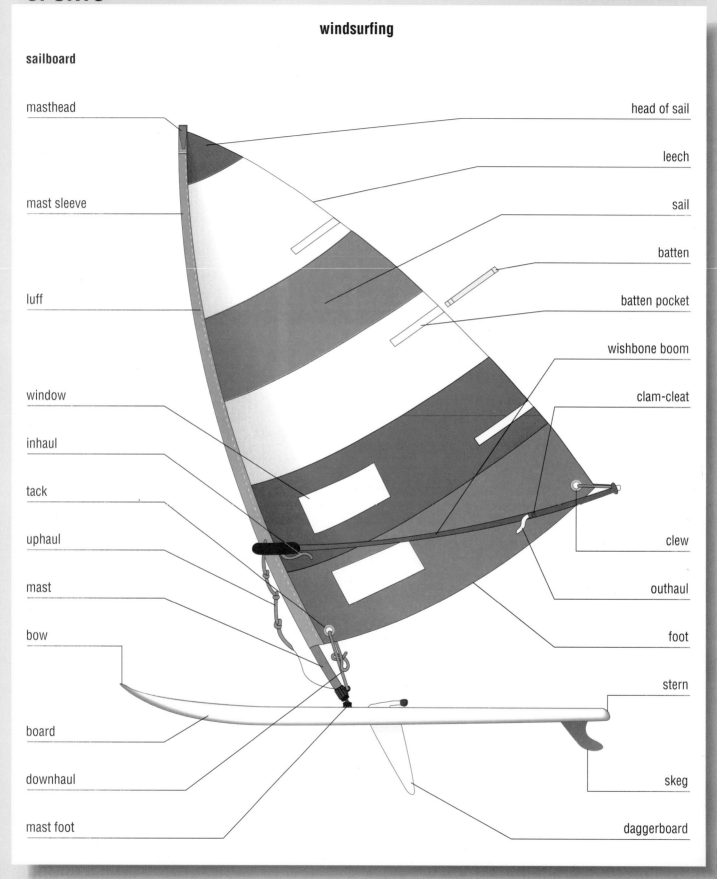

masthead

head of sail

mast sleeve

leech

sail

batten

luff

batten pocket

wishbone boom

window

clam-cleat

inhaul

tack

uphaul

clew

mast

outhaul

bow

foot

stern

board

downhaul

skeg

mast foot

daggerboard

darts

dart

dartboard

barrel

shaft

flight

point

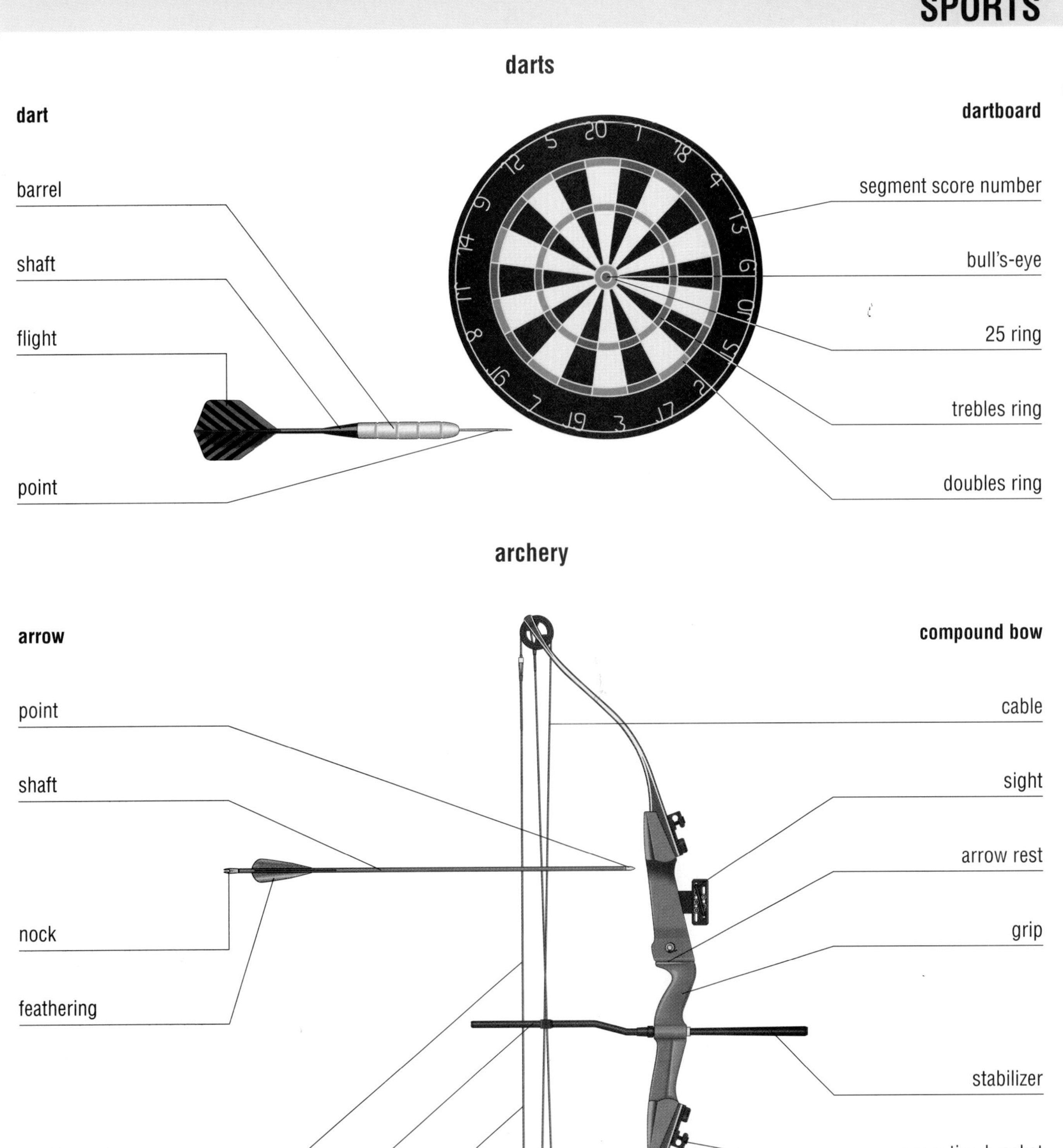

segment score number

bull's-eye

25 ring

trebles ring

doubles ring

archery

arrow

compound bow

point

shaft

nock

feathering

nocking point

cable guard

bowstring

cable

sight

arrow rest

grip

stabilizer

mounting bracket

limb

wheel

camping equipment

tent

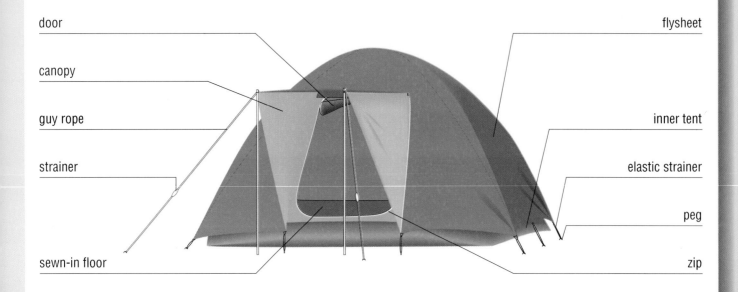

door

canopy

guy rope

strainer

sewn-in floor

flysheet

inner tent

elastic strainer

peg

zip

family tent

canvas divider

living room

guy rope

room

peg loop

frame

window canopy

screen window

wall

elastic strainer

camping equipment

Swiss army knife

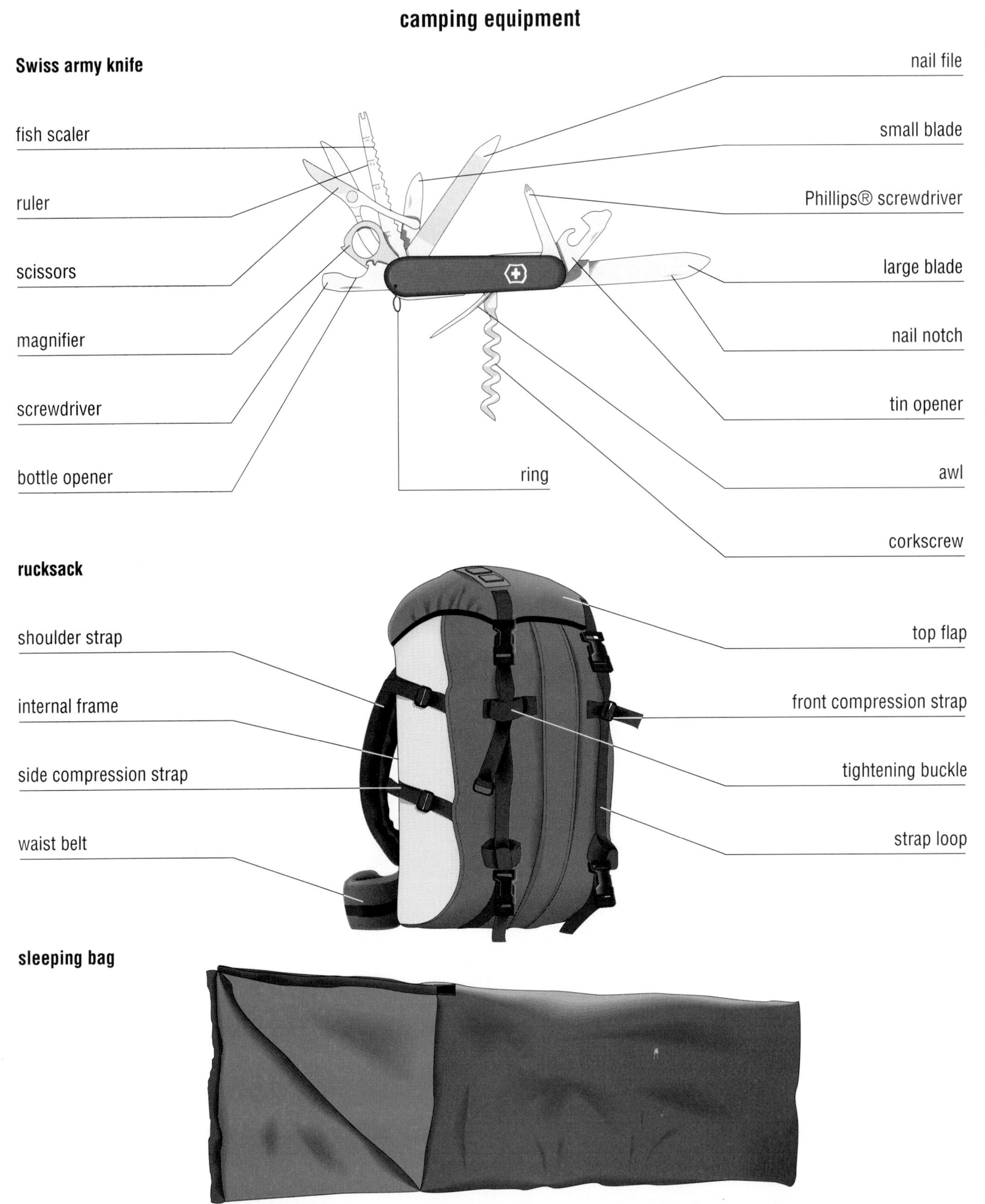

fish scaler

ruler

scissors

magnifier

screwdriver

bottle opener

ring

nail file

small blade

Phillips® screwdriver

large blade

nail notch

tin opener

awl

corkscrew

rucksack

shoulder strap

internal frame

side compression strap

waist belt

top flap

front compression strap

tightening buckle

strap loop

sleeping bag

indoor games

backgammon

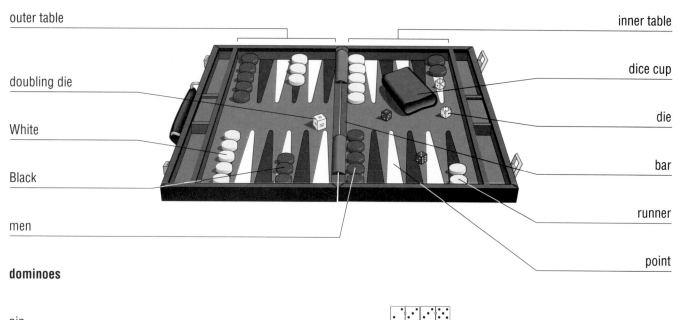

outer table

inner table

doubling die

dice cup

White

die

Black

bar

men

runner

point

dominoes

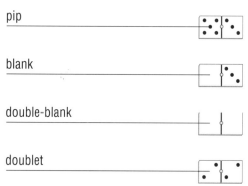

pip

blank

double-blank

doublet

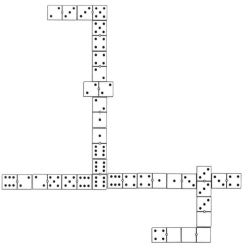

card games

Joker Ace King Queen Jack

 diamond   heart

 spade   club

measure of time

sundial

gnomon

dial

shadow

hourglass

glass bulb

neck

sand

kitchen timer

stopwatch

reset button

minute hand

1/10th second hand

lanyard

start button

stop button

second hand

case

55 5
50 10
45 15
40 20
35 25
30

25 MIN 5
20 10
15

1/10 SEC

analogue watch

hand

dial

11 12 1
10 2
9 3
8 4
7 6 5

digital watch

liquid-crystal display

10:42:55

MEASURING DEVICES

measure of weight

Roberval's balance

dial

pointer

pan

beam

base

electronic scales

display

weight

platform

unit price

function keys

total

numeric keyboard

product codes

ticket

bathroom scales

weighing platform

display

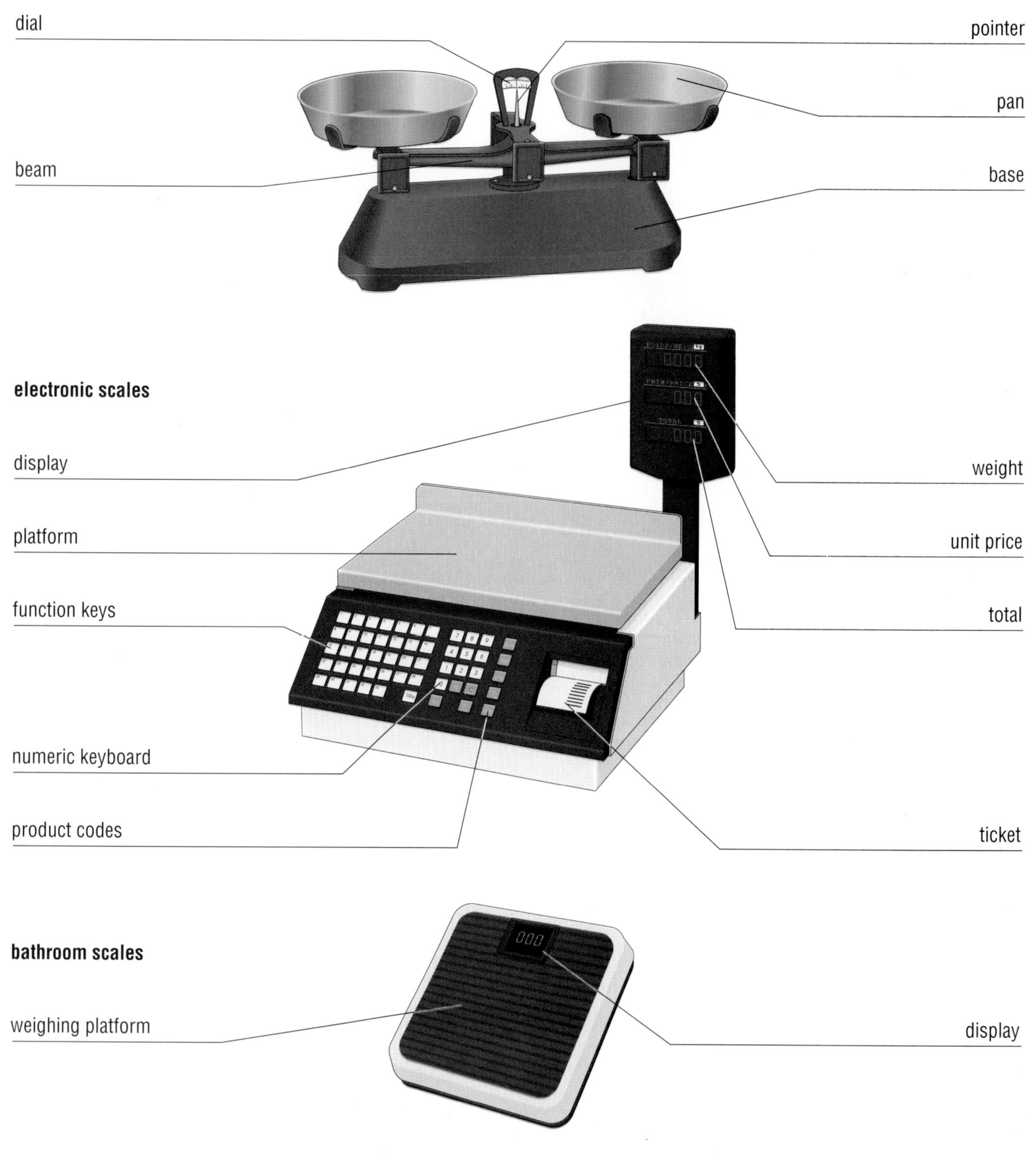

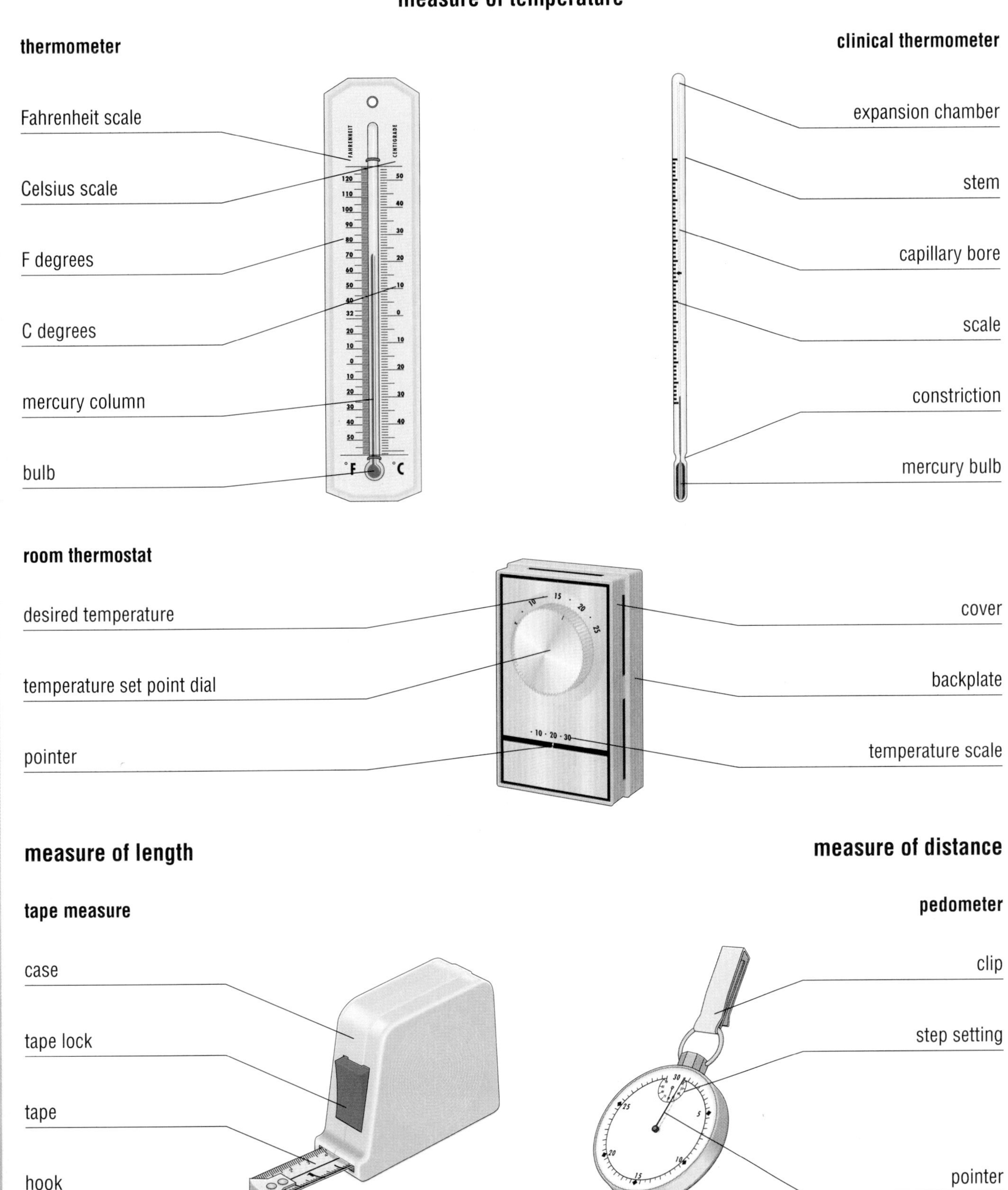

measure of temperature

thermometer

clinical thermometer

Fahrenheit scale

Celsius scale

F degrees

C degrees

mercury column

bulb

expansion chamber

stem

capillary bore

scale

constriction

mercury bulb

room thermostat

desired temperature

temperature set point dial

pointer

cover

backplate

temperature scale

measure of length

tape measure

case

tape lock

tape

hook

measure of distance

pedometer

clip

step setting

pointer

OPTICAL INSTRUMENTS

binoculars

eyepiece

focusing ring

zoom adjustment

body

focusing mechanism

objective lens

hinge

bridge

binocular microscope

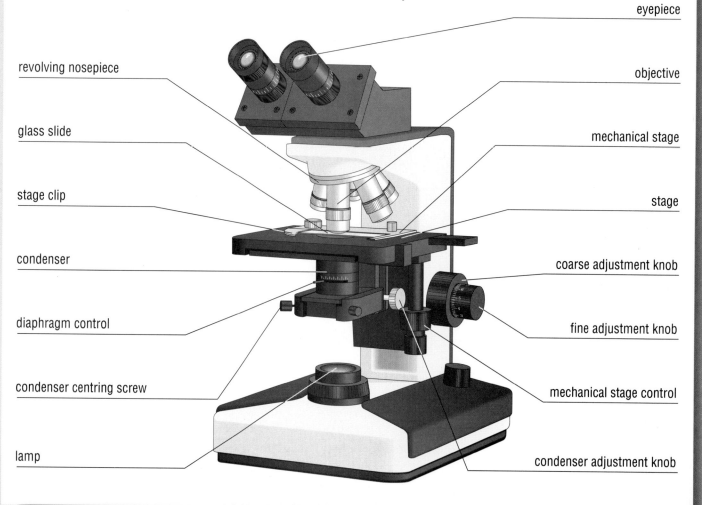

eyepiece

revolving nosepiece

glass slide

stage clip

condenser

diaphragm control

condenser centring screw

lamp

objective

mechanical stage

stage

coarse adjustment knob

fine adjustment knob

mechanical stage control

condenser adjustment knob

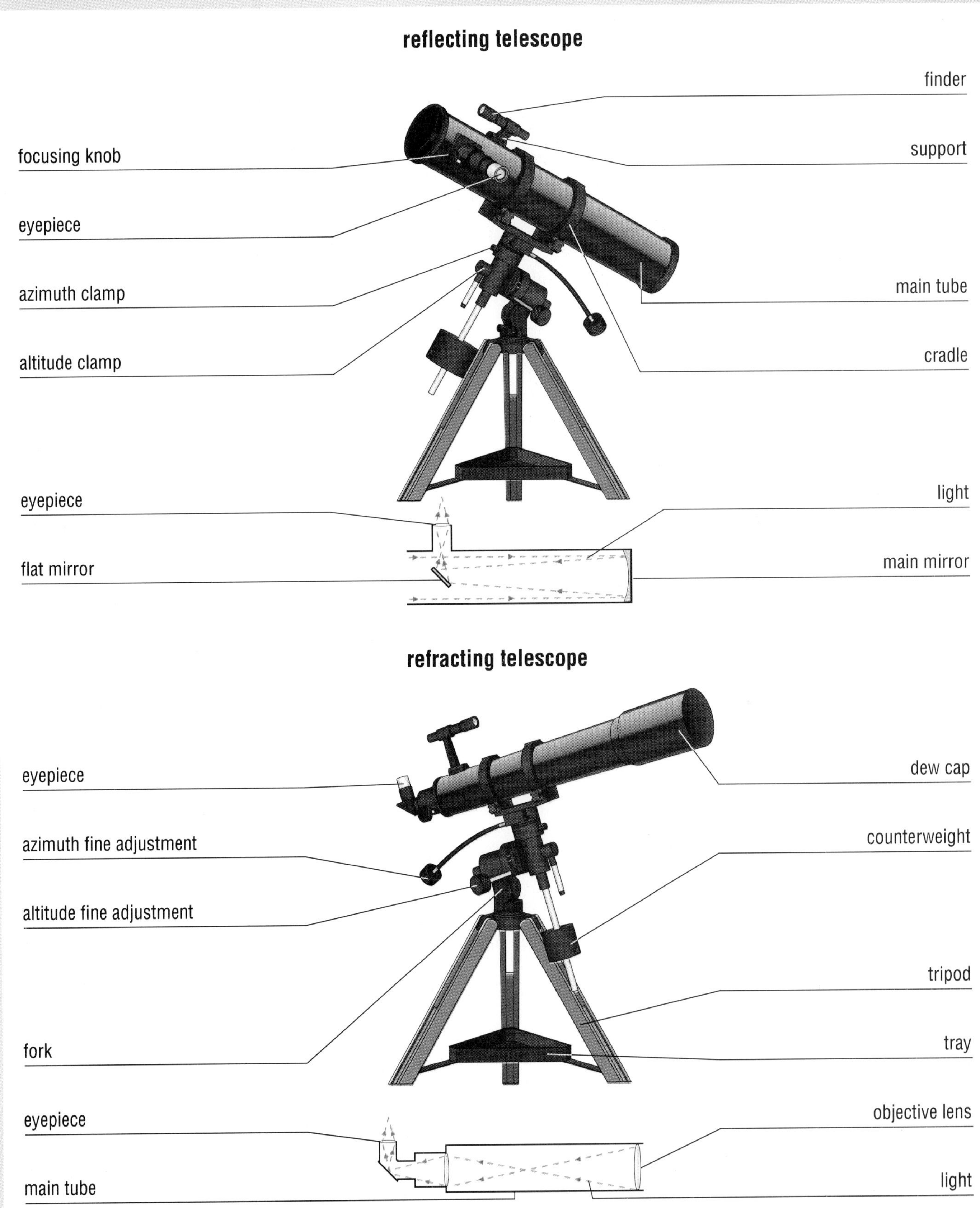

reflecting telescope

finder

focusing knob

support

eyepiece

azimuth clamp

main tube

altitude clamp

cradle

eyepiece

light

flat mirror

main mirror

refracting telescope

eyepiece

dew cap

azimuth fine adjustment

counterweight

altitude fine adjustment

tripod

fork

tray

eyepiece

objective lens

main tube

light

fire engines

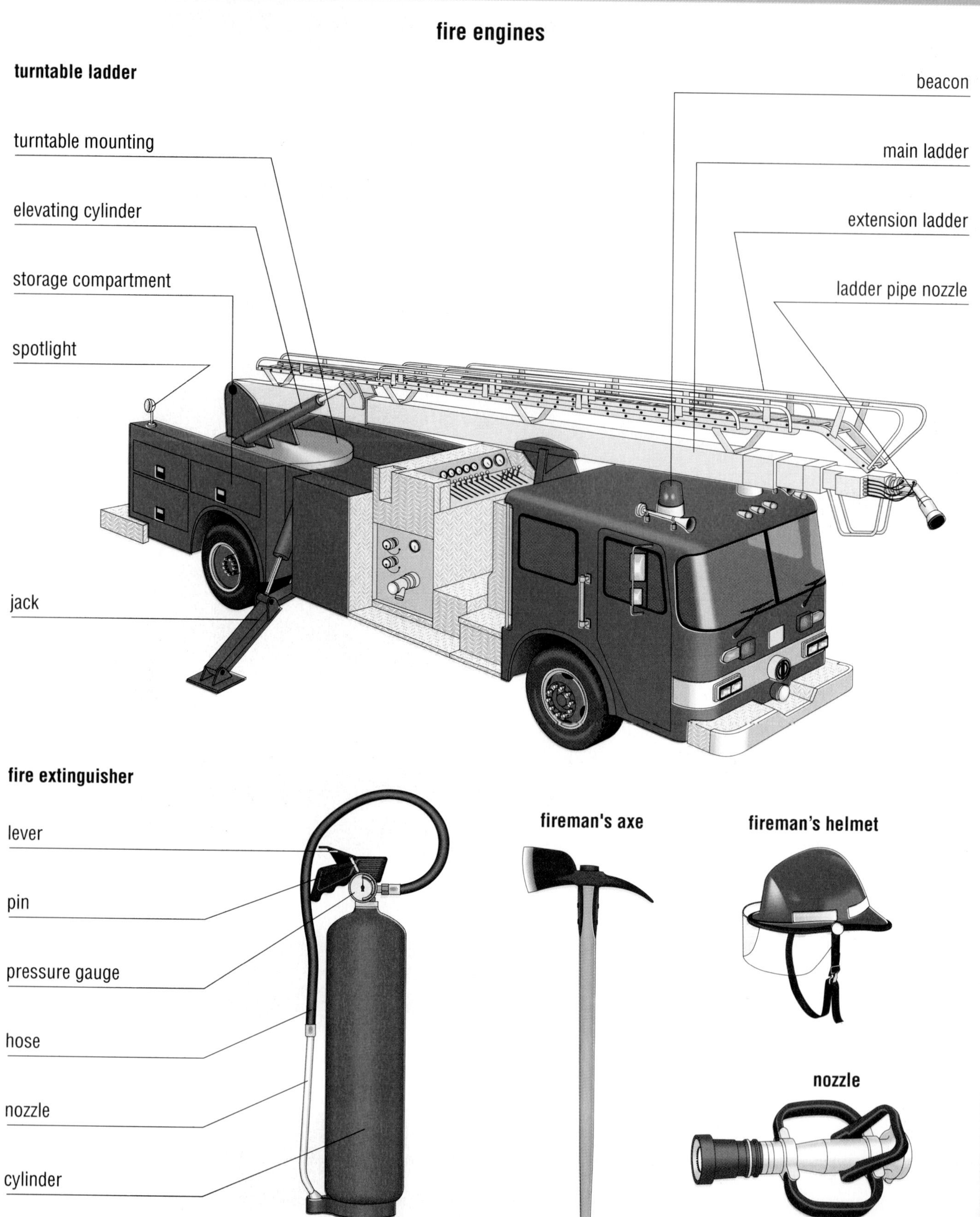

turntable ladder

turntable mounting

elevating cylinder

storage compartment

spotlight

jack

beacon

main ladder

extension ladder

ladder pipe nozzle

fire extinguisher

lever

pin

pressure gauge

hose

nozzle

cylinder

fireman's axe

fireman's helmet

nozzle

fire engines

water tender

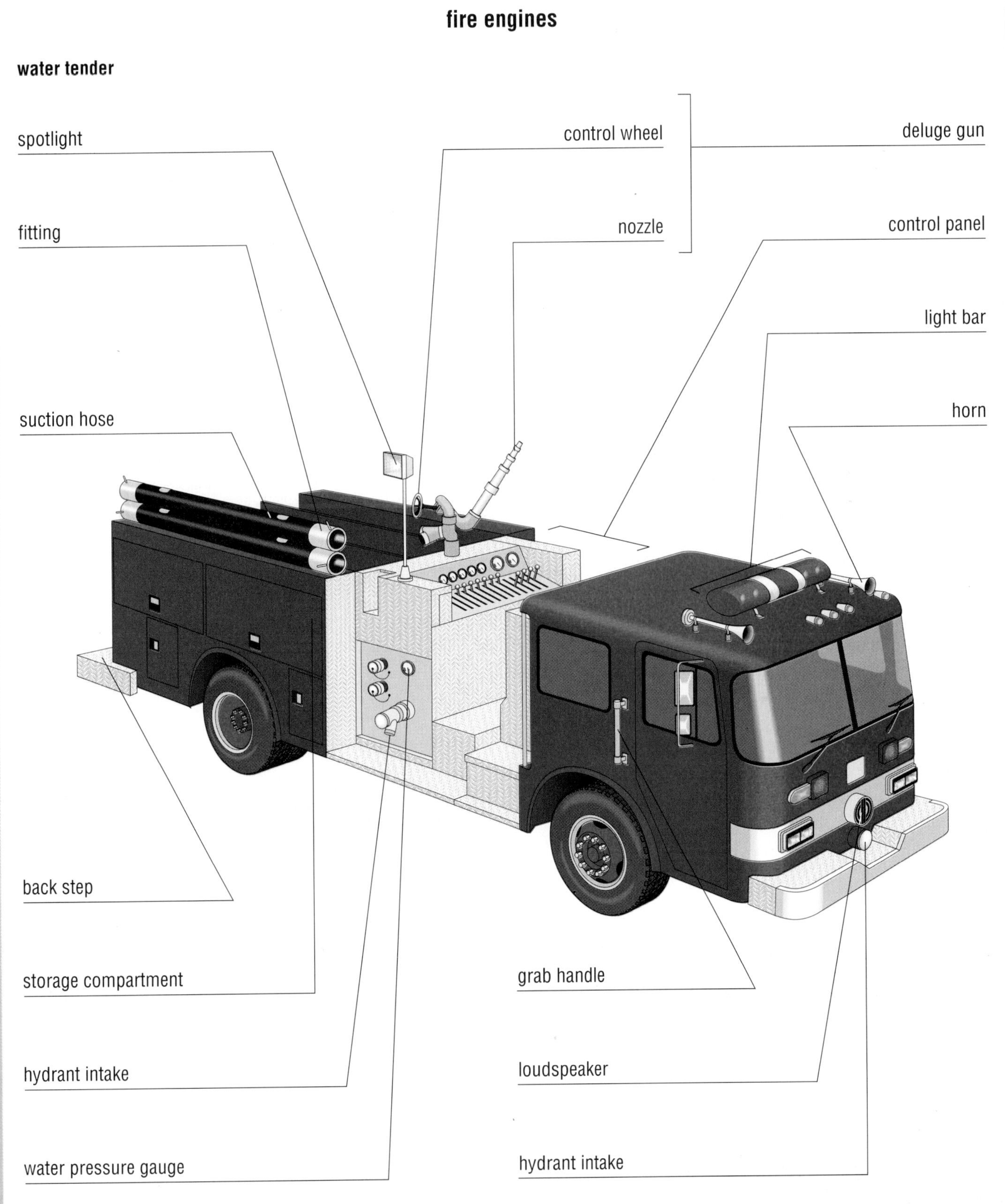

spotlight

fitting

suction hose

control wheel

nozzle

deluge gun

control panel

light bar

horn

back step

storage compartment

hydrant intake

water pressure gauge

grab handle

loudspeaker

hydrant intake

HEAVY MACHINERY

freight handling

tower crane

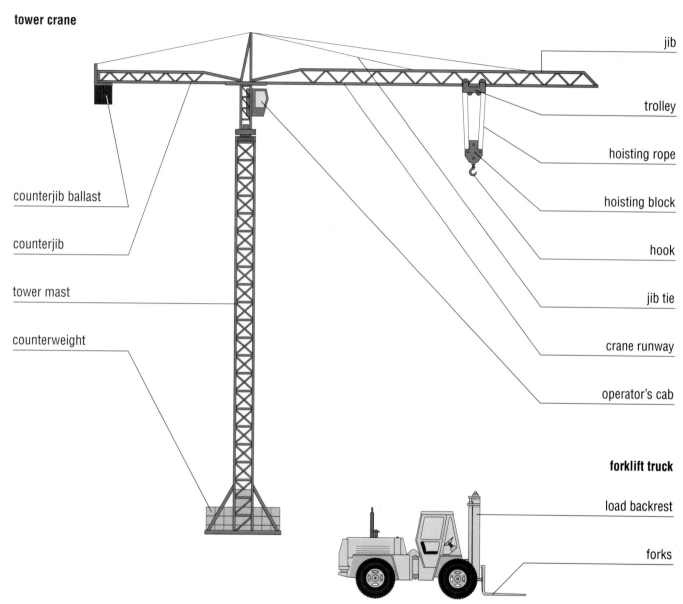

jib

trolley

hoisting rope

counterjib ballast

hoisting block

counterjib

hook

tower mast

jib tie

counterweight

crane runway

operator's cab

forklift truck

load backrest

forks

truck crane

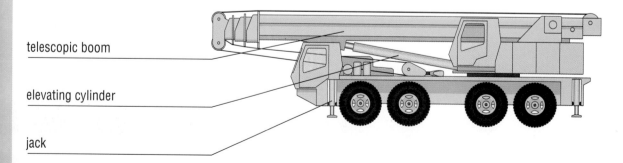

telescopic boom

elevating cylinder

jack

bulldozer

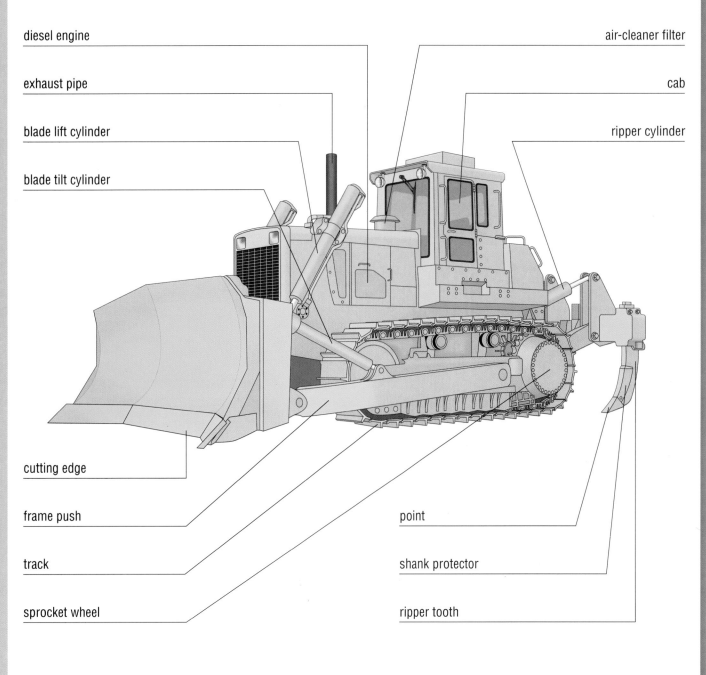

diesel engine

exhaust pipe

blade lift cylinder

blade tilt cylinder

air-cleaner filter

cab

ripper cylinder

cutting edge

frame push

track

sprocket wheel

point

shank protector

ripper tooth

blade

crawler tractor

ripper

wheel loader

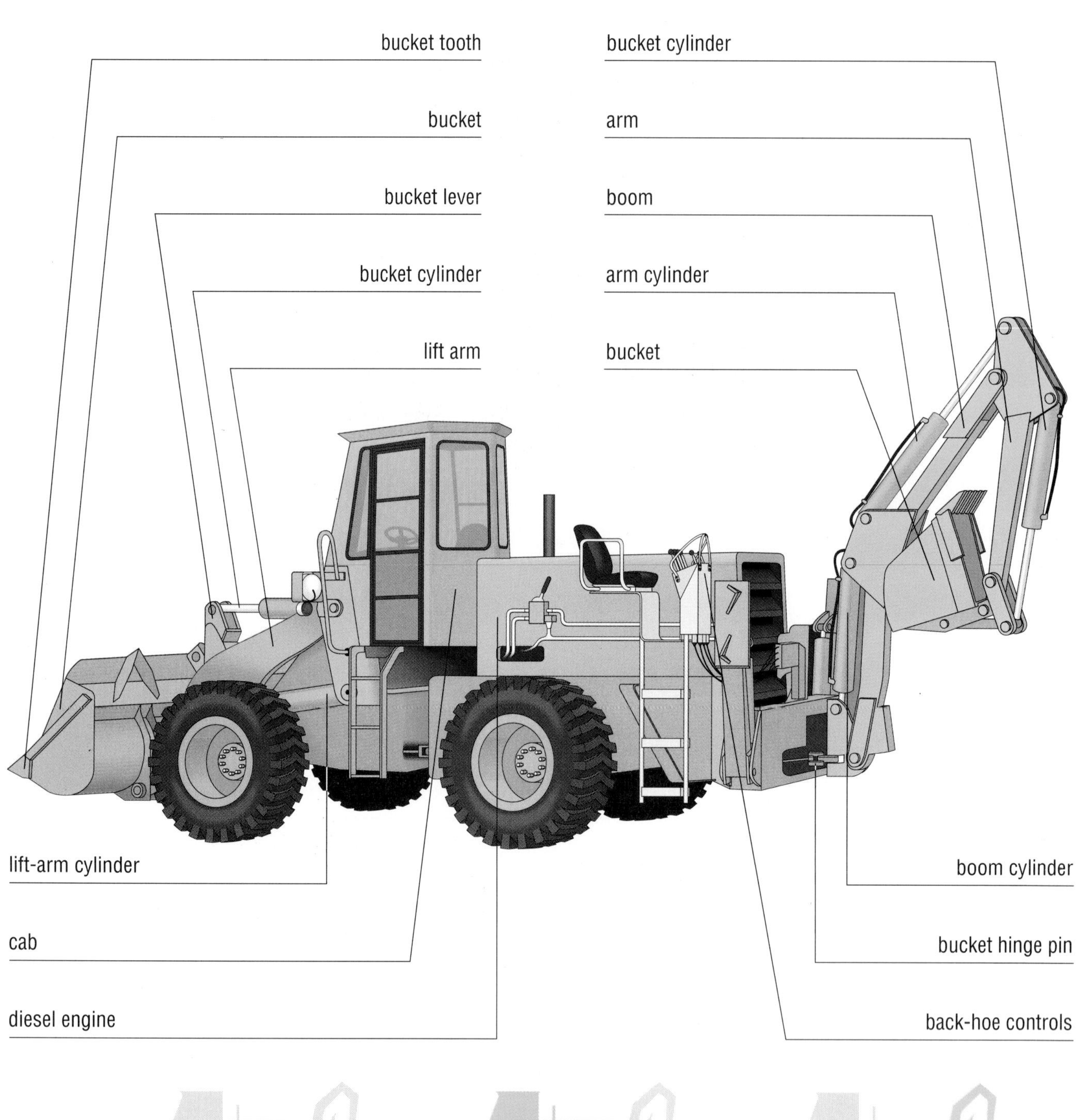

bucket tooth

bucket cylinder

bucket

arm

bucket lever

boom

bucket cylinder

arm cylinder

lift arm

bucket

lift-arm cylinder

boom cylinder

cab

bucket hinge pin

diesel engine

back-hoe controls

front-end loader

wheel loader

back-hoe

dumper truck

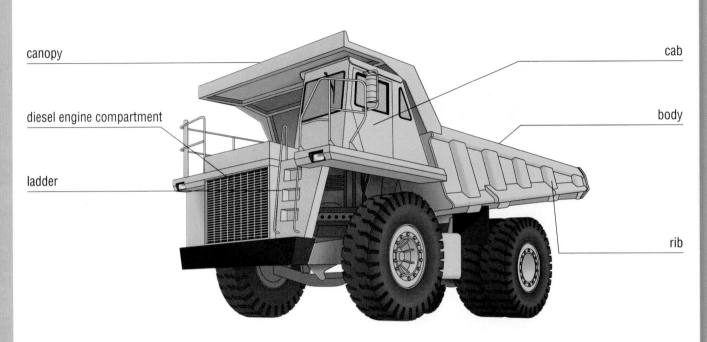

canopy

cab

diesel engine compartment

body

ladder

rib

hydraulic shovel

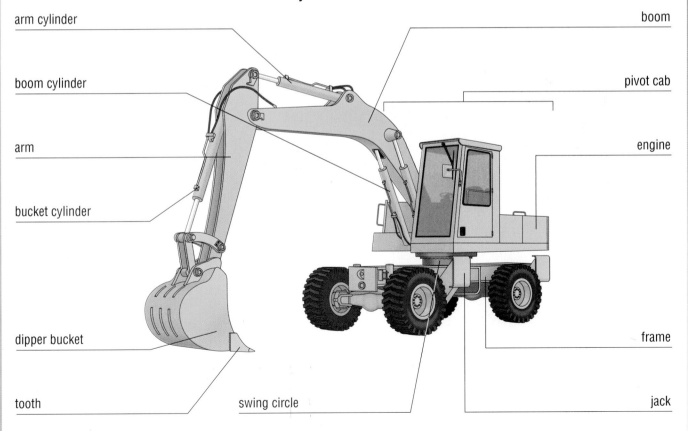

arm cylinder

boom

boom cylinder

pivot cab

arm

engine

bucket cylinder

dipper bucket

frame

tooth

swing circle

jack

SYMBOLS

public signs

telephone

information

disabled

no smoking

toilets

service station

restaurant

hospital

poison

flammable

explosive

electrical hazard

road signs

speed limit

no parking

no entry

stop

one-way traffic

bicycle lane

right bend

give way

school

traffic lights

danger

pedestrian crossing

1/10th second hand 141.
1-metre springboard 134.
1st valve slide 115.
2nd valve slide 115.
3-metre platform 134.
3-metre springboard 134.
3rd valve slide 115.
5-metre platform 134.
5-yard line 119.
6-yard box 118.
7.5-metre platform 134.
10-metre platform 134.
10-yard line 119.
25 ring 137.
25-yard line 119, 125.

A

a 112.
abdomen 24, 25, 26, 31.
abdominal segment 24.
abutment 97.
acanthus leaf 61.
accelerator pedal 91.
accessory shoe 89.
accidentals 112.
Ace 140.
action assembly 113.
add in memory 74.
add key 74.
adhesive tape 72.
adjusting screw 76.
aerial 86, 90, 111.
Africa 12.
after hydroplane 103.
air conditioner 93.
air hole 25.
air hose 135.
air inlet 105.
air line 96.
air lock 103.
air unit 78.
air-cleaner filter 149.
aircraft, long-range 104.
ala 36.
alighting board 25.
all-terrain vehicle 92.
almond 46.
altitude clamp 145.
altitude fine adjustment 145.
AM-FM tuner 86, 89.
American football 120, 121.
American football, strip 121.
ammunition stowage 111.
amphibian 27.
amplifier 89.
anal fin 27.
analogue watch 141.
anchor 102.
ankle 31.
annual ring 18.
Antarctica 12.
antenna 24, 25, 26, 104.
antennule 26.
anther 17.
anti-collision light 104.
anti-slip shoe 77.
anus 26.
apex 26.
apple 43.
apricot 43.
apron 60, 61.
arbour 51.
arch 97.
arch bridge 97.
archery 137.
Arctic 12.
arm 20, 32, 150, 151.
arm cylinder 150, 151.
arm guard 121.
arm pad 127.
arm stump 61.
armchair 61.
armour 108.
armour 111.
armoured plate 111.
armrest 61.
arrow 137.
arrow rest 137.

artichoke 41.
artichoke, Jerusalem 40.
articulated vehicle 94.
ASA/DIN mode 87.
ash layer 13.
Asia 12.
asparagus 39.
asteroids 9.
Atlantic Ocean 12.
aubergine 42.
audio system 91.
auricle 35.
auricular 22.
Australia 12.
auto reverse 86.
autofocus on/off switch 87.
auxiliary handle 76.
avocado 45.
awl 139.
awning channel 93.
axle 99, 128.
azimuth clamp 145.
azimuth fine adjustment 145.

B

b 112.
back 20, 21, 22, 32, 60, 65, 75.
back judge 120.
back pad 127.
back step 147.
back-hoe 150.
back-hoe controls 150.
backboard 129.
backcourt 130.
backgammon 140.
backguard 69.
backstay 128.
backstroke turn indicator 134.
bag, shoulder 84.
baggage compartment 105.
baguette 37.
bail 124.
bailey 55.
ball bearing 72, 128.
ball, rugby 119.
ball, baseball 123.
ball, cricket 124.
ball, hockey 125.
ball, soccer 118.
ball, tennis 131.
ballast 100.
ballpoint pen 72.
ballroom 102.
baluster 58.
banana 45.
banknote compartment 84.
bar 110.
bar line 112.
bark 18.
barn 49.
barrel 110, 137.
base 62, 142.
baseball 122, 123.
baseball, ball 123.
baseline 130.
basement 56.
basement window 56.
basin unit 59.
basket 129.
basket 67, 68, 129, 132, 133.
basketball 129.
basketball court 129.
basketball ring 129.
basketball, game 129.
bass clarinet 117.
bass drum 116.
bass drum 117.
bass pick-up 116.
bassoon 117.
bat, baseball 123.
bat, cricket 124.
bath 59.
bath platform 59.
bathroom 59.
bathroom scales 142.
batsman 124.
batten 136.
batten pocket 136.

batter 123.
batter 122.
batter's helmet 123.
battery 89.
battery warning light 91.
batting glove 123.
battlement 55.
bay window 56.
bayonet 109.
bayonet fitting 63.
beach 13.
beacon 146.
beam 142.
bean sprouts 39.
bean, green 42.
beans, broad 39.
bearing 97.
beater 68, 116.
beater ejector 68.
beaver 108.
bed 62.
beetroot 40.
bell 115.
bell brace 115.
belly 20, 22, 114.
belt 79, 83.
belt buckle 79.
belt loop 80.
berries 44.
bib 83.
bicycle 98, 99.
bicycle lane 152.
bidet 59.
bill 22.
bills, major types of 23.
binding 79, 133.
binocular microscope 144.
binoculars 144.
bird 22.
bird of prey 23.
bird of prey 23.
bird, aquatic 23.
bird, aquatic 23.
bird, insect-eating 23.
bird, perching 23.
bird, seed-eating 23.
bird, wading 23.
Black 140.
Black Sea 12.
blackcurrant 44.
blade 149.
blade 17, 65, 75, 125, 127, 128.
blade lift cylinder 149.
blade tilt cylinder 149.
blank 140.
blanket 62.
blender 68.
blind-side flanker 119.
blouse, classic 82.
blouses 82.
blue 71.
blue line 126.
blueberry 44.
board 136.
boarding step 105.
boards 126.
body 90.
body 93, 114, 115, 144, 151.
body flap 107.
body guard moulding 93.
body pad 127.
body, front view 31.
body, rear view 32.
bogie 100.
bogie frame 100.
boiler 103.
bolster 62, 65.
bolster pillow 62.
bolt 76.
bolt 109.
bolt guide 109.
bonnet 90.
boom 150, 151.
boom cylinder 150, 151.
boot 90, 128, 133, 135.
bottle opener 66, 139.
bottom 132.

bottom line 134.
bottom rail 57.
bow 114.
bow 102, 109, 136.
bow deck 102.
bow thruster 102.
bow window 56.
bowl 65.
bowl, cereal 64.
bowl, salad 64.
bowl, serving 64.
bowl, soup 64.
bowl, sugar 64.
bowler 124.
bowling crease 124.
bowstring 109, 137.
brace 77.
brake cable 98.
brake lever 98.
brake light 92.
brake pedal 91.
brake van 101.
branch 18, 39.
branches 18.
bread 37.
bread guide 68.
bread, American corn 37.
bread, black rye 37.
bread, caraway seeded rye 37.
bread, cottage loaf 37.
bread, crak rye 37.
bread, Danish rye 37.
bread, farmhouse 37.
bread, French 37.
bread, German rye 37.
bread, Greek 37.
bread, Indian chapati 37.
bread, Indian naan 37.
bread, Irish soda 37.
bread, Jewish chollar 37.
bread, milk 37.
bread, pita 37.
bread, pumpernickel 37.
bread, Russian pumpernickel 37.
bread, Scandinavian crak 37.
bread, sesame seeded pita 37.
bread, sliced white 37.
bread, unleavened 37.
bread, Vienna 37.
bread, whole meal 37.
bread, whole wheat 37.
breast 22, 31.
breast pocket 83.
breast welt pocket 80.
breastplate 108.
bridge 84, 103, 113, 114, 144.
bridge assembly 116.
bridge fin 103.
bridges 97.
brim 79.
bristles 77.
broad welt side pocket 79.
broccoli 41.
brood chamber 25.
brush 77.
brush 73.
brussels sprout 38.
bucket 150.
bucket cylinder 150, 151.
bucket hinge pin 150.
bucket lever 150.
bucket tooth 150.
buckle 83.
bud, axillary 16, 17.
bud, terminal 16.
buffer 100.
bulb 39, 63, 143.
bull 50.
bull's-eye 137.
bulldozer 149.
bullet 110.
bumper 90.
bundle 39.
buoyancy compensator 135.
bush 51.
butt 110, 131.
butt end 127.

The terms in **bold type** indicate the title of an illustration.

153

butter compartment 70.
butterfly 24.
buttock 32.
buttoned placket 83.
buttonhole 81.

C
c 112.
c clef 112.
C degrees 143.
cab 149, 150, 151.
cabbage lettuce 38.
cabbage, Chinese 38.
cabbage, green 38.
cabbage, white 38.
cabin 105.
cabinet 88.
cable 76, 86, 137.
cable guard 137.
cable sleeve 76.
calf 32, 50.
Callisto 9.
calls indicator 85.
calyx 17.
cambium 18.
camel 30.
camera 87.
camera body 87.
camping equipment 138, 139.
canine 34.
cannon 20, 111.
canopy 84, 138, 151.
cantaloupe 42.
cantilever bridge 97.
cantilever span 97.
canvas divider 138.
cap 79.
cap 19, 72.
capillary bore 143.
captain's quarters 102.
car 90, 91.
car bodies, types of 92.
car coat 82.
car lights 92.
car wash 96.
carapace 26, 28.
caravan 93.
card games 140.
cardigan 81.
cardigan, V-neck 81.
cardoon 39.
Caribbean Sea 12.
carpentry 75.
carpus 33.
carrier 98.
carrot 40.
cartridge 72.
case 113, 141, 143.
cash readout 96.
cashew 46.
casing 96.
cassette 86.
cassette deck 89.
cassette eject button 88.
cassette holder 86, 89.
cassette loading slot 88.
cassette player 86.
cassette player controls 86.
castanets 117.
castle 55.
castle 55.
cat 21.
cat's forepaw 21.
cat's head 21.
catch glove 127.
catcher 123.
catcher 122.
catcher's glove 123.
catenary 100.
caterpillar 24.
cauliflower 41.
cave 14.
cave 13.
CD player 89.
celeriac 40.
celery 39.
celeste felt 113.

cell 25.
cello 117.
Celsius scale 143.
Central America 12.
central processing unit 74.
centre 120, 126, 129.
centre back 118.
centre circle 118, 129.
centre console 91.
centre face-off circle 126.
centre field 122.
centre fielder 122.
centre flat 118.
centre forward 118, 125.
centre half 125.
centre line 125, 126, 129.
centre mark 130.
centre service line 130.
centre span 97.
centre spot 118.
centre stand 95.
centre strap 130.
cephalothorax 26.
cereal field 49.
chain 98, 99.
chain guide 99.
chain mail 108.
chain stay 98.
chain wheels 99.
chair, dining 60.
chair, formal 61.
chandelier 63.
channel scan buttons 88.
channel selector control 88.
chapel 55.
chard, Swiss 39.
charlotte 48.
cheek 21, 31, 75.
cheese, blue 47.
cheese, Camembert 47.
cheese, Chèvre 47.
cheese, cottage 47.
cheese, Danish blue 47.
cheese, Emmenthal 47.
cheese, Gorgonzola 47.
cheese, Gruyère 47.
cheese, hard 47.
cheese, Muenster 47.
cheese, Parmesan 47.
cheese, petit suisse 47.
cheese, processed 47.
cheese, processed Emmenthal 47.
cheese, processed Gruyère 47.
cheese, ricotta 47.
cheese, soft 47.
cheese, Stilton 47.
cheese, tome au raisin 47.
cheese, unripened 47.
cheeses 47.
cherimoya 45.
cherry 43.
chest 20, 31.
chest protector 121, 123.
chestnut 20, 46.
chick 50.
chick-peas 39.
chicory 38.
children's clothing 83.
chilli pepper 42.
chimney 56.
chimney pot 56.
chimney stack 56.
chin 22, 31.
chin strap 121.
China Sea 12.
chive 41.
chrysalis 24.
chuck 76.
cinema 102.
circle 71.
cistern lid 59.
citrus juicer 66.
clam-cleat 136.
clarinet 117.
classical guitar 114.
claw 21, 22, 24, 26, 28, 75.
claw hammer 75.

clear key 74.
clear-entry key 74.
cleated shoe 121.
clefs 112.
clew 136.
cliff 13, 14.
climbing plant 51.
clinical thermometer 143.
clip 73.
clip 72, 143.
clock 91.
clock operator 129.
clock timer 69.
cloud 15.
cloud of volcanic ash 13.
club 140.
clutch pedal 91.
coach's box 122.
coarse adjustment knob 144.
coastal features 13.
coats 82.
cob 39.
cobbler 48.
cock 50.
cockleshell 61.
coconut 46.
coffee maker, filter 68.
coin pocket 84.
coin return button 85.
coin return chute 85.
coin slot 85.
colander 66.
collar 16, 78.
collarbone 33.
column 14.
coma 11.
comet 11.
command module 106.
commander's seat 111.
commando knife 109.
compass 135.
compass bridge 102.
competitive course 134.
compound bow 137.
compressed-air cylinder 135.
condenser 144.
condenser adjustment knob 144.
condenser centring screw 144.
conductor's podium 117.
cone 13, 71.
constellations 11.
constriction 143.
container 68.
continents 12.
contrabassoon 117.
control column 105.
control knob 69.
control panel 87, 147.
control panel dial 87.
control room 103.
control wheel 147.
convection zone 10.
convertible 92.
cooker, electric 69.
cooking utensils 67.
cor anglais 117.
core 10.
corkscrew 66, 139.
corn salad 38.
corner arc 118.
corner flag 118, 125.
corner tower 55.
cornet 117.
cornice 56, 57.
corolla 17.
corona 10.
counter 78.
counterjib 148.
counterjib ballast 148.
counterweight 145, 148.
coupé 92.
courgette 42.
court 130.
couter 108.
cover 123, 143.
covered parapet walk 55.
cow 50.

cowshed 49.
cradle 145.
cranberry 44.
crane runway 148.
crank 99, 109.
crater 13.
crawler tractor 149.
crease 80.
credit-card compartment 84.
crème caramel 48.
crenel 55.
crêpe suzette 48.
crest 14.
crew neck 81.
cricket 124.
cricket, ball 124.
crisper 70.
crockery 64.
crocodile 29.
croissant 37.
crook 115.
cross rail 60.
cross-country ski 133.
cross-country skiing 133.
crossbar 98.
crossbow 109.
crosspiece 60.
crotchet 112.
crotchet rest 112.
croup 20.
crown 18, 22, 79.
crustacean 26.
cube 71.
cucumber 42.
cuff 127.
cuisse 108.
culottes 82.
cultivator, small hand 52.
cup, coffee 64.
cup, tea 64.
curly kale 38.
currant 44.
curtain wall 55.
curved jaw 76.
cushion 128.
cushion, square 62.
cutlery 65.
cutting blade 68.
cutting edge 65, 149.
cylinder 71, 110, 146.
cymbals 117.

D
d 112.
dagger 109.
daggerboard 136.
dairy 49.
dairy compartment 70.
dandelion 38.
danger 152.
dart 137.
dart 83.
dartboard 137.
darts, game 137.
dashboard 91.
data display 89.
date 43.
dead ball line 119.
death cap 19.
decimal-point key 74.
deck 97.
deer, white-tailed 30.
defensive 120.
Deimos 9.
deluge gun 147.
demi-semi-quaver 112.
demi-semi-quaver rest 112.
denture, human 34.
depth gauge 135.
desired temperature 143.
desserts 48.
dew 15.
dew cap 145.
dewclaw 21.
dial 141, 142.
diamond 140.
diaphragm 89.
diaphragm control 144.

The terms in **bold type** indicate the title of an illustration.

dice cup 140.
die 140.
diesel engine 149, 150.
diesel engine compartment 151.
diesel-electric locomotive 100.
digit 21, 27.
digital watch 141.
dining room 102.
dipped 92.
dipper bucket 151.
disabled 152.
disc 95.
disc brake 95.
dish, butter 64.
dish, casserole 67.
dish, hors d'oeuvre 64.
disk drive 74.
diskette 74.
dispenser 72.
display 74, 142.
display panel 88.
distance, measure of 143.
divide key 74.
diving 134.
dog 21.
domestic appliances 68.
dominoes 140.
door 70, 90, 93, 104, 138.
door handle 90.
door lock 90.
door mirror 90, 94.
door open warning light 91.
door shelf 70.
door, exterior 57.
doorknob 57.
dormant volcano 13.
dorsum 36.
double bass 117.
double boiler 67.
double-blank 140.
double-breasted buttoning 79.
doubles pole 130.
doubles ring 137.
doubles sideline 130.
doublet 140.
doubling die 140.
doughnut, ring 48.
downhaul 136.
downhill skiing 132.
downpipe 56.
draining spoon 66.
drawbridge 55.
drawer 60, 69.
drawing pins 73.
drawstring 84.
drive shaft 105.
drive wheel 111.
driver's cab 100.
driver's seat 111.
drums 116.
drumskin 116.
dry gallery 14.
dual seat 95.
duck 50.
dumper truck 151.
dune 13.
dungarees 83.
dust tail 11.
duvet 62.
dynamo 98.

e 112.
ear 35, 60.
ear canal 35.
ear loaf 37.
eardrum 27, 28.
earpiece 84, 86.
Earth 9.
eclair 48.
edge 128, 132.
edging 51.
egg tray 70.
elastic strainer 138.
elastic waistband 80.
elbow 20, 21, 32.
elbow pad 121, 127.
electric drill 76.

electric guitar 116.
electrical hazard 152.
electrified fence 49.
electronic scales 142.
electronic viewfinder 89.
electronic viewfinder controls 89.
elephant 29.
elevating cylinder 146, 148.
elevator 104.
elevon 107.
end line 129.
end pin 114.
end wall 134.
end zone 120.
endive 38.
endive, broad-leaved 38.
engine 95, 111, 151.
engine room 102, 103.
engines 107.
entrance 25.
entrance slide 25.
epaulet 79.
equals key 74.
equipment 52, 53.
eraser 72.
eraser 72.
eraser holder 72.
estate car 92.
Europa 9.
Europe 12.
exhaust pipe 94, 95, 105, 149.
expansion chamber 143.
explosive 152.
exposure mode 87.
extension ladder 77.
extension ladder 146.
eye 22, 26, 28, 35, 75.
eye, compound 24, 25.
eye, simple 24, 25.
eye, stalked 26.
eyeball 27.
eyebrow 35.
eyecup 89.
eyelash 35.
eyelet 78, 84, 128.
eyelet tab 78.
eyelid 28.
eyelid, lower 27, 35.
eyelid, upper 27, 35.
eyepiece 144, 145.

f 112.
f clef 112.
'f' hold 114.
F degrees 143.
F-1 engine 106.
face 31, 75.
face mask 121, 127.
face-off circle 126.
face-off spot 126.
faces 75.
faculae 10.
Fahrenheit scale 143.
fairing 95.
family tent 138.
farm animals 50.
farm buildings 49.
farmhouse 49.
farmyard 49.
fast forward 88.
fast-forward button 86.
fauces 34.
fauld 108.
feather 22.
feathering 137.
feet, major types of 23.
femur 33.
fence, paling 51.
fennel 39.
ferrule 65, 77.
fetlock 20.
fibula 33.
fig, Indian 45.
figure skate 128.
filament 10, 17, 63.
filler neck 94.
film advance mode 87.

film rewind 87.
filter 67.
fin 105.
fin, first dorsal 27.
fin, pectoral 27.
fin, pelvic 27.
fin, second dorsal 27.
finder 145.
fine adjustment knob 144.
finger 123.
finger, index 36.
finger, little 36.
finger, middle 36.
finger, third 36.
fingerboard 114.
fingernail 36.
fire engines 146, 147.
fire extinguisher 146.
fireman's axe 146.
fireman's helmet 146.
first base 122.
first baseman 122.
first quarter 10.
first space 129.
first stage 106.
first violin 117.
first-class cabin 104.
fish 27.
fish scaler 139.
fish slice 66.
fitting 147.
fixed jaw 76.
flagstone 51.
flammable 152.
flank 20, 22.
flanking tower 55.
flap 84.
flap pocket 80.
flare 10.
flash light 87.
flashgun, electronic 87.
flat 27.
flat mirror 145.
flews 21.
flight 137.
flight deck 104, 105, 107.
flipper 135.
floor, first 56.
floor, ground 56.
flower 16.
flower bed 51.
flower bud 16.
flower, parts of a 17.
flowers, clump of 51.
flush handle 59.
flute 117.
fly 80, 83.
fly agaric 19.
flysheet 138.
fob pocket 83.
focusing knob 145.
focusing mechanism 144.
focusing ring 87, 144.
fog 15.
fog lamp 92.
folding door 59.
foliage 18.
food mixer 68.
foot 22, 26, 32, 136.
foot fault judge 130.
foot pocket 135.
football 121.
football, equipment 121.
footboard 62.
footbridge 55.
fore leg 24, 25.
fore wing 24, 25.
forearm 21, 32.
forecourt 96, 130.
forehead 22, 31.
forest 14.
fork 65.
fork 98, 145.
fork, garden 52.
fork, hand 52.
forklift truck 148.
forks 148.

forward slide button 87.
foul line 122.
fountain pen 72.
fourchette 79.
frame 25, 76, 95, 131, 138, 151.
frame push 149.
free-throw lane 129.
free-throw line 129.
freewheel 99.
freezer compartment 70.
freight handling 148.
freight hold 104.
freight wagon, types of 101.
French horn 117.
fret 114, 116.
fridge-freezer 70.
frog 27, 114.
front brake 98.
front brake lever 95.
front compression strap 139.
front derailleur 98, 99.
front leg 60.
front lights 92.
front pocket 84.
front sight 110.
front top pocket 80, 83.
front-end loader 150.
fruit 16.
fruit salad 48.
fruit, citrus 44.
fruits, stone 43.
fruits, tropical 45.
fryer, deep-fat 67.
frying pan 67.
fuel indicator 91.
fuel tank 94, 95, 100, 105, 111.
fulcrum 134.
full back 119.
full moon 10.
fullback 120.
fumarole 13.
fume extractor 111.
function keys 142.
funnel 66, 102.
fuselage 104.

g 112.
g clef 112.
G-clamp 76.
gable 56.
gable vent 56.
galaxy 11.
galley 104.
Ganymede 9.
garage 56.
garage driveway 56.
garden 51.
garden light 51.
garlic 41.
gas tail 11.
gaskin 20.
gastropod 26.
gateau 48.
gateleg 60.
gauntlet 108.
gear cable 99.
gear lever 91, 98, 99.
gearchange pedal 95.
genital pore 26.
geyser 13.
gibbous moon 10.
gill 19.
gill cover 27.
giraffe 29.
give way 152.
glass bulb 141.
glass cover 70.
glass slide 144.
glottis 28.
glove 123.
glove 127, 132, 133, 135.
glove compartment 91.
glove finger 79.
gloves 79.
glue stick 73.
gnomon 141.
goal 118, 119, 120, 125, 126.

The terms in **bold type** indicate the title of an illustration.

goal crease 126.
goal judge 126.
goal line 118, 119, 120, 125, 126.
goalkeeper 127.
goalkeeper 118, 125, 126.
goalkeeper's pad 127.
goat 50.
gong 117.
goose 50.
gooseberry 44.
gorge 14.
grab handle 93, 94, 147.
granulation 10.
grape 44.
grapefruit 44.
graphic equalizer 89.
grass bag 53.
grater 66.
gravy boat 64.
greave 108.
green 71.
greenhouse 49.
grille 90.
grip 137.
groin 31.
groove 132.
growth line 26.
guard 58.
guard iron 100.
guard rail 70.
guardhouse 55.
guava 45.
gun flap 79.
gunner's sight 111.
gusset 84.
gutter 56.
guy rope 138.

hail 15.
hailstone 15.
hair 32, 114.
halfway line 118, 119.
hammer 75.
hammer 110, 113.
hammer rail 113.
hand 32, 36, 141.
handbrake 91.
handkerchief 83.
handle 53, 65, 68, 69, 70, 75, 76, 77, 84, 86, 123, 124, 12**5, 131.**
handlebars 98.
handrail 58.
handsaw 75.
handset 85.
handset cord 85.
hanger loop 81.
hanging basket 51.
hanging pendant 63.
harness 135.
harp 117.
hat, crown 79.
hat, felt 79.
hatband 79.
hatch 107, 111.
hatchback 92.
haunch 20.
hazelnut 46.
head 11, 24, 25, 26, 32, 39, 75, 76, 114, 116, 131.
head linesman 120.
head of sail 136.
headband 86, 131, 133.
headboard 62.
headland 13.
headlight 90, 95, 100, 111.
headlight/indicator signal 91.
headphone jack 86.
headphones 86.
hearing, organ of 35.
heart 140.
heartwood 18.
heat shield 107.
heater controls 91.
hedge 51.
heel 32, 78, 114, 123, 127.
heel piece 132.
height-adjustment lever 53.

helicopter 105.
helium sphere 106.
helix 35.
helmet 108, 121, 127.
hemi-demi-semi-quaver 112.
hemi-demi-semi-quaver rest 112.
hen 50.
hen house 49.
hi-fi midi system 89.
high-speed train 100.
highlighter pen 72.
hill 14.
hind leg 24, 25, 27.
hind toe 22, 23.
hind wing 24, 25.
hinge 57, 144.
hip 32.
hip pad 121.
hip pad girdle 127.
hipbone 33.
hitting area 123.
hive 25.
hive body 25.
hob 69.
hob edge 69.
hock 20, 21.
hockey 125.
hockey skate 128.
hockey, ball 125.
hockey, field 125.
hoisting block 148.
hoisting rope 77, 148.
home plate 122.
honeybee 25.
honeycomb 25.
hood 135.
hoof 20.
hook 57, 128, 143, 148.
hooker 119.
horn 91, 94, 147.
horns 26.
horny beak 28.
horse 20.
horseradish 40.
hose 146.
hose nozzle 53.
hose trolley 53.
hose, garden 53.
hospital 152.
hot shoe 87.
hourglass 141.
house 55.
house on stilts 54.
house, exterior of a 56.
housing 76.
hub 98.
hubcap 90.
huckleberry 44.
humerus 33.
husk 39.
hut 54.
hut, grass 54.
hydrant intake 147.
hydraulic jack 93.
hydraulic shovel 151.

ice cream scoop 66.
ice cube tray 70.
ice hockey 126, 127.
ice hockey player 127.
igloo 54.
ignition switch 91.
image sensor 89.
in goal 119.
incisors 34.
incoming message cassette 85.
Indian Ocean 12.
indicator 92, 95.
indicators 88.
indigo 71.
indoor games 140.
infield 122.
information 152.
inhaul 136.
inner table 140.
inner tent 138.
inside bowl 65.

inside centre 119.
inside linebacker 120.
inside-leg snap-fastening 83.
instrument panel 91.
instrument panel 91, 95.
instrument unit 106.
internal frame 139.
internode 16.
Io 9.
iris 35.
iron frame 113.
isba 54.

J-2 engine 106.
Jack 140, 146, 148, 151.
jacket 82.
jacket, casual 80.
jacket, single-breasted 80.
jacket, single-breasted 80.
jamb 57.
jaw 76.
jeans 83.
jersey 121.
jib 148.
jib tie 148.
jockey roller 99.
Joker 140.
jug, coffee 68.
jug, cream 64.
jug, water 64.
Jupiter 9.

kangaroo 30.
kernel 39.
kerosene tank 106.
key 113, 115.
key signature 112.
key-bed 113.
keyboard 74, 113.
keyboard cable 74.
King 140.
kiosk 96.
kitchen timer 141.
kitchen utensils 66.
kiwi fruit 45.
knee 20, 31.
knee pad 121, 123, 127.
knee sock 133.
kneecap 33.
knife 65.
knife 135.
knit shirt 81.
knob 123.
knurled bolt 77.
kohlrabi 40.
kumquat 44.

labial palp 24.
lace 123.
ladder 93, 151.
ladder pipe nozzle 146.
ladle 66.
lagoon 13.
lake 14.
lamb 50.
lamp 144.
lamp, standard 63.
lamp, table 63.
lampshade 63.
lampstand 63.
land, ploughed 49.
landing 58.
landing light 105.
lane 134.
lane number 134.
lane rope 134.
lanyard 141.
lapel 80.
large blade 139.
last quarter 9.
launch escape system 106.
lava flow 13.
lava layer 13.
lawn 51.
lawn edger 52.
lawn mower 53.
lawn rake 52.

lead 72.
leaf 16, 39, 60.
leaf, parts of a 17.
leather skin 124.
ledger lines 112.
leech 136.
leek 41.
left back 118, 125.
left cornerback 120.
left defence 126.
left defensive end 120.
left defensive tackle 120.
left field 122.
left fielder 122.
left forward 129.
left fullback 118.
left guard 120, 129.
left half 125.
left halfback 120.
left inner 125.
left midfield 118.
left safety 120.
left service court 130.
left tackle 120.
left wing 118, 119, 125, 126.
leg 22, 28, 32, 53, 60, 62, 116.
legs 24.
lemon 44.
length, measure of 143.
lens 87.
lens hood 89.
lentils 39.
leotard 82.
lettuce, cos 38.
levelling- adjustment foot 87.
lever 68, 96, 146.
lid 67, 68.
lifeboat 102.
lift arm 150.
lift-arm cylinder 150.
ligature 115.
light 145.
light bar 147.
light bulb 63.
light, ceiling 63.
light, on/off indicator 68, 69.
light, outdoor 56.
light, strip 63.
light, wall bracket 63.
lighting cable 93.
lightning 15.
lightning conductor 56.
lights 63.
limb 18, 137.
line 112.
line judge 120.
line of scrimmage 120.
linen 62.
linesman 118, 126, 130.
lining 78.
lion 29.
lip 20, 21.
lip, lower 34.
lip, upper 34.
lips, commisure of 34.
liquid hydrogen tank 106.
liquid oxygen tank 106.
liquid-crystal display 141.
litter bin 96.
Little Bear 11.
little finger hook 115.
livestock van 101.
living room 138.
load backrest 148.
loading gate 110.
lobate toe 23.
lobe 23, 35.
lobster 26.
lock 57.
lock forward 119.
lock rail 57.
lock ring 87.
locking device 77.
loins 20, 32.
lookout tower 55.
loophole 55.
loose-head prop 119.

The terms in **bold type** indicate the title of an illustration.

loose-leaf pad 73.
loudspeaker 89.
loudspeaker 147.
lounge 102.
lower chord 97.
lower rudder 103.
luff 136.
lug 116.
luggage compartment 100.
luggage rack 93.
lunar module 106.
lunule 36.
lychee 45.

M machete 109.
machine gun 111.
machine heads 116.
machinery store 49.
magazine 110.
magazine base 110.
magazine catch 110.
magma 13.
magma chamber 13.
magnetic gasket 70.
magnifier 139.
main beam 92.
main engines 107.
main ladder 146.
main landing gear 104.
main mirror 145.
main tube 145.
main vent 13.
maintenance area 96.
mallet 75.
mandarin 44.
mandible 24, 25, 27.
mane 20.
mangetout 39.
mango 43.
manoeuvring engine 107.
manual focusing dial 87.
margin 17.
marker light 94.
marker pen 72.
marrow 42.
Mars 9.
mask 123, 135.
mast 136.
mast foot 136.
mast sleeve 136.
masthead 136.
mattress 62.
mattress cover 62.
maxilla 27.
maxillipeds 26.
meadow 49.
measure of distance 143.
measure of length 143.
measure of temperature 143.
measure of time 141.
measure of weight 142.
measuring cap 68.
meat keeper 70.
mechanical stage 144.
mechanical stage control 144.
Mediterranean Sea 12.
memo book 73.
memo pad 73.
memory cancel 74.
memory index 85.
memory recall 74.
men, backgammon 140.
men's clothing 79, 80.
Mercury 9.
mercury bulb 143.
mercury column 143.
merlon 55.
message delay selector 85.
message length selector 85.
message playback button 85.
metacarpus 33.
metatarsus 33.
microcomputer 74.
microphone 89.
microprocessor 74.
middle leg 24, 25.
middle linebacker 120.

middle sole 78.
midrange 89.
midrange pick-up 116.
midrib 17.
mileometer 91.
Milky Way 11.
minibus 92.
minim 112.
minim rest 112.
minute hand 141.
mirror 59, 95.
missile 103.
missile tube 103.
mist 15.
mixing bowl 68.
moat 55.
mode selectors 86.
molars 34.
Moon 9.
Moon, phases of the 10.
morel 19.
motor 53.
motor home 93.
motor unit 68.
motorcycle 95.
mound 122.
mountain 14.
mountain slope 14.
mountain torrent 14.
mounting bracket 137.
mounting foot 87.
mouse 74.
mouth 26, 27, 34.
mouthpiece 115, 135.
movable jaw 76.
mud flap 94.
mudguard 95, 98.
mug 64.
multiply key 74.
muntin 57.
mushroom, deadly poisonous 19.
mushroom, edible 19.
mushroom, parts of a 19.
mushroom, poisonous 19.
musical notation 112.
muskmelon 42.
muzzle 20, 21, 110.

N nail 75.
nail file 139.
nail notch 139.
name plate 76.
nape 22, 32.
natural 112.
natural arch 13.
navel 31.
navigation light 104.
nebula 11.
neck 20, 28, 31, 65, 114, 141.
neckroll 62.
nectarine 43.
Neptune 9.
net 130.
net 129.
net cord 130.
net judge 130.
neutral zone 120.
new crescent 10.
new moon 10.
newel post 58.
nipple 31.
no entry 152.
no parking 152.
no smoking 152.
nock 137.
nocking point 137.
node 16.
nonstriker 124.
North America 12.
North Star 11.
nose 20, 36, 104.
nose landing gear 104.
nose leather 21.
nose, bridge of 36.
nose, tip of 36.
nosepad 84.
nostril 20, 22, 27, 28, 36.

notch 80.
note book 73.
note symbols 112.
nozzle 146.
nozzle 106, 146, 147.
nucleus 11.
number 8 119.
number key 74.
number plate light 92.
numeric keyboard 142.
nut 76, 109, 114.
nut, Brazil 46.
nuts 46.

O objective 144.
objective lens 144, 145.
oboe 117.
observation window 107.
Oceania 12.
octave mechanism 115.
offensive 120.
officials' bench 126.
oil warning light 91.
okra 42.
old crescent 10.
olive 43.
on-deck circle 122.
on/off 86.
on/off light 85.
on/off switch 74, 85.
on/off/volume 86.
one-way traffic 152.
onion, Spanish 41.
onion, spring 41.
open-air terrace 102.
open-side flanker 119.
operator's cab 148.
orange 44, 71.
orchard 49.
orchestra 117.
ostrich 30.
outer table 140.
outfield 122.
outhaul 136.
outlet 93.
output jack 116.
outside centre 119.
outside half 119.
outside linebacker 120.
outsole 78.
ovary 17.
oven 69.
oven control knob 69.
overcoat 82.
overflow 59.
ovule 17.

P Pacific Ocean 12.
paint roller 77.
paint tray 77.
painting upkeep 77.
paints, watercolour 73.
palate, hard 34.
palate, soft 34.
palm 36, 123.
palmar pad 21.
palmette 61.
pan 142.
pane 57.
panel 57.
pannier bag 99.
pans, roasting 67.
pantograph 100.
pants 121, 123.
papaya 45.
paper clips 72.
parallelepiped 71.
parallelogram 71.
parapet 97.
parapet walk 55.
parsnip 40.
pass 14.
passenger cabin 104.
passenger coach 100.
passenger liner 102.
pastern 20.
pasture, permanent 49.

patch pocket 83.
patera 61.
path 51.
patio 51.
pauldron 108.
pause/still 88.
payload 106.
payload bay door 107.
payphone 85.
peach 43.
peak 14, 79.
peanut 46.
pear 43.
peas, green 39.
pecan nut 46.
pedal 98, 99, 116.
pedal rod 113.
pedestrian crossing 152.
pedicel 17.
pedometer 143.
peg 114, 138.
peg box 114.
peg loop 138.
penalty arc 118.
penalty area 118.
penalty bench 126.
penalty spot 118.
pencil 72.
pencil sharpener 73.
pencil, propelling 72.
pencils, colouring 73.
penis 31.
pepper pot 64.
pepper, sweet 42.
per cent key 74.
pergola 51.
periscope 103.
periscopic sight 111.
perron 56.
persimmon, Japanese 45.
personal articles 84.
petals 17.
petiole 17.
petrol flap 90.
petrol pump 96.
petrol pump 96.
petrol pump hose 96.
petrol station 96.
phases of the Moon 10.
Phillips® screwdriver 139.
philtrum 36.
phloem 18.
Phobos 9.
photoelectric cell 87.
piano 113, 117.
piccolo 117.
pick-up selector 116.
pickguard 116.
pickling onion 41.
pickup truck 92.
pie 48.
pier 97.
pig 50.
pigsty 49.
pillow 62.
pillowcase 62.
pin 146.
pine nut 46.
pineapple 45.
pip 140.
pistachio nut 46.
pistil 17.
pistol 110.
pistol grip handle 76.
pit 28.
pitch 124.
pitcher 122.
pitcher's plate 122.
pith 18.
pivot 128.
pivot cab 151.
plane surfaces 71.
planets of the solar system 9.
plant, parts of a 16.
plastron 28.
plate, dinner 64.
plate, salad 64.

The terms in **bold type** indicate the title of an illustration.

157

plate, side 64.
plateau 14.
platform 77, 142.
platform ladder 77.
platter 64.
platter, fish 64.
play 88.
play button 86.
player's number 121.
player's stick 127.
players' bench 122, 126, 129.
playing field 119.
playroom 102.
plug 76.
plum 43.
plum, Japanese 43.
Pluto 9.
pneumostome 26.
pocket 83.
pocket calculator 74.
pocket handkerchief 80.
pocket, hand warmer 80.
point 65, 75, 128, 137, 140, 149.
pointer 142, 143.
poison 152.
polar bear 30.
polar lights 11.
pole grip 132, 133.
pole shaft 133.
pole tip 133.
poleyn 108.
pollen basket 25.
pome fruits 43.
pomegranate 45.
pond, garden 51.
popping crease 124.
port 102.
port sail plane 103.
portable shower head 59.
porthole 102.
position marker 114, 116.
pot hole 14.
potato 40.
potato masher 66.
potato, sweet 40.
power cable 53.
power car 100.
power train 99.
power-off slide-select bar 87.
practice pedal 113.
pre-set buttons 88.
premolars 34.
preset buttons 88.
pressure bar 113.
pressure cooker 67.
pressure gauge 146.
pressure regulator 67.
price per litre 96.
printed document 74.
printer 74.
prism 71.
proboscis 24.
product codes 142.
profiterole 48.
prolegs 24.
promenade deck 102.
prominence 10.
prong 65.
prop stand 95.
propane gas cylinder 93.
propeller 102, 103.
protective cup 121, 127.
protective helmet 99.
protector strip 90.
pubis 31.
public signs 152.
puck 127.
pulley 77, 109.
pulley block 109.
pulse button 68.
pump 98.
pump nozzle 96.
pumpkin 42.
punch hole 78.
pupil 35.
purfling 114.
purge valve 135.

purse 84.
push buttons 85.
push-button 72.
pyramid 71.

quarter 78.
quarterback 120.
quaver 112.
quaver rest 112.
Queen 140.
Queen Anne leg 61.
queen excluder 25.
quince 43.

rack 67, 69.
radar 104.
radar mast 102, 103.
radiation zone 10.
radiator grille 94.
radio mast 103.
radio/cassette player 86.
radish 40.
radius 33.
raglan sleeve 79.
rail 100.
rain 15.
rainbow 15.
raindrop 15.
rake 52.
ramekin 64.
rampart 55.
rapier 109.
reactor 103.
reactor compartment 103.
rear brake 98.
rear derailleur 98, 99.
rear footrest 95.
rear leg 60.
rear light 92, 98.
rear lights 92.
rear sight 110.
rearview mirror 91.
receiver 130.
receptacle 17.
record 88.
record button 89.
recorder on/off switch 88.
rectangle 71.
red 71.
Red Sea 12.
reed 115.
referee 118, 120, 126, 129.
reflecting telescope 145.
refracting telescope 145.
refrigerator compartment 70.
refrigerator van 101.
remote control 88.
remote control 87.
remote control detector 88.
remote control terminal 87.
remote-control arm 107.
removable blade 77.
repair shop 96.
rerebrace 108.
reservoir 68.
reset button 141.
rest symbols 112.
restaurant 152.
restaurant car 100.
restricted area 129.
retractable step 93.
return crease 124.
reverse slide button 87.
reversing light 92.
revolution counter 91.
revolver 110.
revolving nosepiece 144.
rewind 88.
rewind button 86.
rhinoceros 29.
rhombus 71.
rhubarb 39.
rib 33, 39, 84, 151.
rib pad 121.
ribbing 81, 83.
ridge 14.
right back 118, 125.

right bend 152.
right cornerback 120.
right defence 126.
right defensive end 120.
right defensive tackle 120.
right field 122.
right fielder 122.
right forward 129.
right fullback 118.
right guard 120, 129.
right half 125.
right halfback 120.
right inner 125.
right midfield 118.
right safety 120.
right service court 130.
right tackle 120.
right wing 118, 119, 125, 126.
rim 84.
rinceau 61.
rind, natural 47.
rind, red 47.
rind, white 47.
ring 19, 84, 115, 139.
ring binder 73.
rink 126.
rink corner 126.
ripper 149.
ripper cylinder 149.
ripper tooth 149.
riser 58.
river estuary 13.
rivet 128.
road signs 152.
Roberval's balance 142.
rock 13.
rock garden 51.
rocket 106.
roller cover 77.
roller frame 77.
roller skate 128.
roof 25, 56.
roof vent 56, 93.
room 138.
room thermostat 143.
root 16.
root 16, 65.
root cap 16.
root hairs 16.
root, lateral 16.
root, primary 16.
root, secondary 16.
root-hair zone 18.
roots 18.
rose 53.
rosette 114.
rotor blade 105.
rotor head 105.
rotor hub 105.
rucksack 139.
rudder 102, 104, 107.
rugby union 119.
rugby, ball 119.
ruler 72.
ruler 139.
run 124.
rung 77.
runner 140.

sabaton 108.
sabre 109.
saddle 98.
safety chain 93.
safety rail 77, 100.
safety valve 67.
sail 136.
sailboard 136.
salad spinner 66.
saloon 92.
salsify 40.
salsify, black 40.
salt cellar 64.
salt marsh 13.
sand 141.
sand island 13.
sapwood 18.
sash-frame 57.

Saturn 9.
saucepan 67.
saucer 64.
saxophone 115.
scale 112.
scale 23, 27, 28, 143.
school 152.
school supplies 72, 73.
scissors 139.
scorer 129.
scraper 77.
screen 88.
screen print 83.
screen window 138.
screw 75.
screw 114.
screw fitting 63.
screwdriver 75.
screwdriver 139.
scroll 114.
scroll foot 61.
scrum-half 119.
seal 30.
seam 79, 124.
seat 60, 61.
seat post 98.
seat-belt warning light 91.
second base 122.
second baseman 122.
second hand 141.
second space 129.
second stage 106.
second violin 117.
seed leaf 16.
segment score number 137.
semi-breve 112.
semi-breve rest 112.
semi-quaver 112.
semi-quaver rest 112.
semi-trailer 94.
semicircle 129.
sepals 17.
server 130.
service line 130.
service module 106.
service station 152.
set of utensils 66.
set square 72.
set-in sleeve 81, 83.
settee, two-seater 61.
sewn-in floor 138.
shadow 141.
shaft 127, 131, 137.
shallot 41.
shank 75, 84.
shank protector 149.
sharp 112.
shears, hand 52.
sheath 17, 21.
shed 51.
sheep 50.
sheet, fitted 62.
sheet, flat 62.
shelf 70, 77.
shelf channel 70.
shell 26, 28.
shield 28.
shin guard 121, 123.
shin pad 127.
shirt 83.
shirt 80, 131.
shirt cuff 80.
shirt tail 80.
shock absorber 95.
shoe, trainer 78.
shoelace 78.
shoot 16, 18.
shooting star 11.
shop 96.
shorts 83.
shortstop 122.
shoulder 20, 21, 31, 131.
shoulder blade 32, 33.
shoulder pad 121, 127.
shoulder strap 84, 139.
shovel 52, 132, 133.
shower cubicle 59.

The terms in **bold type** indicate the title of an illustration.

shower head 59.
shutter 57.
shutter release button 87.
shutter, louvre 57.
sickle 52.
side 65, 114.
side compression strap 139.
side light 92.
side line 125.
side rail 77.
side span 97.
side vent 13, 93.
side wall 134.
sideline 129.
sight 137.
sight, organ of 35.
signal light 67.
silage store 49.
silk 39.
silo tower 49.
simple-span beam bridge 97.
singles pole 130.
singles sideline 130.
sink 59.
sink hole 14.
siphon 14.
skate 127.
skating 128.
skeg 136.
skeleton 33.
ski boot 132.
ski goggles 132.
ski hat 132, 133.
ski pole 132, 133.
ski stop 132.
ski suit 132, 133.
ski tip 133.
skid 105.
skimmer 66.
skin 27.
skin diving 135.
skirt 131.
skirt, pleated 82.
skirt, straight 82.
skirting board 58.
skirts 82.
skull 33.
skylight 56.
sleeper 100.
sleeper-cab 94.
sleeping bag 139.
sleeping quarters 103.
sleepsuit 83.
sleeve strap 79.
sleeve strap loop 79.
sleeveless 81.
slide 110.
slide projector 87.
slide tray 87.
slides 87.
sliding roof 90.
slip joint 76.
slip joint pliers 76.
slit 79.
slot 65, 68, 75.
slow-motion 88.
small blade 139.
smell, organ of 36.
smoke-grenade launcher 111.
snail 26.
snake, venomous 28.
snap fastener 80.
snap-fastening front 83.
snare 116.
snare drum 116.
snare drum 117.
snare head 116.
snare strainer 116.
snorkel 135.
snort exhaust 103.
snort induction 103.
snout 27.
snow 15.
snow crystals 15.
snow, perpetual 14.
soap dish 59.
soccer 118.

soccer ball 118.
soccer, field 118.
sock 121, 131.
sofa 61.
soft pedal 113.
soft ray 27.
soft-drink dispenser 96.
solar cell 74.
solar system, planets of the 9.
sole 128.
sole plate 100, 128.
solid body 116.
solids 71.
solleret 108.
sorbet 48.
sorrel 38.
soufflé 48.
soundboard 113, 114.
soup tureen 64.
South America 12.
Southern Cross 11.
sow 50.
soybeans 39.
space 112.
space shuttle 107.
spacelab 107.
spade 52, 140.
spanner, adjustable 76.
spatula 66.
speaker 85, 86.
speaker volume control 85.
spectrum 71.
speed control 68.
speed limit 152.
speed skate 128.
speedometer 91.
sphere 71.
spicules 10.
spiked shoe 123.
spinach 38.
spindle 60.
spiny ray 27.
spiracle 24.
spit 13.
splat 61.
split end 120.
spoiler 95.
spoke 98.
spoon 65.
spoons, measuring 66.
spores 19.
sports car 92.
spotlight 146, 147.
spreader 84.
sprinkler, arm 53.
sprinkler, revolving 53.
sprocket wheel 149.
spur 14, 116.
square 71.
square root key 74.
squash, autumn 42.
stabilizer 137.
stabilizer fin 102.
stabilizing fin 106.
stables 49.
stack 13.
staff 112.
stage 144.
stage clip 144.
stairs 58.
stake 51.
stalactite 14.
stalagmite 14.
stalk 39.
stalk vegetables 39.
stamen 17.
stanchion 128.
stand 68, 116.
stapler 73.
staples 73.
starboard 102.
stars 11.
start button 141.
starting block 134.
stateroom 102.
steering column 91.

steering wheel 91.
stem 16.
stem 16, 19, 98, 143.
step 77, 94, 100.
step setting 143.
stepladder 77.
stereo control 86.
stern 102, 136.
stern deck 102.
sternum 33.
stick 125.
stick 114, 116, 127.
stick eraser 72.
stick glove 127.
stiffening girder 97.
stigma 17.
stile 57, 60.
sting 25.
stipule 17.
stirrup 109.
stirrup sock 123.
stitch 78.
stitches 123.
stitching 123.
stock pot 67.
stop 21, 88, 152.
stop button 141.
stopwatch 141.
storage compartment 87, 93, 94, 146, 147.
storage door 70.
strainer 138.
strap 83, 123.
strap loop 139.
stretch-limousine 92.
stretcher 60.
striker 124.
striking circle 125.
string 114.
stringing 131.
strings 113.
stud 78.
stump 18.
stump 124.
style 17.
submarine 103.
submersible watch 135.
subterranean stream 14.
subtract from memory 74.
subtract key 74.
suction hose 147.
summit 14.
Sun 10.
Sun 9.
sun visor 91, 93.
sun's atmosphere 10.
sun's surface 10.
sundeck 102.
sundial 141.
sunglasses 84.
sunspot 10.
super 25.
support 60, 63, 145.
support leg 93.
surface element 69.
surface of the water 134.
suspended span 97.
suspender 97.
suspension bridge 97.
suspension cable 97.
sustaining pedal 113.
swallow-hole 14.
sweaters 81.
swede 40.
sweetcorn 39.
swimmerets 26.
swimming 134.
swimming pool 134.
swimming pool 102.
swing circle 151.
Swiss army knife 139.
Swiss roll 48.
switch 68.
switch lock 76.
switch, on/off 53, 76, 87, 88.
swivel head 76.

steering wheel 91.
T-shirt 83.
tab 84.
table top 60.
table, gateleg 60.
tack 136.
tag 78.
tail 20, 21, 22, 27, 28, 104, 132, 133.
tail boom 105.
tail fan 26.
tail light 95.
tail plane 105.
tail rotor 105.
tailpiece 114.
talon 23.
tang 65.
tank 111.
tanks 107.
tap 59.
tap connector 53.
tape 123, 125, 143.
tape lock 143.
tape measure 143.
taproot 18.
tarsus 33.
tart 48.
tartlet 48.
tasset 108.
taste, organ of 34.
team shirt 123.
teapot 64.
teeth 75.
telephone 152.
telephone answering system 85.
telephone, cordless 85.
telephone, portable cellular 85.
telephone, push-button 85.
telephones 85.
telescopic boom 148.
telescopic front fork 95.
television 88.
television set 88.
temperate set point dial 143.
temperature control 67, 68.
temperature indicator 91.
temperature scale 143.
temperature, measure of 143.
tendon guard 128.
tennis 130, 131.
tennis ball 131.
tennis player 131.
tennis racquet 131.
tennis shoe 131.
tenor drum 116.
tension rod 116.
tension roller 99.
tension screw 116.
tent 138.
tepee 54.
thermometer 143.
thermostat control 70.
thigh 21, 32.
thigh pad 121.
third base 122.
third baseman 122.
third stage 106.
thorax 24, 31.
thread 75, 76.
three-quarter backs 119.
threshold 57.
throat 22, 76, 131.
throat protector 123, 127.
throttle handgrip 95.
thumb 36, 79, 123.
thumb hook 115.
thumb rest 115.
thumbscrew 76.
tibia 33.
ticket 142.
tie 80.
tie closure 84.
tight end 120.
tight-head prop 119.
tightening buckle 139.
tiller 109.
tilt-back head 68.
time signature 112.
time, measure of 141.

The terms in **bold type** indicate the title of an illustration.

159

INDEX

timekeeper 129.
timer 67.
timpani 117.
tin opener 66, 139.
tinted lens 84.
tip 17, 39, 65, 75, 84, 132.
Titan 9.
toaster 68.
toe 21, 22, 23, 31, 75.
toe box 128.
toe clip 98.
toe pick 128.
toe piece 132.
toe stop 128.
toilet 59.
toilet bowl 59.
toilet cistern 59.
toilet lid 59.
toilet roll holder 59.
toilets 152.
tomato 42.
tone control 116.
tone controls 86.
tone selector 85.
tongs 66.
tongue 28, 34, 78, 128.
tongue sheath 28.
tonsil 34.
tool tray 77.
tools 52, 53, 76.
tooth 28, 34, 151.
top 18.
top collar 80.
top flap 139.
top rail 57.
top stitching 83.
torch 135.
torpedo 103.
torpedo room 103.
total 142.
touch line 118, 119.
touch, organ of 36.
tow bar 93.
towel rail 59.
tower 97.
tower crane 148.
tower mast 148.
towing hitch 93.
track 111, 149.
track link 111.
tractor unit 94.
tractor unit 94.
traditional houses 54.
traffic lights 152.
trailer caravan 93.
trailer mount 94.
tramlines 130.
trapezoid 71.
tray 53, 145.
tread 58.
tread, bullnose 58.
treble pick-up 116.
trebles ring 137.
tree, parts of a 18.
trellis, fan 51.
tremolo arm 116.
trench coat 79.
triangle 71, 117.
trigger 89, 109, 110.
trigger guard 110.

trip mileometer 91.
tripod 145.
tripod stand 116.
Triton 9.
trolley 148.
trombone 117.
trousers 80.
trousers 127.
trowel, hand 52.
truck 128.
truck tractor 94.
truck crane 148.
truck tractor 94.
trumpet 115.
trumpet 117.
trunk 18, 32.
trunk, cross section of a 18.
tub 51.
tuba 117.
tubular bells 117.
tuning pin 113.
tuning slide 115.
tuning switch 86.
tunnel 107.
turbine 103.
turbofan jet engine 104.
turkey 50.
turn-up 80, 83.
turning wall 134.
turnip 40.
turnover 48.
turntable 68, 89.
turntable ladder 146.
turntable mounting 146.
turret 111.
turtle 28.
turtleneck 133.
turtleneck 81.
TV on/off switch 88.
TV/video button 88.
tweeter 89.
twig 16, 18.
two-handed sword 109.
two-way collar 79.
type of fuel 96.
tyre 90, 98.

'U' lock 99.
ulna 33.
umbrella 84.
umpire 120, 130.
umpire-in-chief 122.
underpass 97.
undershirt 123.
unit price 142.
uphaul 136.
upper chord 97.
upper deck 104.
upper rudder 103.
upright piano 113.
Uranus 9.
uvula 34.

V-neck 81.
valance 62.
valley 14.
valve 98.
valves 115.
vambrace 108.
vamp 78.
vanity mirror 91.

vegetable bowl 64.
vegetable garden 49.
vegetable steamer 67.
vegetables, bulb 41.
vegetables, fruit 42.
vegetables, inflorescent 41.
vegetables, leaf 38.
vegetables, root 40.
vegetables, seed 39.
vegetables, tuber 40.
vein 17.
Velcro® closure 84.
venom conducting tube 28.
venom fang 28.
venom gland 28.
vent 91.
ventilating fan 100.
Venus 9.
vertebra 33.
vertical pupil 28.
video camera 89.
videocassette recorder 88.
vine leaf 38.
vinyl grip sole 83.
viola 117.
violet 71.
violin 114.
visor slit 108.
visual display unit 74, 96.
volcanic bombs 13.
volcano 13.
volume control 86, 88, 116.
volume readout 96.
volva 19.
vulva 31.

waffle 48.
wagon, bogie 101.
wagon, bogie car-carrying 101.
wagon, bogie flat 101.
wagon, bogie tank 101.
wagon, bogie well 101.
wagon, bulkhead flat 101.
wagon, container flat 101.
wagon, gondola open 101.
wagon, hopper 101.
wagon, piggyback flat 101.
waist 32.
waist belt 139.
waistband 80, 83.
waistband extension 80.
waistcoat 80.
walking legs 26.
Walkman® 86.
wall 138.
wall string 58.
wallet 84.
walnut 46.
warming plate 68.
warning lights 91.
warning plate 76.
watch pocket 80.
water bottle 98.
water bottle clip 98.
water key 115.
water level 68.
water pressure gauge 147.
water table 14.
water tender 147.
watercress 38.

waterfall 14.
watering can 53.
watermelon 42.
weapons, thrusting 109.
weather 15.
weatherboard 57.
web 23, 27, 123.
webbed toe 23, 27.
weeder, hand 52.
weighing platform 142.
weight 142.
weight belt 135.
weight, measure of 142.
welt pocket 81.
wet suit 135.
wheel 53, 111, 128, 137.
wheel loader 150.
wheel rim 95, 98.
wheelbarrow 53.
whiskers 21.
white 35, 140.
white light 71.
wicket 124.
wicket keeper 124.
wigwam 54.
wild animals 29, 30.
willow 124.
wind deflector 94.
window 57.
window 69, 90, 104, 136.
window canopy 138.
window sill 57.
windscreen 90.
windscreen wiper 90.
windshield 95.
windsurfing 136.
wing 22, 24, 90, 104, 107.
wing vein 24.
wiper switch 91.
wire cutter 76.
wisdom tooth 34.
wishbone boom 136.
withers 20, 21.
women's clothing 82.
wood ray 18.
woofer 89.
wrap-over top 82.
wrest plank 113.
wrist 21, 32, 36.
wrist strap 132, 133.
wristband 131.

xylophone 117.

yellow 71.
yule log 48.
yurt 54.

zebra 29.
zip 138.
zoom adjustment 144
zoom lens 89.
zoom lever 89.